YOUR LOVING SON, ANDREW

MICHAEL L. TYLER

Palmetto Publishing Group
Charleston, SC

YOUR LOVING SON, ANDREW

First Edition

Printed in the United States

ISBN-13: 9781641114509
ISBN-10: 1641114509

YOUR LOVING SON, ANDREW

It was a beautiful day, the sun warm but not too hot like it usually was on most summer days in Haymarket, warm on the face with a cool breeze that signaled that it was going to be a great day. The kind of day when you'd expect to be out in a field playing ball with the family, or having a picnic with your best gal. There were so many things that would spring to Andrew's mind on a day like today. To some, it would have been odd that Andrew and his family would decide to be standing in the middle of a nowhere town like Haymarket waiting for a stinky bus. There must certainly have been a reason for them to all be standing on the side of a dusty dirt road in rural Virginia. And indeed, Andrew was about to embark on the adventure of a lifetime. But looking at the faces of his parents reminded him so vividly of what he was going to miss when he was gone. The laughing, the hugs—and of course no one can forget Mom's homemade meals. Her mashed potatoes and gravy were legendary, and Andrew was going to miss them on those cold nights of eating only beans.

"Mom, please!" said Andrew. "Dad, can you please get Mom off of me?"

Andrew knew that his leaving wasn't going to be easy for her, but he didn't imagine for a moment that she would be acting like one of those eco nuts tying themselves to a redwood to save its mighty bark. She was clinging to him like his socks do when he forgets to put a static sheet in the dryer.

Mike grabbed his wife Marie by the arm and pried her off of their son. He was no happier about their boy going into the armed forces than she was, especially with so many going overseas to fight in the Middle East. But it was his decision, not theirs. He knew what he was doing when he signed on the dotted line. There was a war going on, and as terrified as he was of his boy possibly going over there to fight, he couldn't deny feeling just as equally proud of him. He and his father had seen action in Vietnam and Korea, and he had a sneaking feeling that Andrew didn't want to break tradition of fighting for his country.

Andrew stepped back and gave his father a wink. He didn't want either of his parents to know that he was about to blubber like a three-year-old. His guts were in knots. Part of him wanted his mother to hold on even tighter and never let him go, but the other half knew that this decision was right for him. He could have easily broken down just by looking at his mother's unhappy face. Everything about her expression screamed, "Please don't go." It broke his heart to hurt her so badly.

He heard his father's gruff soldier-like voice in his head: "*For every sociopath* who *comes* *back with cool war stories to tell his buddies, there are thousands* who *come back with their lives ruined.*" He heard that and a million other tidbits of wisdom play over and over in his head, but to stay home would mean that he was okay with his life, and unfortunately he wasn't. He loved his parents more than life itself, but there were things out there that he wanted to see before milking cows for the rest of his days. He wanted to see London; he wanted to see Tokyo; he wanted to see something besides the undercarriage of their cow, Sophie.

His father approached him, and as a joke, snatched him close to hug him but at the last second pushed him away and said in a loud military tone, "Army men don't hug, boy!" He stepped back a half-step and saluted his son. He waited for a reply before lowering his hand. "Obviously they'll have to work with you on your saluting skills," he said.

Andrew loved his father's weird sense of humor and nodded in agreement. He was going to be nineteen in a few months, and he figured that by the time he came home, he would be bigger, stronger, and be a real man that his parents could be proud of. And besides, he knew that Donna Jones would eat her heart out when he came home all big and buff. She'd wish she had gone out with him when she had the chance.

"I swear, I will write as often as I can, Mom," said Andrew. "I swear."

He couldn't help getting a bit emotional himself, but he choked the tears down. He didn't want the last thing they saw before he left to be him blubbering like a baby.

Andrew's mother and father walked their son the last few yards to where the bus smelling of diesel was waiting with open arms for the green recruits. Andrew wasn't the only kid from Haymarket, Virginia to want to prove something to family and friends. He, just like the others, was petrified and fearful, but also anxious to be one of those men talked about by the old folks. He loved hearing the stories at the barber shop where his dad got the few hairs he had left cut once a month. He loved the stories about those heroes of past who had helped keep this country safe, and how they did so much for other countries as well. How they helped industrialize nations and get rid of the very bad people running the show. He would be proud to add his name to that list.

The decrepit bus driver bellowed, "*Let's ride!*"

A few seconds later, Andrew stepped up into the bus and found himself a seat inside facing the dirty fingerprinted window through which he could see his mom and dad one more time. He could see his mother crying, and if he looked hard enough, he could see tears in his father's eyes as well. He had never known his father to be emotional, but he knew all of their thoughts because he'd thought them himself a million times since he signed up. He could read both their minds just as easily as he could read the stop sign that they were standing next to.

His parents waved to their son as the bus roared to life and started moving forward. Andrew turned and reciprocated with a wave himself. After only a few seconds, they became smaller and smaller until the stop sign next to them was the only thing he could make out.

He saw a few acquaintances from school on the bus, but no one that he really hung out with regularly. Mostly jocks from high school and college. The bus trip was going to be over two hours to Camp Aberdeen, where he would be doing his basic training. To help pass the time, he grabbed his pad out of his knapsack and opened up his writing tablet. He wanted his mom to understand why he was doing this, but she would never understand the look that his dad gave Mr. Andrews and Mr. Johnson when they went to get their hair cut, that look of respect and gratitude and appreciation for their service. He wanted so badly to be in that club, but his mom would never understand his reasons for that. He just hoped his dad would explain it in terms his mom could grasp.

He wanted to write his mom something, anything—a letter to help ease his guilt for leaving. He clicked his pen.

Dear Mom and Dad,

Mom, I know you will be the one reading this to Pop, so let me say first that I love you both very much. I'm sitting on the bus, we just got on the highway, and I wanted to let you know that I didn't want to leave, but actually, the opposite is true. I wanted to stay and help Pop with the tractor and plant the seeds, but I think that this is something I have to do so that I'll know that helping out on the farm is not all I'm good for, you know? I think Dad can explain it to you better than I can. Just ask him about the barbershop. I think I should help someone besides myself, you know? Anyway, I just wanted to let you know that in no way am I running away to get away from either of you, or our tiny one-cow town. I may not even get sent to Iraq or Afghanistan or anywhere dangerous. Some guys get sent to Bumfart, Georgia to pick peaches all day, after all. But if they do send me over there, I promise to make you both proud. I think that's all I have to say for now, so I'll write more after I get settled in.

Your Loving Son, Andrew

Andrew placed his tablet back in his knapsack and looked at his watch. *That killed fifteen minutes,* he thought to himself. He didn't want to take a nap or mingle with the fellas. He just wanted to ponder where he would end up, or who he would become, or how his life would turn out after this experience. He knew that he could possibly be killed, but he obviously hoped that that wouldn't happen. He had no brothers or sisters to help out Mom and Dad if anything happened to him, so he had to make it back. He just had to.

He peered out the window with his cheek upon the cool glass. It was a nice, sunny day, and if he had been in a car with a girl at his side, it would've been a great day, a perfect day. Unfortunately, he was on a bus full of rowdy teenagers hooting and hollering about how many ragheads they were going to kill. He didn't share that mentality on killing anything. He didn't even like killing bugs just minding their own business. That was another thing that he kept thinking of, too: *what if I'm face to face with someone who was trying to kill me? Would I have the stones to blow his head off?* That was something he hoped he'd never have to do, but if he did get deployed to the Middle East, he would have to face the fact that it might happen.

Without warning, the guy in the seat across from Andrew said, *"Andrew, right?"*

"Uh, yeah, Andrew Knox," he said. "I know I've seen you in school, but I'm sorry, your face is all I know."

"The name is Donald, Donald Birch. I guess you and I are about to get a wake-up call about what's really out there, huh?"

Donald extended his hand. He didn't seem much into the hooting and hollering, either. Of course, Andrew would gravitate towards the one other guy who, like him, wasn't screaming like an idiot.

Andrew was always making new friends, and it was no different with Donald. He knew him from around school. He couldn't tell anyone a thing about the guy, but he'd never heard a bad word about him. He deduced that he too was in "the middle," like Andrew was. Not necessary a cool kid, but not in the nerd section, either. He shook Donald's hand, and at the same time asked, "What made you join up? Killing a bunch of ragheads like those jackasses?"

He pointed to the rowdy bunch up front who thought they were real life GI Joes because they wanted to kill them some foreigners and mount them on their trophy wall at home.

"No, not really," said Donald. "I just wanted to do something besides live my life in that one-horse town and have a bunch of regrets about what I could've done or should've done, you know? I didn't want to wake up one morning at sixty-eight and say 'what if.'"

Andrew knew all too well. "You're wrong about one thing," he said. "It's a one cow town." He waited for proper response to his funny joke, and after a broad smile sprung up on Donald's face, he continued. "I do, too. Are you in my head or something? I know it's gonna make my dad proud, and I know it will be good for me in a lot of ways, but I don't want to live my life thirty years from now thinking that I chickened out."

He paused for a second, and then said, "What do your parents think of all this?"

"I'm sure they're both looking down on me saying they're very proud of me, no matter what I do."

Andrew gulped a big wad of spit down his throat. All this time he seen him around, he never knew he was an orphan. "Dude, I'm sorry to hear about your parents."

Donald just simply said, "These things happen."

Andrew changed the subject. If he had lost his parents, he probably wouldn't want to talk about it either. He and his folks were closer than two front teeth, as his father liked to say.

"I bet basic training is going to be a real ball buster," he said. "I hear they make you do sit-ups it the mud and eat bugs and shit."

Donald had to admit that he liked Andrew a lot more than he would've liked those wannabe jarheads up front. He was scared to death about going, and even more scared of not going. He had seen so many war movies about how war scars a man and how pulling the trigger isn't as easy as you'd think, but the "what ifs" would have haunted him, and he knew it.

"Yeah, I guess, but I don't care," he said to Andrew. "I guess if it makes me a tougher s.o.b. then bring it on. You're not going to survive over there being a namby pamby girly man," he finished, accentuating the last phrase with his best Arnold impression.

Andrew grinned from ear to ear. "That was pretty good. I haven't heard anyone use 'namby pamby' in like fifty years, but it's okay, just don't use it too often. I guess I see your point, though. If basic is going to toughen you up, then you should want it to be hard."

"Exactly! I don't think we're going to love our drill instructor or anything, but they say you love him later when you're out in the field and something he taught you saves your life."

"Were you writing your girlfriend earlier?" said Donald.

Andrew smiled. "No, it was a letter to my parents."

"You just left them twenty minutes ago!"

"Yeah, I know. But I didn't feel like sleeping or listening to those guys up there, so I wrote a letter. I told them I would write." At the mention of parents, Andrew tried to change the subject. "Do you have a girlfriend?"

Donald figured Andrew was changing the subject to be nice, which made him a nice guy, but still a momma's boy. He'd lost his parents years ago, but he did have a few people he could write to if he wanted.

"No, I don't have a girl waiting for me to come back, unless you want to consider Sister Agatha at the orphanage my girl," said Donald. "She's nice and all, but I think she's married to God or something. I don't think it would work out between us."

Andrew liked Donald's warped sense of humor. "Was she fat and barking orders around all the time, and carrying a belt strap?"

"No, she was about thirty-something I'd guess, and skinny and very nice. She always said I was going to be somebody someday. I remember one time when I was a kid, she snuck me in some snacks after bedtime. I was sick and I hadn't eaten any dinner. I don't think they would have horse-whipped her or anything, but she seemed to always be there when I was feeling down."

Donald paused for a second, his mind obviously elsewhere.

"She sounds nice," said Andrew. "Do you still talk with her? I mean, do you still keep in contact?"

"I have her information, but when I went away to college, she kinda got lumped up into the whole dustbowl, nowhere town that I wanted to forget."

"You came back here, though. Why?"

Andrew had to admit that he would've enrolled at whatever college Donald was at. He knew they would've had a lot of fun.

"I came back because I wanted to say goodbye to a few people I knew, like the Sister, I guess. Just in case the worst happened, maybe. I just didn't fit in over at that one-teacher hillbilly college outside Manassas. It wasn't easy dropping out. I thought about it for a long time. Nothing seemed to be what I wanted to do, or to be. Then I started to think about being a soldier, so I talked with the recruiter here, and he said that I could get Uncle Sam to pay for my college and maybe get a degree to go anywhere in the world I wanted. The community college just wasn't going to offer me that. The only thing it really gave me was a maxed-out credit card. I would have never been able to afford a four-year college, you know? I could barely pay for the crummy community college."

"Yeah, I heard the recruiter talk about that, too," said Andrew. "I'm also going to look into that. I want to be a mechanical engineer. I want to work at NASA or someplace like that. I want to build rockets and shit, something that is gonna land on an asteroid and find some Andrewonium or something."

Donald sat back in his chair and just looked up at the ceiling of the bus, wondering what he really wanted to do with his life. He wanted to know exactly what he wanted to be, just like Andrew, but unfortunately all he knew for sure was that he wanted to help people. He wanted to get his shit together and be like a big brother to a kid like him, someone who was completely lost, a basket case. He would have given anything to be like the other kids, but the truth was that he was an orphan who no one wanted. Parents want cute little babies, not a ten-year-old smartass. His mouth always seemed to get the better of him and make him undesirable to prospective parents. And he had come to the realization many years ago that he didn't want another mom or another dad. He wanted his real parents back.

Andrew saw that his new friend had drifted into la la land. "You okay?" he asked.

Donald shook the cobwebs out of his head along with the self-pity. He wasn't going to live in the past anymore. He was always so envious of people who looked genuinely happy, like they had found the thing that he was always searching for. He was going to put all of that garbage in a bag and tie it up, sling it over a bridge and let it be gone forever. He was going to try, anyway. "Yeah, I'm fine. Just old ghosts is all."

"Anything you want to talk about?"

"I just think about shit that could have happened once in a while; you know? What if my parents had lived? What if I'd been adopted? That kind of shit."

"Wow, that's some heavy stuff. Have you ever talked with anyone to just get the crap off your chest and deal with it?"

"Yeah, the Sister," said Donald, "but she was all just 'everything is going to be fine' and 'God loves you' and 'everything happens for a reason.' I don't think that helped as much as she thought it did."

"But what if they give you a psych test at the base and decide you're unfit? Then what?"

"I don't think that's going to be an issue. I'm not so crazy that it keeps me up at night. I just wonder sometimes what my life would've been like if it had taken a different road, is all."

"We all think about that, though. What if my parents were rich bankers, instead of poor farmers? What if I was super smart and finished high school at twelve?"

"You really wanted to graduate at twelve?"

"No, I just mean the crazy stuff you think of when you're wondering 'what if,' that's all."

"Then the doctor should assume I'm perfectly normal if everyone does it, right Andy? Can I call you Andy?"

Andy had to admit that he had a point. "Yeah, it's my name Donny. I guess it's pretty normal. As long as you don't think about it to the point of snapping and killing all your bunkmates in their sleep!"

"I think you're safe, Andy."

Don appreciated Andrew's sense of humor as well. They were only a year apart in age, so they could've even been friends in high school. Don wondered what they would've done, what adventures they might've gotten themselves into. But like everything else, he figured, no one would ever know. Then he said to himself, "*Why not start now? We can be good friends starting now.*" He laughed and said aloud, "I wonder what stupid shit we would have done if we had met ten years ago."

The thought had crossed Andrew's mind as well only a moment ago. "I don't know," he began, "but I bet we would have been good at being bad. Like my dad says, '*If you can't be good, then be good at it.*' I always played pranks on my parents. I loved scaring my mom, and she would chase me with a rolling pin or a rag or sometimes just a bare hand. Every once in a while, she would catch up to me, but all she did usually was grab my face and smoosh it between her fingers and tell me to stop being so damn bad."

"That's the stuff I miss because of not having had parents for such a long time."

"Being chased by your mother and getting your cheeks smooshed?"

"No, dink," said Don with a laugh. "Having memories to look back on. I don't admit this to many people, but sometimes I have trouble remembering what my mom and dad looked like. I try to remember my mom's face, but it seems to be different every time."

Don couldn't explain it, but he felt as if he were talking to someone, he'd known for much longer than an hour and a half. He didn't usually open up to people about anything.

'I don't mean to be nosey," said Andy, "but how did they die? You don't have to talk about it if you don't want to."

He had the sneaking feeling that Don was a dam ready to burst, but was he really ready to be this guy's psychiatrist?

"They died when I was nine," said Don. "They got into an accident and the car caught on fire, and neither one got out alive."

Andy could see on the other boy's face the heartache, the longing, and the remorse of a young boy hating his parents for leaving him all alone.

"Were you in the car with them?"

"No, I was at the babysitter's house a few doors down from ours. They woke me up and told me that my mom and dad had been in a car crash, and that they were dead." Don stopped abruptly. He felt like a babbling baby crying about all of his woes to a complete stranger.

"Didn't you have any family that would take you in?" said Andy.

"None came forward, let's just say." He had an uncle, but he had never offered to take care of him, and as far as he knew, no one begged him.

"I'm so sorry," said Andy. "No one in the whole family came forward? What a bunch of jerks."

"Yeah, I thought that for a while too, but the truth is, I can't assume anything about anyone else's financial or mental situation. I can't tell anyone else that they owe it to me, or to my parents, or that it's the right thing to do and they should do it so I don't have to grow up in an orphanage. They did what they thought was best for their family, and I don't hate any of them for it. I mean, I don't hate them anymore."

The truth was that he had a tough time accepting the garbage that he'd just spewed out. He had hated everyone for the longest time, even the people that tried to help. He knew that he had his chances to get adopted, but he sabotaged them, and it was his own self-destructiveness that he had to live with. It wasn't easy, and the regrets never went away.

"I don't care," Andy persisted. "They should have taken you in, and if they didn't, then they're just jerkwads."

"I like to think of it as the hand I was dealt and all that junk, and as long as I'm happy, and am kind to my fellow man, and live a hate-free life, then I will be okay."

Andy had to wonder if this guy was full of shit, or if it was just Sister Agatha talking. He knew for a fact that he would have grown up and visited each one of them and slit all their tires, maybe even poured a few pounds of sugar down their gas tanks for good measure. "I'm not one hundred percent sure that you're as okay with it as you say you are," he said finally, "but I know what I would've done if they'd left me in that hole to rot."

Don leaned forward. "Would you have visited them in the dark of night and bashed their heads in with baseball bats? Would you have set their houses on fire? Would you like to take a butcher knife and stick it through the tops of their heads?"

"Yes, I think we are on the same wavelength," said Andy. "I would've probably done all those things and more."

"But where would it have gotten you, or me? It would have just put you in another hole worse than the one you were in. I had to channel that anger and rage and self-pity into something besides just planning their executions. By the way, I think I thought of every possible way to shish kabob a live human being, in case you wanted to know. And I think you now know more about me than you ever wanted to. So what about you?"

"What about me?"

"What's your story?"

"Well," Andrew began, "I'm a farmer's boy who thought there must be more to life than cows and string beans. I love my parents, I'd love to be rich and buy them a house so they wouldn't have to work so hard every day. I would love to come back a tough, buff son of a bitch who can lift car engines with one hand, but we both know the truth about that. With this body, the best I can come back with is a buff Pee Wee Herman maybe."

"Why can't you be the next Mister Universe?"

"Let's go down the list, shall we? My Legs look like broomsticks, my arms look like candlesticks, and my chest is as wide as an oak leaf. Since my arms, my legs, my chest, and my shoulders are off a twelve year old boy or maybe a sixteen year old girl, maybe ,if we take away all that and transplant them with another person's limbs, I might have some hope."

Don laughed.

"What's so funny?" said Andy.

Don could see Andy with big broad shoulders instead of a chest as wide as a dinner plate. "I just think you'd look totally different. The army could make you a buff son of a bitch, I guess."

Don didn't want to say what he was really thinking. He was envisioning Andy with muscles so big that he couldn't even wipe his own butt.

Andy gave him a strange stare, but it just made him value his new— though be it odd—friendship even more. Don was very jovial, and he had a definite streak of mischief in him. "Yeah, right! You were probably thinking about me being crushed under that engine block."

"How did you know?"

The banter between the two young men went on back and forth until they both felt the jolt of the bus leaving behind the nicely paved streets to veer a dirt road covered in pot holes. They both turned to the window and took in the wide-open range. Neither could see anything except corn stalks, and they both figured that they were in corn country somewhere.

Eventually, after the bus shook and rocked with every pothole, they could see the camp looming bigger and bigger in the distance. Andrew wondered if he would have to be treated for whiplash when he got there. He was bouncing around like a lottery ball. "Damn, I think this bus driver is drunk," he said between gritted teeth.

Don shook his head in agreement. "I think the pot holes out here are bigger than the bus."

"I hope this roller coaster ride is over soon, because I think I'm about to have internal bleeding."

Soon afterwards, the bus slowed until it eventually came to a complete stop. They were parked in front of a huge building, but it didn't look like many buildings that any of these Virginia kids had ever seen before. It was dome-shaped and made out of aluminum, no bricks and no wood, just shiny aluminum. Andrew was in awe—or, to be more precise, he was intimidated, to say the least. He saw recruits running around as if someone was chasing them with a machine gun or something, men screaming at other men, men doing push-ups and sit-ups and chin-ups. He didn't really want to do any of these things ever in his life.

"Holy shit, Don," said Andy. "I think we are so fucked."

Don could not deny that the churning in his stomach was due to agreeing heartily with Andy's statement. "Uh yeah, that would be a big *duhh*." He saw what looked like a bunch of guys being tortured in broad daylight. He knew what to expect from war movies, but seeing it up close and personal was a totally different matter. "I think I want your mommy," he joked.

Andrew just bobbed his head up and down in agreement.

They both stood up as the bus driver opened the door. The driver told everyone to get out and form a line. Andrew and Don were at the back of the bus, so they didn't hurry to get out. The yahoos in front acted like they weren't scared, but Andrew and Don both knew that they had a load in their pants just like the two of them did.

They got off the bus and formed the last two in the line, which was anything but uniform. They didn't say anything. They didn't even move. They both just stood there and, in unison, prayed to God that they would make it back to Haymarket alive.

There was a very unpleasant officer who popped up out of nowhere, and who just started shouting at Andrew and the rest of the guys lined up, "Any iPad, any iPhone, any Iwatches are mine if you are caught using them. There is no Wi-Fi out here, and any material brought to me will only further my daughter's savings account. Any contributions are definitely appreciated. I will help you kids get through your detoxification of social media, and being on the internet twenty three hours of the day. I have a great big shoulder you can lean on when you start to shake." Andrew tried to tune his screaming out. Andrew knew this guy would have snapped his neck if he tried to get near his shoulder, and mostly he knew he was not going to like it here. "*Oh shit*", he whispered under his breath.

BASIC TRAINING

Dear Mom and Dad,

Well, like I said in my last letter, I'm at Camp Aberdeen, and it's not like home at all. I have guys yelling at me twenty-three hours a day, and when they aren't yelling, they're making me clean toilets or they're making me run around the camp with fifty pounds of crap tied to my back. I can honestly say that I'm in the best shape I've ever been in, though. No pain, no gain, right Pop? I can do more push-ups, sit-ups, and chin-ups than I ever thought possible. I'm still hanging with Don most of the time on my downtime. We don't have much of that here unfortunately, but when we do, I mostly play cards or backgammon with Don. He has helped me out a lot here, Mom, and I don't think I could've made it through this without him pushing me.

Tell Pop that I'm doing good and that I will be home in no time. Tell Peanut to be a good dog and that I will see him soon. I still have a few weeks of basic, but after that, I'm not too sure about where I go next. I will write to you again soon, and just know that I am safe and becoming a better man, and that by the time I get home, I will be able

*to run around the farm like one of those jack rabbits. I
have to go for now, but I will write again soon.*

Your Loving Son, Andrew

After Andy shoved his notebook back under his pillow, he rolled over to the other side of his bunk to where Don was laying down relaxing. "Up for a game of cards?" he said.

Don had been sitting there not oblivious to the fact that his buddy was writing to his parents again. Andy must have sent them ten letters in the past two weeks. When he said that he and his parents were close, he really meant it, Don thought.

"I think I'm just going to hang here and chill out," said Don. "That last round of PT was brutal, and it really did me in. Everything in and out of my body is sore. I think even my nostril hairs are sore from panting so hard." He groaned. "I think I should be left alone to just die. I think that is the only thing left for me to do, just sit here until they can bury me out back by the dumpsters."

"First of all, *ewww..*," Andy began, "and secondly, don't say that. How on earth would I get through these PTs if you weren't there? You being so shitty at it keeps the Sarge off the rest of our asses."

Don said, loud enough so that the whole platoon could hear, "I think Private Andy here has a point. I think you all owe me something for keeping the hardass off your butts. How about ten from each of you, and we'll call it even."

Most of the platoon mumbled something about "in your dreams" and "yeah right," and even one or two "kiss my asses." Andrew threw a ten onto Don's bunk and said, "Keep up the good work, soldier. There may be another ten in it if you can keep me from running around this damn camp again in full gear. That shit is getting heavy."

"That's called exercise, dink. The only reason the Sarge pushes you is because he wants you to be fit and strong, just in case. I understand why he's an asshole to me, but you ain't no valedictorian when it comes to peak fitness."

"Yeah, I know, but you do admit that he's an asshole, right?"

"Yeah, but I bet you'll kiss his ass one day after he saves your life," said Don. "I bet you come back here and plant one right on his pimply, hairy ass. You would probably French his ass hole while you were down there, too."

Andrew played it off as if he was really mortified by the comment. "You have a point, but how would I do that if your head was already wedged up there?" With a wave of his hand, he continued, "Come on, you have to admit you're always sucking his dick, and that's the real reason he's on you all the time. He's trying to rub out that brown nosing shit spot you have on your nose. I think everyone here knows it but you."

"I admire and respect him," Don began, "but that's not kissing his ass. I know that the stuff he shows us is to make us better soldiers."

"Do you hear yourself right now?" Andy tossed a wad of paper over at his bunkmate across from him. "Hey Ray, am I right or am I right?"

Ray Reynolds just gave Andrew a smirk. He wasn't much for Andrews foolery. He was a serious soldier. Not one who thought of cracking jokes all day. He preferred to be left alone. He did not associate with too many of his bunk mates.

"What's wrong big guy? What's got all those muscles so wound so tight?"

Ray just looked at him as if to say, *huh? Whatever.* "Look, Andy, I don't want to get into you all's marital argument. I think you both kiss each other's asses way more than the Sarge's."

Andrew and Don looked at each other as if to say *you rotten son of a bitch.* "Ray, how could you say that about us, buddy?" said Andy. "I thought we were friends? I thought we were teammates? I thought we were simpatico?"

Ray walked over to the two other young men. He loved messing with them, as did most of the guys. Truth be told, he liked both of them. They were good guys, but sometimes they gave off the impression that they shared everything with each other, even their asses.

"We are, Andy," said Ray. "I was just trying to say that neither of you can kiss his ass if you have your heads stuck up each other's'. You feel me, right, Andy?"

Andy looked at Ray in a way that said *I'll kick your ass,* but he didn't act on it. He knew better. Ray was a musclebound freak of nature. He was tough when he got there, and was ten times tougher now.

"I think you better sit down and not write checks your ass and Don's can't cover," said Ray.

"What does Don's ass have to do with it? I can take care of my own battles, Ray Ray," he said in response. Andy knew it was all in good fun. They did this kind of thing at least ten times a day. Sometimes you were the cast, and sometimes you were the audience.

"What I meant, *An-Dee,* was that since Don owns half of your ass, you might not want to get his half in jeopardy, is all."

Don busted out laughing. He couldn't help it. That was a good one, and it was this that was going on right now that helped burn the day away. Anything besides running, jumping, saluting, and scrubbing floors was a welcome change.

"What the fuck, Don?" said Andy. "I thought you were on my side?" But he wasn't really upset. He had almost busted out laughing himself. That had been a pretty good burn.

Don straightened up. "Don't get your vagina in a twist," he said. "Hey fellas, did you all meet my mistress, Andrina?"

Most of the squad was cackling and giggling at his remark. Andrew interrupted him, but no one paid him any mind. Don continued, "You know I still love you, sweetheart. On our next hike, I'll pick you some wild flowers. Will that make your pussy stop crying?"

The whole barracks was waiting for Andrew's comeback. This was what was called entertainment around here. There was no television or pool table or air hockey. A verbal battle was as good as it got.

Andrew wasn't going to let Don have the last good burn. "You weren't saying that last night while you were licking my pussy, now were you? All I saw was the balding spot on the top of your head, and all I heard was you eating like you were in a pie-eating contest. If you had of had a TV on that balding spot you would have been the perfect date."

Andrew flipped Don the finger to punctuate the burn, and Don smiled back. This was why they got along so well. Neither man had any malicious intent towards the other, and they both knew that they would have each other's back in a pinch. This was as close as either of them would get to having a brother.

"Oh, I meant to tell you," Don continued. "While I was down there, I could detect a hint of a yeast infection."

"So why did you stay down there?"

"I was hungry."

Everyone busted out laughing, but Andy laughed loudest and hardest. "I think that's why I love you so much, darlin'. You are one sick, twisted, freakish individual. You know this, right?"

After Don stopped laughing himself, he wiped the tears from his eyes and said, "Yeah, I know, but I wasn't like that before I hung around with you. I was a good Christian boy who was kind and generous and never said a naughty word."

"You mean you were a good Catholic schoolgirl who dropped her skirt for every boy or priest who passed by. I know about you Catholics."

"Dink, I never wore a skirt, and if any guys came by, they sucked on my long shlong just like you did last night. No, they were actually a lot better than you were last night."

"I didn't have a lot to work with, to be truthful."

Don was getting ready to say something else when Private Reynolds shouted, "Sergeant on deck." He turned his head to see ballbuster Bob Burnside walking through the door. He jumped to his feet and leapt in front of his bunk, looking straight ahead. He could see the sergeant inspecting the recruits as well as their bunks. He would stop and scream in the private's face about how his bunk looked like it had been made up by a blind Seeing Eye dog and then move on to the next one. Now it seemed to be Don's turn.

"So how are you doing, Birch?" said the Sergeant. "Did you get enough exercise yesterday? I heard you came in here whimpering like a beaten dog? Is that true?"

The whole time, he was screaming at the top of his lungs less than two inches from Donald's nose.

"No, Sir! I was not whimpering at all, Sir," he responded, screaming at the top of his lungs in return.

"Are you saying that my information is incorrect, Birch? Are you saying that the guy who comes and tells me everything about this mud hut is lying, Birch!?"

"Yes, Sir! He is lying to you, Sir!" Don was yelling at the top of his lungs, trying to get the Sergeant to move on down the line and hassle someone else. But Sergeant Burnside looked into Don's eyes and said almost softly in comparison, "Okay, I'll let him know that he was wrong."

Don didn't move or speak. He was just glad that it was over. Burnside was on his way to torment Andrew now. Everyone believed that this was the sergeant's form of masturbation. By the time he got off, he had some kid wetting his pants. Don knew that he would never give him that satisfaction, no matter how many laps he had to do around this godforsaken camp.

Andrew stared ahead hoping that Burnside would just mosey on past, but no such luck. As he was screamed at belligerently, he knew he was just one of Burnside's fun activities on his daily to-do sheet. Andy thought back to the farm and helping his dad. It was a trick he used that really helped him when Burnside took out his anger on him. He stared straight ahead, and in his mind he was smashing open a ripe watermelon and eating the core. He was a million miles away.

But the Sergeant noticed the glazed look in Andy's eyes, as though he weren't listening to a word he was saying. "Are you listening to me, princess?!" Then he screamed louder, "Oh, princess? Am I bothering you, princess?"

Andy snapped out of his daydream, and with an ear-piercing screech, he yelled, "No, Sir, I'm hanging onto your every word, Sir!"

His smartass comments didn't usually go over well with the officers, but in this case, the sergeant gave him a break.

"I'm so glad, Knox, because I was pretty sure I was being ignored, and that hurts my feelings!"

"No, Sir! I would not ignore you, Sir!"

"Are you tired, princess?"

"No, Sir!"

"I thought you might be, because I heard a bunch of laughing in here a bit ago, and guess whose screechy, twangy voice resonated over everyone else's? That's right, Knox, it was yours. Why do you think that was, Knox?"

In actuality, Burnside thought that Knox was a pretty good soldier, but his mouth seemed to be the death of him. He was the class clown, and Burnside hated class clowns. They got people killed.

"Probably because my voice is still changing, Sir!"

There was a low murmur among the cadets. They all tried to hide their laughter under the guise of coughing and clearing their throats.

Burnside ran over to Doug Harrison, who was still trying to cover up his laughter. "I think we have an epidemic of some sort in here," he said. "What do you think, Harrison?"

Doug knew that he couldn't tell Burnside what he really thought. He couldn't tell him that he was a mouthy piece of shit that liked pushing little boys around for fun. He also couldn't tell him that he was thinking a good fist down his throat might cure him of that. He just wimped out and said, "I think you're right, Sir!"

"You think I'm right about everything, don't you, Harrison?"

Still screaming at the top his lungs as well, Doug replied, "Yes, Sir!" But what he really wanted to say was something along the lines of, "Eat shit and die," or, "Kiss my ass, you prick," but he refrained. He'd been there long enough to see that people like Burnside sat in their little offices and played God just to cope with their inadequacies in other areas. It made him feel a little better to know that his inadequacies were not in the same areas at all.

Burnside spun around. "Okay, girlfriends, I think that we need some fresh air and to do some exercise to get those nasty coughs out of your system." He turned back and got in Andrew's face again. "And guess who's going to lead them in those exercises, Knox?"

"You are, Sir!"

Andrew knew better. Burnside was going to pin this shit on him and make him hated by every eyeball in this hut.

"Uh, that would be a big fat negative, Knox!" Burnside took a deep breath and then continued, "That would be your monkey ass, Knox. You're going to get to lead your men in a grueling, cough-extracting regimen while I sit in my chair and see what kind of leader you really are. Do you think you're a good leader, Knox?"

Still using his high-pitched, cracking voice, Andy bellowed, "Yes, Sir, I think I am, Sir!"

"Good, Knox," said Burnside. "I know you can make me and your mommy so proud of you by the time we get done today. Your men are going to love you just like they love me when you get back to where you're standing right now. Aren't you excited at this opportunity?"

He got a "yes, Sir" in response, and then Burnside continued, "So, have your sick men get geared up and meet you outside in ten. Can you do that, Knox?"

"Yes, Sir!"

Andy knew he was screwed. Everyone was going to kick his ass in the showers later.

"Good, Knox. I hope you're laughing as loud as you were earlier, Private Knox, because we are gonna have some fun tonight. Right?"

"Yes, Sir!"

"Move out, unless you want me to shove a Howitzer up your ass to motivate you girls!"

Burnside had to admit that snot nosed smartasses like Knox were great to have at happy hour, but in the field, when bullets were grazing your earlobes, it was guys like Private Reynolds who you would be huddled around to help get you home alive. He wished they were all like his prized pupil Raymond Reynolds.

Andrew waited to see Burnside leave the barracks before uttering, "Sorry guys, but you know he would have come in here with any excuse to screw us." He hoped that would ease the beating he expected to get later.

But the guys didn't respond. They just got their gear together and headed out the door. Don walked past Andy and gave him an evil stink eye as he walked past. "When are those balls going to drop with that voice of yours?" he said.

Andy had a big lump in his throat. He hated that he was the one who everyone else was angry at. He liked it much better when it was Thomas or Jacobs who bore the brunt of the guys' ire. This was his first time in the hot seat.

As they all found themselves outside in formation, they stood still waiting for Sergeant Burnside to come out. But he never did. They waited two minutes, then five, then ten, but no Burnside. They just stood there like someone had nailed their boots to the asphalt.

Raymond Reynolds knew exactly why the sergeant wasn't coming out. He said that they were Andy's to command, and just as he figured, Andy had more piss in his shorts than balls. He looked over at Andy, who was staring blankly into space. "Hey, Corporal Knox," he said. "What do you want us to do?" The question was more of an insult.

Andrew snapped back to reality. He understood now. He was in charge, and he was flunking big time. He had to show the guys and Burnside that he could lead, even if his stomach said otherwise. He walked a few paces ahead so that he was in front of his men, and then bellowed, "Platoon, attention!" He tried to emulate Burnside as best he could, but he could tell that he paled in comparison.

However, the platoon still snapped to attention. They all knew that this was going to be more of an exercise in futility than anything they'd seen before, and they waited for their fearless leader to lead them in whatever he could come up with.

Don watched as his friend stood squirming in front of everyone. He could see that Andy was obviously not much of a leader. He thought it was like going to the bridge of the Titanic on its last voyage and finding

Daffy Duck at the wheel. But he could only stand there and silently wish his friend luck.

Private Knox spanned the platoon, but he saw no friendly faces. In fact, he saw mostly disgust, anger, and extreme disdain. He took a deep breath and did the best he could, calling out, "Attention!"

The platoon straightened up. They were told to do all the twists and turns that were involved in basic drills. He had them right face and left face and about face, but he hadn't gotten to the point of maneuvers as of yet. It was hot, impossibly muggy, and the last thing anyone wanted to do was walk five miles with sweat pouring out from every part of their body and every muscle screaming in agony. The dirt felt like concrete, and the dust that would be kicked up as they marched would do nothing for morale, either.

"Forward, March!" said Andy, figuring he'd be hoarse by the time he got back into bed tonight.

As they walked past the officer's hut, they saw Burnside leaning up against the doorframe with a sadistic look on his face that told everyone watching that he had all the power. "Good luck Knox," he said with a sneer. "If you make it back, you can get yourself and the fellas some chow."

Andy saluted Burnside as he walked by, as did the others.

Burnside watched as the privates marched up the hill. He had a sly grin at the prospect of them taking Knox out in the field and stripping him down to his birthday suit and making him hike back in the buff.

Andy put one foot in front of the other, bellowing out a good ol' Army tune to help his boys stay in step. He could just see them stopping and busting his ass and turning around. He knew that if he ever was going to be any kind of leader, it would have to begin today, and right now. Maybe he did joke around too much, but right now he was dead stern. He was sober and solemn, and his tone was serious. He wanted to show his troops, his sergeant, and himself that he was more than just a punch line.

Only time will tell, he thought to himself.

DOWN ON THE FARM

Mike and Marie Knox were both overjoyed when they received one of their boy's letters in the mail. Every day they waited to see if one of Andy's letters was sitting in the mailbox. Sometimes Marie was at the mailbox waiting when the mail lady drove her little car up to their house. It was a joyous occasion for her when she looked inside and saw a letter with Andrew's handwriting on the front.

Today was no exception. Marie was at the end of the driveway, and Mike was working on the mower with one eye watching Marie's reaction, when Gladys the mail lady handed Marie the mail. He was every bit as excited as Marie, but he just didn't show it outwardly as much as she did. With one eye on his project at hand and one eye on Marie, it was difficult to say which was the more important thing he was focusing on.

Mike saw the mail car coming down the road. It was Gladys, all right. No other car made that *I'm on my last leg* sound more prominently than Gladys' car. She stopped up the road first at the Glenn house, and then at the Thomas house. In a moment, it would be their turn, and he would either have a happy wife or a miserable one. And he was really hoping for a happy wife. The food at dinner tasted much better coming from a happy wife.

Gladys' car puttered and sputtered its way down Crain Road on its way down to the Knox farm's mailbox. It seemed as though Gladys was going as slow as she possibly could. " Let's get this over with," Mike thought to himself. "Am I getting a meal or a sandwich tonight?"

It seemed like an eternity was passing before him, but the old rickety car finally made it to where Marie was standing by the mailbox. A bundle was handed to her, and then she was off again. A few seconds after Gladys departed, Mike could see his wife waving a letter in her hand. He knew then that he was going to eat good tonight.

Marie hooted and hollered. "Mike, we have two letters today," she exclaimed. "We have two."

She couldn't have been any happier than if she had hit the lottery. She ran into the house and waited for her husband to come in, too. After a few seconds, she opened the door. Mike wasn't moving fast enough for her.

"Are you coming in or what?" she said.

Mike hopped off the mower and moseyed up to the main house. He was excited, too, but he wasn't going to put on a spectacle like Marie just had. He walked into the house and found himself staring at Marie, who was now sitting at the kitchen table. She was waiting like a kid at Christmas for her father to allow her to open up her presents.

"Are you ready?" She motioned for him to have a seat. She didn't want to read the letters to someone looming over her shoulder.

He pulled his chair out, sat down, and waited. "Go ahead and read the damn letter," he said. "What are you waiting for?"

Marie smirked. "I think I will let that one pass, only because I'm in too good of a mood to let your negativity bring me down."

"Negativity? What negativity? I'm just asking you to read the thing before he gets back home." Mike waved his hand as if to dismiss her foolishness.

Marie ripped open the first of the two envelopes. It had the oldest postmark of the two. "Okay, here we go," she said, and she started reading aloud to a very attentive Mike Knox.

Dear Mom and Dad,

Well, I'm still at Aberdeen, and I wish I could talk to you in person, but the best I can do for now is write to you. The other guys are teasing me because I write so many letters. But I don't pay any attention to them. Don rags on me a lot about my mom sewing an awful long apron string, and that you must be one great seamstress. I tell him to go jump in a lake. You know that he grew up in an orphanage, and that he lost his parents, but when we get back home we're going to open up a hardware store or landscaping company, or maybe a construction business or something like that together. We have already talked about it, and we are going to be big.

I hope that everything there is going well. I got your last letter, and it sounded like you and Pop are doing good. I know it's different there without my smart butt running around and making trouble. I will be home before you know it, though. Tell Peanut to stop crapping on the porch. We have acres of grass to crap on, and he wants to crap there? That dog is getting lazier and lazier. Kick him in the butt the next time he does that.

Tell Pop to just leave all the stuff in the barn alone and we'll get it straight when I get back. None of that stuff is worth hurting his back over. If Don comes back the same time I do, then the two of us can do it for him.

They've been working us like dogs here, Mom, and I don't like it one bit. I think they are trying to kill us before we leave here, but I can say I'm in the best shape of my life. Mom, you won't even recognize me. I look like a very handsome gorilla, with muscles popping out everywhere.

Got to go for now, Mom and Pop, but I will write you again tomorrow.

Your Loving Son, Andrew

Marie stopped reading there. She looked up at Mike with tears streaming down her face. "He is a good boy, Mike, he really is," she said.

"Yep."

She grabbed the hem of her apron and wiped her face. "Let's read the second one, shall we?"

"I think that is a *mawvelous* idea, Mrs. Knox," he said with a British James Bond accent. Not a good impression, but it was an attempt at one, as Marie liked to describe it.

Marie ripped open the second letter and a single page was inside. She unfolded the paper and began to read its contents aloud.

> **Dear Mom and Dad,**
>
> *I am almost done with basic, and we will be learning where we're being shipped soon. No one knows where they are going yet. We could be in Korea, I'm told. We could be in the States. Some are going to Germany, and some may be going to the Middle East. No one knows, but we should know in about two weeks. I will let you know as soon as I know. It was good talking with you the other night on the phone. I was beginning to think that they didn't even have a phone around here. I guess they didn't want any of us to get all homesick in the beginning. And I guess I can understand that.*
>
> *I just wanted to say hi and tell you that I was thinking about you guys. Kick Peanut in the butt for me, and tell him to be good. I love you guys.*
>
> **Your Loving Son, Andrew**

Marie began to cry all over again. She missed her little boy so much that her heart ached. She missed him, she feared for him, and she wanted him home where he belonged.

Mike got up and walked around to his wife's side of the table. He put his arm around her shoulders. "He is going to be home before you know it," he said. "In a couple years, he is going to be a man. A man that we are both going to be so proud of. He will have benefits from the Army that we could never give him. We're just going to have to suck it up and support him and have faith that everything will be okay. We can be the kind of parents who remind him every day that we are proud of him, and we miss him, and that we love him."

Mike knew he was right, but it didn't make swallowing all of the crap he had just spewed any easier.

Marie knew that he was right, too, but she would throw all that away just to have Andrew home right now. She had heard too many bad things about kids coming home battered, bruised, and missing limbs or screwed up in the head. She didn't want that for Andrew. She wanted him home and not having flashbacks about buddies getting blown up or twitching every time a car backfired.

She watched as Mike went out the door mumbling something about getting back to work. In reality, she knew he just wanted to be alone when he shed his tear or two.

Mike did not turn around as he walked out of the house. Getting these letters from Andrew was a double-edged sword. It made Marie happy, but at the same time made her miserable, which in turn did not make Mike very happy at all. Her fears were valid fears. They both had friends who had lost someone who they loved in this stupid war. Mike had a friend who lost a brother and a son in a country that he had never even heard of before last year.

He walked into the barn, and as he picked up the shovel to excavate some manure from the barn, he just let the tears fall down his cheeks. He was so mad at having to be brave and having to act like he was okay. He wasn't okay. He wanted his son home, and he wanted him safe. He knew with the way things were going over there that there was a better chance that Andy would end up over there than not. They talked about low numbers on the news almost every night, and that only meant that the boys who did sign up were almost destined to go over there. He knew that Andy was not a fighter. He was doing this to make his father proud, and for that, a heavy burden of guilt lay upon Mike's shoulders like a cinderblock.

He shoveled and cried, shoveled and wiped his face and cried some more. He could see the droplets hitting the concrete. He could feel a sticky, clammy moisture covering his cheeks. He was not above shedding a tear, but if he believed in the stupid war, he knew it would have been different. But he didn't. He didn't think Americans should be over there at all. He knew that those people would be fighting over something a thousand years after he was long gone, and it burnt him up to think that the government thought that it was okay to lose our children for a cause that we had no right butting our noses into.

He wiped his face and eyes and leaned the shovel back up against the stall. He wanted to believe in the war, he really did. He believed in his country and all that it stood for, but this time he thought the government was dead wrong, and it made sending his son off to fight in it all the worse. This war was all about money, and who could get the most of it. He understood fighting the Nazis, and he understood fighting the Civil War, but this he did not believe in. He would never fully understand having the balls to tell another country how to live their lives if the only people they were hurting was themselves. He was not a prejudiced or racist man, which made this smear propaganda he heard on the news every night a hard thing to take. He didn't want his son lumping every Persian or Pakistani up in the same raghead mentality no more than he wanted them lumping every American into the KKK. There was so much that he and Andy still had to enjoy before he became worm food. He wanted his boy home, and he wanted him home *now*.

But he forced himself to shake off the cowl of self-pity. He was acting as if Andy was already dead. He had to stop that right now, because Marie would surely pick up on it, and he knew his wife very well. She would feed off of it until it drove her crazy.

As he exited the barn, he shook off the tears and the doubt and threw back on his happy face, his *everything is going to be okay* face. He had to do it for Marie, even though he could barely keep from crying some days.

There was too much work that needed to be done. He walked over to the mower and picked back up where he'd left off before the mail lady had arrived.

Marie could see Mike walking around outside through the kitchen window. He looked as though he was deep in thought, trying to remember what the hell he was even trying to do. She wondered if he truly thought that she couldn't see the redness in his eyes or hear the coarseness in his throat. She knew all too well the signs of someone who had been crying, or who was about to. *Does he really think he had to hide it?* she thought to herself. She loved him for his attempt, but at the same time, she wanted to be there for him just like he was for her. He was her rock, and he was just as lost to her as Andy was, as far as she was concerned. She had shed many a tear for the both of them.

Mike tried to keep his mind off of everything else in this unfair world except for this old Briggs and Stratton riding lawn mower that he was trying to revive again. A temperamental piece of equipment if ever there was one. It wanted to run only when it wanted to. Many a time, it was like playing rock, paper, scissors with it. Sometimes the farmer won, and sometimes the mower won.

He yanked on the pull cord, but a single spark of life was all he got out of the ancient relic. He had a small patch of grass in front of the house that he liked keeping tidy for Marie, but every year it was getting harder and harder to do so.

He primed the carburetor, but still no luck. He was about to give up, when finally, on the seventh or eighth pull, the mower stayed running. He figured he'd better get this grass mowed before it died again. With the mower at full throttle, he walked it over to the small patch of grass. He thought about how many times he would look over and see Andy riding this piece of crap. The mower was almost as old as Andy was, in fact. It seemed like Andy was just seven or eight years old when he'd started riding this thing around.

Mike was in another world. It was true that in the real world, he was mowing grass, but his mind was a million miles from home. He envisioned his son in uniform trying to keep his head down. He saw his boy trying to save another guy's life after he was hit in the leg by a sniper rifle. He saw everything as clear as if it were happening to him. He had seen action back in Korea, and he'd witnessed the very things that Andy might be in store for. But he could never share these things with Marie. It would give her nightmares for a month, or maybe even longer.

He knew what it was like to see a buddy's arm nowhere near the rest of him, or to try and drag a dead, lifeless body out of the line of fire. To see that look in a comrade's eyes, a look that got Mike choked up to this very day. The look that told him they'd just realized that tomorrow is not a word in their vocabulary anymore. He had seen horrific acts that no man should ever see. And he didn't want those things for Andrew. He tried to block them out, but he knew in his gut that his son was not going to be the same when he got home. No one knew this better than him. He could pray that he wouldn't see any action, but in the pit of his stomach, he knew that Andy would see something that would change him forever before he got home.

Marie watched as Mike made zigzag lines in the grass. She could tell that he had no idea that he wasn't going in a straight line. But she figured some grass mowed was better than none, and she left him alone. Going out there to try and comfort her husband wouldn't do any good. He was a very proud man, and breaking down and crying was not an option. She let him be. She knew Mike, and she knew that leaving him alone was the best thing that she could do for him right now.

Marie reached up to the top of the refrigerator and pulled out her spiral notebook and pen, and then walked slowly over to the kitchen table. The notebook had Andrew's name written across the front of it in big bold letters with blue marker. She couldn't pour her heart out to Mike, so Andrew was the next best thing. She pulled out the chair and sat down. There were tears welling up in her eyes, but she pushed them back. She took her thumb and index finger and squeezed the bridge of her nose, straightened up her back, and held the pain at bay. She flipped the pad open, and with strong feelings pouring through her head, she allowed them to be transferred from there to the blue ballpoint pen and finally to the paper. She wanted Andrew to know those feelings as well.

She clicked the pen and began writing.

Dear Andrew,

We all miss you around here, but I know you already know that. I miss you so much that it hurts me to think about it. It's not easy for a mother to come to grips with what Washington is asking of me, but I'm trying so very hard, son, I swear it.

I see your face everywhere. I hear your voice everywhere. I think even Peanut hears you sometimes. On occasion, he will perk his ears up and I could swear that he thinks he hears you coming down the drive. And yes, on occasion I will peek my head up and look out the curtain, too. I know, I know, I ain't sane. I can only say it's because I miss you in so many ways, but I don't think I have enough paper to write all of them down. If anything happens to me before you get back, there are a few things I just want you to know. It was an honor being part of your life, and no mother had a better son. I mean that with all my heart. You are a great son, and your compassion, your generosity, and your heart has always been something that I could count on. I just wanted you to know that.

Your Loving Mother

Marie broke down and sobbed. She couldn't go any further with all the things that she wanted to say. Images of her son flooded her thoughts. The tears fell on the paper like raindrops, and she saw so many scenarios of her son's return home, but she still couldn't shake that uneasy feeling. She was so scared for her boy. He was in such danger, or he would be soon, and she saw the evidence every day on the television that good boys were dying or coming back with half of their bodies gone. And she knew that it didn't matter how hard you prayed—they still were not like the boys they'd been when they left. Thousands of mothers were never going to get to see their little boys again, and it's all because those big shots in Washington can't play nice.

She wanted to go and kick every one of them in the behind. She got a brief smile on her face at the thought of lining each one of those good-for-nothing politicians up against a wall and kicking the tar out of each and every one of them. She was not a fan of the majority of the people who stood on Capitol Hill. There were no more honorable people left in Washington. There were only greedy, money-grubbing snakes, if you were to ask her opinion. They cared about one thing and one thing only—money, money, and more money.

She straightened up and dried her eyes with a napkin on the table. This wasn't the first nor the last time she would sit here and sob, and the scariest thing of all to her was holding onto hope. Hope that Andy would not go overseas, or hope that he would come back exactly as he had left. She knew that it was not realistic. She could tell in his letters that he was becoming more and more independent, and even though his letters told of how much he loved them both, it seemed as though each one got shorter and shorter. She could see the writing on the wall, and it said that he was becoming a man and didn't need his mother as much anymore. It made her so mad, but as Mike had said, it was inevitable.

She left the letter on the table and got up to look out the window at Mike. He was still mowing the same postage stamp of grass. She tried not to make this all about her, but she still thought, *why did this have to happen? Why did they have to do this to her?* She hated this war, and she hated the bullies running it just as much.

She stared out the window and just watched her husband mow the grass. She hoped that he wouldn't run into a tree. In the daze that he seemed to be in, it wouldn't surprise her in the slightest if he did.

She wiped her hands on her apron and walked out the door. It was time to put a stop to this foolishness before he ran himself into the side of the barn.

I MISS YOU TOO, MOM

Andrew sat in his bunk and read his mom's most recent letter. It was a long one this time. She must have had a lot to get off her chest, or maybe there were more exciting events than usual happening on the farm. The latter, he doubted.

He read the letter once, and then twice, and then even a third time. He knew in his heart that she wasn't referring to whether something might happen to her—she was referring to whether something might happen to *him*. It didn't take a rocket scientist to figure out that she was terrified that something was going to happen to him. He knew all too well the different scenarios that could play out. He could wind up pushing paper at the Pentagon or pushing up daisies in Afghanistan. And what would happen to his parents if he weren't around, he wondered? He actually knew all too well what would happen. His mother and his father would become hermits. His mom would break down at every little thing, and his Pop would spend all his time out in that damn barn finding things to do so that he wouldn't think about it all the time. He was sure of it. He saw his parents every day until now, and he knew them almost as well as they knew themselves.

He broke out of his daydream when one of the guys came in. Francisco was a clown like Andy was. He loved to make the guys laugh while he told his stories from when he lived in New York City. His stories were funny, mostly because of that thick Brooklyn and Long Island accent of his. Everything he said sounded like it came right out of a Bogart gangster film. He would tell the bumpkins about all the hookers and drug dealers and stuff like that that he saw every day.

Most of the guys there in basic were indeed country bumpkins, and they knew how to milk a cow better than how to unsnap a bra with one hand. Andy included himself in that category as well. He knew his experience with women peaked at getting a feel from Gina Rolono out on the playground playing softball. It wasn't on purpose, but he remembered how nice and soft she felt when she fell on top of him. He remembered that day fondly. He always wished he had had the nerve to ask her out that day, but his courage didn't blossom until after she had left for Wyoming or somewhere with her parents. That was one thing he knew he would always regret.

Francisco—or, as they called him, Frisco—came over to ask why he was in the barracks all by his lonesome. "Why you here all by yourself?" he said. "It ain't like they give us too much time to enjoy for ourselves. Why don't you come over?"

Frisco knew why he was here. He was pining over his mommy. It didn't take a genius to figure out what he was reading. He and the guys would have thought that it was a girlfriend, the way he reads the letters, but he wasn't the only one missing a mother. A lot of the guys secretly shed a tear into their pillow two or three times a week.

"I'm cool, Frisco," he said. "I'm just writing a few letters. I've been neglecting my duties to my adoring public." Truthfully, he was sad. And he was scared. He was wondering if he should have stayed his ass home and worried about taking care of his parents instead of doing jumping jacks in the middle of nowhere. After reading his mother's letter, he was sick to his stomach. Even though she was referring to him not coming home, he still had to think about the vague possibility that *she* might not be there when he came home. That thought hadn't crossed his mind until now, and he hated himself for leaving her.

A cold sweat washed over him, nothing but guilt. He was drenched in it. He felt like he was a self-involved little twit who was only thinking of himself, and he knew that that wasn't the real him, but it didn't make the guilt go away any easier.

Frisco could see that he was about two seconds away from crying, so he just backed off. He went back over to his bunk, three bunks down.

"I hear ya, boy," he said. "You tell all those girls that you're bigger now, and so is your peter. Tell them to stay faithful until you get back to them."

Frisco knew that Andy was reading his mom's letter, but he figured it would make him feel better if he thought that the guys figured he had a bunch of girls waiting on him. Frisco was sure this kid was a virgin, and probably hadn't seen any hair pie except in magazines.

"Yeah, I see you've been eyeing me up in the showers again," said Andy. "I've been telling them all that. I told them that it's hard to hold in one hand nowadays. I think they know it was big enough before, and now I don't want to scare them, but to tell the truth, I'm scared I may hurt them bad."

"That's what you think, huh?" said Frisco with a smile.

"Yeah, I mean if I have to whip it out, I will. I'm pretty sure I could pole vault with this thing. I don't want you to get jealous or anything, though."

Andrew liked bullshitting with Frisco. He was a pretty cool guy to just trash talk with. He never took it too far, unlike some of the guys here, who seemed to be all pumped up on their own egos.

"Okay, whip it out," said Frisco, "but if it's bigger than mine, I'm going to rip it off so I can still have the biggest one. Go on, stand up and show it to me."

In reality, he knew that this guy probably had to jerk off with tweezers.

"Let me get back to writing my letter, you pervert," said Andy. "I always knew you wanted to handle my junk. I don't want to see you sneaking around my bunk late at night trying to get a peak."

"If I did, Andy, it would only be to smother you with your own pillow. Keep that in mind, you big-petered freak you."

Frisco punched him in the arm on the way out. As he got close to the door, Andrew called out, "Don't be jealous! Yours might get bigger, too."

Frisco turned and simply said, "Tweezers, little man, tweezers," and then walked out through the barracks door.

Andrew wasn't quite sure what that meant, but he assumed it meant something about needing tweezers to find his dick. When in fact he knew where it was, but just wished there was more to see.

Andrew rolled over and stretched out on his stomach. He got out his notepad and started writing. He figured he had to do something for his mom so that she knew that he missed her, too, and that they would see each other soon. Then he got a spark of creativity. He would write her a poem, and that would make her feel better. Mothers always liked when their kids did something creative to show their love. He remembered the one time he had made his mom a birdhouse to stick outside the front window. She went on and on about that birdhouse like it had been crafted by Bob Villa or something.

There was a time where everything that he made got put up on the refrigerator, or the knick-knack shelf. He was sometimes surprised that he didn't see some bronzed poopy diapers up on the mantle. He remembered one time when his dad got in trouble for taking the works of art off the fridge so that he didn't have to keep bending down to pick them up every time he opened the door. And he remembered his mom acting like he had defiled the *Mona Lisa*. It did make him feel good, but at the same time, it made him realize that his mother was plum crazy, as he liked to think of her. He loved her craziness, though, and anyone who would say a word against her would have to deal with him.

He smiled at the thought of someone actually thinking that he intimidated anyone.

He sat back and thought of things that rhymed with *mom* or *dad* or *love* or *missing you.* He went through them in his head: *love, dove, stove, move, nove, rove. You, moo, coo, noo, soo, too, flu.* This was not going to be easy.

He went over all of the things that made up a good poem. *I love you. I miss you.* What would make his mom cry with joy, he wondered? Then he stopped writing poetry and just started writing. He figured the words would come to him.

Hey Mom,

It's been five or six weeks since I've seen you, but my God, it seems like so much longer. I can't remember the

*last time I had a really good home-cooked meal. I mean,
one of your famous pork chops would really hit the spot
right now. Oh yeah, and your mashed potatoes, too.
Hmm, I can taste them now, all smothered in gravy. God,
I miss you and Dad. I know you will be fine until I get
home. I mean, if you aren't there, me and Dad will starve
to death. Just don't help Dad with anything too heavy or
dangerous, and you will be just fine. I feel kind of guilty
about not writing in a few days, but they've been keeping
us really hopping here. I now know how to strip a rifle
and put it back together with my eyes closed. I'm getting
bigger, too. I have muscles on top of my muscles. I mean,
if you compare me to five weeks ago...*

*I wrote you a poem to show you how I feel. Don't be too
harsh; I'm not the best poet.*

> *I can't wait to talk with you on the phone*
> *it helps me to feel not so totally alone*
> *No matter where they send me, or for how long*
> *you have to keep living and staying strong*
> *If you're not with me, there will be no reason*
> *To have a happy and joyful holiday season*
> *that I've been proud to be your son, every single day.*
> *You are my best friends, and you always took care of me*
> *every time I had a cough, or just skinned my knee.*
> *I know you and Dad will never know how much fun*
> *it is for me to be your ever-loving son.*

Your Loving Son, Andrew

He sat and reread the letter and poem a dozen times. It sounded about
as good as he could come up with. He knew that he'd never be an Ernest
Hemingway, but it didn't sound too bad. And as he was folding the letter,

he could hear the guys coming back. He hurried to put the letter in the envelope and seal it shut. He didn't want the guys to see him writing to his mommy.

Before the guys could come in, he had slipped his letter under his pillow. He would mail it tomorrow.

As Donny came in, he could see his friend sitting on his bunk, just relaxing. He knew he had to cheer him up. He could tell in the past few weeks that Andy was racked with guilt and fear. Not being afraid of the war, or getting hurt, but fear of never seeing his parents again. It didn't take Sigmund Freud to diagnose what was going on in this kid's head. The kind of fear that you have when you have a feeling in your gut and you don't know why it's there, but you can't get rid of it all the same. No amount of Pepto or Rolaids can quench that kind of nausea. Don knew it all too well. Not now, of course, but there had been a day when he too had that exact same gnawing at the pit of his stomach.

He flopped down next to Andy. "What you doing there, Wilma Lee?"

Andrew was appreciative of the attempt at humor, but today he just didn't have it in him. For the first time, he really, *really* realized how he had been so selfish and hadn't thought things through. He'd left his parents all alone, and it was only himself that should have been hurt by his decision. He thought someone should take a baseball bat to his face and just keep whaling away at him until he was someone else altogether. It wasn't rational, but he couldn't help it. No poem or phone call was ever going to make up for the rash, foolish thing that he had done to his parents.

"Not much, Roxie," he finally managed. "Just sitting here thinking about where we're headed next. Am I going to Pennsylvania to help control the Amish population, or am I going to Kaderbwewshgstan in the middle of some forgotten wasteland?"

"Where?" said Don with a stupid look on his face.

"You know what I mean. I can't roll my tongue properly to say most of those places over there. I can say Baghdad, I can say Iran, but most of the other names hurt my tongue."

"Do they now?" said Don. "I thought you were this smart kid who got straight A's in high school, and all the jocks beat up for being such a nerd?"

"It's true that I was that guy, but weren't you the guy behind all the jocks picking up all their dirty underwear?"

"That's the best you got, Wilma? I mean, *really*. I thought you were better than that? I bet even slowpoke Jacobs over there could have come up with something wittier than that."

They both looked over at Private Jacobs, who showed no sign of caring about their conversation. In fact, he looked like he was a million miles away from this place. Don and Andy cracked up laughing , and Don was glad to see that Andy's demeanor had changed a bit. He knew what Andrew could be like if he sunk too low into depression. It wasn't pretty to sit and stare at someone who looked like his dog had just died.

"I bet he is sitting over there thinking about how his life sucks so bad because he is so stupid," said Don, referring to Jacobs.

"Or he's thinking about how long he can stay in here before they realize how stupid he really is, and instead of giving him a gun, they give him the boot out of here."

Andrew was suddenly ashamed of himself. "I'm such a dick," he said.

"Yeah, you really are." Don busted out laughing at the hurt look on Andy's face. "Did I hurt your *whittle feewings* Miss Wilma?"

Andrew wanted to get up and punch him, but it seemed like that was just a bit too much effort to put out for his dumb ass. "You're no prize either, Lucy," he said instead.

"I wanted to talk with you about the letter I got today," said Don. "From some office in D.C. that says I'm going overseas after my time here is up."

Andy had a stupid look on his face again, but this time it had nothing to do with laughter. He was serious this time. "Dude," he began, "why didn't you tell me earlier?"

"I was going to, but you were all into writing home and shit. I didn't want to mess with you."

"Why not?" said Andy.

"Well, sometimes you're bummed out and you don't seem like you want to do stuff," said Don, "so I didn't want to pile more crap on you. I mean, you have your own stuff to deal with."

"I know, but this is big, dumbass. Where are you going? I mean, *when* are you going?"

"I guess we have two more weeks here, and right after that, I guess I'm going to Kabul until I get stationed somewhere else." Don paused for a second and then continued. "You haven't got anything yet?" he asked.

"No, I haven't heard shit. I just wrote my mom telling her the same thing. I thought I would know something by now, but they want to fuck with my head and keep me on pins and needles, I guess. They must have learned their tactics from Bob Burnside. He's the one who probably told them to hold off and let me sweat a few more days. He can be such a dick, you know?"

"That's all well and good, but we're talking about me right now, and I want to bitch about them sending me half way around the world to stand guard on some major's Johnny-on-the-spot so he don't get shot while taking a shit."

"I hear you, brother. I wouldn't be happy either," said Andy. "Kabul—isn't that where all the fighting is? I mean, is there anyone else going there with you?"

"I've heard a few of the guys talk about getting letters, but I think some got them today, and some like you are still waiting," said Don. "I know Doug Harrison is going to Kabul, but I don't know where any of the others are going."

"Hold on a sec."

Andrew stood up on his bunk and addressed the other guys in the barracks. "Excuse me, guys, but who has received their orders for where they're going next?"

Of the ten or so guys in the barracks, about half raised their hands. Harrison, Jacobs, Smith, and Tyler were the closest to him. Andrew asked, "Where are you going, then? Because my papers must be lost in the freaking mail or something."

Doug Harrison spoke first. "I'm on my way to Kabul in about two weeks, but I don't know where everyone else is going."

Don spoke up then. "Yeah, we're both going to Kabul. Any of you guys going there?"

Jacobs and Smith both shook their heads in unison.

Tyler spoke next. "I'm going to some backwater place in Maryland called Fort Meade in Glen Burnie, or some shithole like that. I bet they don't even have a grocery store big enough to put a Humvee in. From my research on the place, I'm going to be the smartest guy there."

Andrew said, "That won't say much for the learning curve in that town, if you are. I mean seriously, Tyler, you're about as smart as a tree frog. No, you're maybe as smart as the bark that the tree frog is pissing on."

Tyler just laughed along with the others. "Well, I guess I would rather be dumb and be carrying around a big dick than an A student and jerkin' a gherkin. I hear there's a lot of protein in your diet there, Andy. No wonder you have such a shiny coat, you dink."

The guys busted out laughing. Don halted his laughter for a moment to say, "I didn't know you were so witty there, Tyler. I thought Andy was right about that leaf and all."

Tyler finished, "I can be witty when I'm in the right company, but hanging around you two would have brought my I.Q. score down thirty points, so I just kept quiet. I know you understand, Don, so explain it to your friend."

"I thought we were friends, Tyler," said Andy. "And this is how you treat me?"

"We are, Knox," said Tyler, "but I'm glad I'm going to Glen Burnie rather than hoping your ass is what's between me and a coffin."

The laughter stopped. They all knew that he was dead serious. It was the opinion of many, but he had just said it aloud. He did like both Andy and Don, but he knew this wasn't a game, either.

Andy just said simply, "Okay, Tyler, I get you. I'm glad too."

He spun around back to Don. "So, it looks like Kabul is the hot spot this year. I hope they have good beaches."

Tyler didn't say anything else, but Andy knew that those kinds of remarks were what he was referring to. The ones that led everyone to believe he was just an immature kid. He hadn't realized until now that he was the weak link and that he was stopping a lot of them from taking things more seriously. He knew that Tyler and the guys didn't hate him, but he knew that they didn't like him much, either.

Don was beginning to see the others' point. Andy was too much of a jokester. He knew in his heart that Andy would have his back no matter what, but was it enough?

"Well," he began, "they don't have to have good beaches as long as I get home safe. I can go to the beach when I get home."

Jacobs and Smith chimed in. "I here you, man," said Jacobs, and Smith said, "That's exactly how I feel, too." They all high-fived each other and tried to conceal the fact that they were scared as shit.

Andrew watched the three guys high-five, and for some reason, he felt left out. It wasn't a club you wanted to be joined up with, unless you were a bit sociopathic or psychopathic. Anyone who would want to go four thousand miles away from home to blow people's heads off had one or two screws loose to begin with.

"I wish they would let me know where I'm going, for God's sake," he said. "This is bullshit, I tell you. I want to know, and I want to know *now*."

Jacobs watched as Andy puffed out his feathers a bit, and he wondered if Andy was as petrified as they were. They kind of assumed that it was worse not knowing. You could be going halfway across the world or be staying in your own back yard. Jacobs knew from his own experience that he was both glad and pissed off at the same time. He would have something to be proud of later, but what if he didn't come home? Or what if he came home without feet or legs or arms? What if he came home throwing himself on the ground every time a car backfired? He wasn't sure that it was fair to put anyone through that, even if it was to protect his country. He figured he was a coward at heart.

Andrew did indeed want the unknown to be over with, but he was aware that as long as he didn't know, the gods could wave their hand and he could possibly get some cushy job in San Francisco or Miami guarding alligators. He didn't realize how scared he would be now when he had started this venture. He wanted his parents to be proud, but the guys heard all the time about other guys who didn't make it home, or guys who came back all fucked up. Andrew was getting messed up just thinking about it, and he hadn't even gone anywhere.

"I just want them to tell me so my mother will stop worrying," he said. "It's not fair to her."

He failed to mention that he was about to poop his pants.

Don spoke up to kill the tension. "I'm sure you'll be told in the next day or two. I think everyone will know in the next few days. Just sit back, little fella, and keep a change of undies on hand."

"It will be just my luck that I end up with Tyler in Glen Burnie peeling potatoes and cleaning out latrines," said Andy. But if truth be told, he would be just fine with that.

"Well, just sit back, and they will give you a plane ticket," said Don. "And if it's someplace you can pronounce, you'll be fine."

Don figured that it was time to change the subject to something a little less gloomy.

BOB BURNSIDE

Bob was not the most liked person on base by any stretch of the imagination, and he knew it. Officers as well as cadets found him a bit abrasive, to say the least. There was not a whole lot to be said for his winning personality, which was mostly because of his disposition. He never laughed. He never found any joke funny, and he very rarely even wanted to have human contact other than a chat with his corporal.

He was sitting in his chair outside his office, looking out over the camp. It was late in the evening, and there was not much stirring at this hour. It was overcast, so there was not much to look at above the horizon, either. These cool evenings were getting darker sooner, and even though it wasn't that late, the darkness made it look much later than it was.

He was tired of being here. No, he was *sick and tired* of being here. He got reports every week, every day, of kids that he trained coming back in body bags or missing limbs. This was not the kind of war he was used to. These people drove up in cars and blew themselves up. He knew that his job was important, or so they told him, and so he tried to tell himself, but at the same time, he just wasn't feeling like being a drill sergeant anymore. There was no way to train people to survive suicide bombs. He wanted to contribute something besides showing snot-nosed kids how to blow their noses without accidently pulling the pin out of their grenade. Truth be told, he wasn't doing much of anything anymore except collecting a check.

He looked out at the vast emptiness which was Camp Aberdeen and he wondered how the hell he got there in the first place, and why the hell he was still there. The place reminded him a hundred different ways every day how much he hated it, but in fact, he mostly just hated himself. He thought someone could probably do a better job than he seemed to be doing. He pictured himself in the trenches actually killing the people that were threatening his country. He knew he should be out with the men who he trained, not here holding recruits' hands while they cried themselves to sleep. He should be in Afghanistan.

Burnside didn't sing the blues very often, but it was usually about this time when all the green horns were getting their papers that he knew for the most part which ones would make it back and which ones weren't ever going to see their mothers again. Every five months, he saw little kids come in and bigger bulkier kids go out. Every one of them just about hated his guts, and that was just how he wanted it. He tried his best to make sure that every single one of them wanted to spit in his face before they left camp. Some got it, but most didn't. And the ones that didn't weren't worth his time anyway.

Something in the distance coming out of the chow hall caught his eye. A couple of guys from barracks three. Mostly dipshits, he thought to himself, but as he knew from experience, not all were good and not all were bad. He saw Smith, Birch, and Harrison walking back to their bunks, and he could only guess that they were dead men walking. Just three dumbass teenagers who had only recently gotten weaned from their mother's teat. He knew that they were all going to the Middle East, and he figured the only way they would survive eighteen months was if they stayed in the latrine. It wasn't fun seeing toe tags walking around camp. But it was a side effect of the job—a job that he thought more and more about turning over to someone different than himself. He was hating this place more and more each day. He wasn't doing a damn bit of good here. He knew he should be overseas where he could do some real good. His boss and his boss knew it too, but just because they wanted a yes man over there meant he had to stay here and wipe snot filled noses. The fact that he didn't tell them all to go to hell ate him up some nights.

He knew mostly who was going where next, and most of this crew was going overseas to relieve the ones who had already been there a while and had earned their points. There were a lot of guys who were close to coming home, but who just didn't hear that last bullet whiz past them. He heard all about it from the officers—the enlisted men who lost a brother, from magazines, from the cute blonde bar maids who were just listening to some customer sob in his beer after losing a brother, cousin, nephew. He knew they weren't all dumbasses, but it seemed as though he only heard about the ones who were.

He laid his head back against the cool window pane and envisioned himself in the trenches with his boys, the ones who he considered worthy of him remembering. These were the ones he considered to be bred for just this kind of mission. He could see them walking into a village, weapons at the ready, and wiping out the people who had killed so many of his friends. He could see himself saving one of his boy's lives who weren't paying close enough attention to the sneaky bastard hiding in the barrel, or the little lump of dirt rising from the otherwise flat roadway. He saw it all as if he had already lived it, and to be stuck here just plagued him.

The rum he was sipping made him more hateful with every swallow. He hated the army for sticking him in this stink hole and telling him he was needed here and that he was doing himself and his country proud. He had to be a true American and fight the urge to go kill and instead train others to do it. He had heard the rhetoric so many times that it made him want to puke all over his captain's shoes. He wasn't needed here. Any blind monkey could do what he was doing. The way he saw it, he was being punished. He'd been exiled by some shit-eating colonel who should have been bitch-slapped instead of promoted, and in his mind, he wanted to be the one doing the slapping.

Burnside took a big swallow from his glass and yelled, "Here, here!"

He had never become an officer—not because he didn't think he deserved it. He knew he deserved it. His problem, which was explained to him on many occasions by those same officers, was that he'd never knew how to play the game. He'd never learned the politics necessary to become an officer. He drank a bit too much. He mouthed off a bit too much. He mouthed off to the wrong people a bit too much. He heard it all, and it was like a skipping record playing in his head. He thought about it long and hard in the wee hours of the night, on some nights just like this one. He couldn't help it if those pansy ass officers couldn't take a real man telling them to get their heads out of their asses.

The only captain he respected was Captain Morgan. He was always there when Burnside needed him, and Morgan agreed with everything that he said. Burnside raised his glass and saluted the ceiling. "Here's to you, Captain. You know exactly what I'm talking about."

He stood up, walked inside and over to the desk next to his bunk, and grabbed the fifth to fill up his "empty soldier," as he called it. After filling up his soldier again, he sat down at his desk and looked over some files describing all the soldiers in his command on this particular time around. He scanned the names, pointed, and almost yelled, "Dead, dead, maybe, maybe dead, most definitely dead," and with each name he perused, he realized that he hated them all. He hated them with a passion. Why not just snap their necks here, and save the plane fare? They weren't going to do anything but go over there and get their fool heads blown off, and there wasn't one thing that he could do about it.

He pulled out Birch's file and looked over the notes that he'd made over the past few months. It was obvious that this guy wasn't going to do anything but come home in pieces. He wasn't a soldier. *He is a moron*, thought Burnside. He hung around that waste of space Knox, and for that reason alone he should be taken out back and shot.

Burnside pushed all the files on the floor. "All you monkey dicks are dead, and you just don't know it yet," he said. He stood up and went back to his bottle, pouring himself another big swig. "All you motherfuckers should wake up and smell the funeral roses."

After that outburst, he was shocked to see his door open quickly and his commanding officer Captain James standing at his door. As drunk as he was, he still tried to muster what resembled a salute. "Yes, Sir!"

Captain James was less than thrilled with his sergeant's condition. "I could hear you all the way outside, Burnside. Is there a reason you hollered for me to come in here?"

"No, Sir!"

Burnside was obviously caught off guard, and with his proverbial pants down. His inner voice was screaming to tell this young fart to go suck on a howitzer, but he caught himself. "I did not call you, Sir!"

Captain James knew that Burnside used to be a good soldier, but now these outbursts were getting too frequent. The cadets could smell the booze, and it was just making a mockery of everything he stood for. James could see that he was just burnt out. He wasn't the first soldier to find solace in a whiskey bottle. He'd been lenient with him about his recent binges, but they were becoming too frequent for his liking. No matter how much pain the man was experiencing, there was no excuse. He realized that he was going to have to do something about Burnside's behavior. He needed a psychiatrist to help him deal with what he was going through, not a bartender.

James knew that Burnside thought he had a monopoly on self-hate and guilt. He too felt like he was raising baby chicks just to ship them off to the market. He felt no shame in admitting that he sometimes felt like drowning his sorrows, but he had a job to do. This job, no matter what his personal thoughts on the matter were, was an order to be completed, and that was that. This wasn't a perfect world where all the kids grow up big and tough and able to take care of themselves. This was a thankless job, and you had to pull yourself out of the self-pitying muck, grab your balls and suck it up until your commanding officer told you to do otherwise. And that was the one thing that his sergeant had seemed to forget.

Knowing that the sergeant was in no shape to listen to a speech, James didn't bother. He just simply said, "What'd your problem, soldier? I mean, I've heard you moan and whine and cry about being here, about pretty much everything except what you're doing wrong. I didn't put you here, nor did I ask for you to stay. You're here because some prick in Washington thinks you should be here, and for that, and that alone, you're going to get your shit together and stop throwing yourself these pity parties. If you don't think you can, then please do us all a favor and retire. Do I make myself clear, Sergeant?"

As much as his initial reflex was to kick this guy's teeth in, Burnside just stood there and said nothing. He wouldn't give this little prick the satisfaction of apologizing or justifying his actions. He just stood stone-faced with the lines of age covering his weather-beaten, hard life wearing brow.

Captain James was much younger than his shitfaced sergeant, but he was still responsible for his actions. He didn't agree with everything that came out of Burnside's mouth, but he did agree with one thing. He had pissed someone off, and that someone was Captain Lewis James.

At the top of his lungs, and inches away from Burnside's face, he screamed, "I'm not going to see this again, or you and I are going to have a serious problem! I'm not someone you want to piss off. Even if I do respect you, I'm not going to let things like this slide. I hope we understand each other, because I'd really hate to be the guy that busted your balls."

As he approached the door, he half-turned back to Burnside without facing him. "Get yourself together, or get the fuck out!" he said before turning again without another word and leaving the sergeant's room. There was nothing left to say.

Burnside watched as Captain James walked out. He gave him the finger to his back. He wanted to shove a hand grenade down his throat, but the finger would have to do for now.

Burnside didn't like being talked to like that, especially from some pimply-faced kid who had sucked on all the right shlongs. He didn't need this shit anymore. He had way more than his twenty in, and he'd felt like telling these people to go shove it up their asses more than once. He decided that he was going to quit first thing in the morning.

He flopped back on his bunk and leaned his head up against his backboard, and a big smirk on his face. He felt good about his decision to not see any more kids come in and have to explain to them why they were stupid for enlisting and that there was no glory in going over and killing someone. There was no Hitler anymore, and you weren't saving an orphanage or a bunch of starving people. You were there for one thing and one thing only, and that was protect the rich man's interests. But that doesn't sell too many books. Signing up didn't make you a bad person—it only meant that you were stupid. Burnside knew that the job had to be done, but not by these kids. It took real, seasoned men to go over and get this job done. Guys like him, guys who knew how to get the hard work done.

He was finished. He was done with this place, and these assholes who couldn't think for themselves, who just want a war story to tell their kids. He needed another drink to forget about the morons he was supposedly training.

He laid back on his bunk and imagined all the things he was going to do when he got out of there. He was going to call his best gal Jennifer and let her know that he was done for good. He was finished with it all, and he was ready to finally marry her. He knew that that would make her happy. He was going to tell her that this time was different. He had told her so many times that he was going to retire, but he never did. This time, though, he was done. He hated this place, these kids, and most of all, he hated that bastard James. He was sure of it this time.

His thoughts became fuzzy. The room started began to spin like a carousel. He was getting a bit groggy, and he didn't want to pass out. He started to see toe tags whirling around like a baby would see a mobile spinning above his crib. He wanted to bitch and whine and cuss some more. He wanted to, but the booze was taking its toll on him. He was out.

He would wake up in the morning with his chin in a pool of his own saliva, and one hell of a hangover pulsing through his head. He was living the life of a functional drunk. He got mad, he got drunk, he passed out, and then he did it all again the next day. And never once would he ever think he was the one with the problem.

RAYMOND REYNOLDS

There were many other guys in barracks nine with him, but Ray felt so alone. He knew the other men were kind of his friends, but truthfully, he knew just as they did that they would not be friends on the street. They were more associates than friends. He would not have fit in with most of these guys in any other context. Ray would've been the guy sitting at the lunch table with all the jocks in letterman jackets. Now he sat there on his bunk and wondered about what was next. He now knew, like most of the fellas, that he was going to Afghanistan. And he knew it wasn't what he wanted. What he wanted to do was shit in his shorts.

He didn't want the other guys to know how scared he was, but he felt so alone that it was almost paralyzing. Up until now, he'd been the prized pupil. He was the biggest and most obedient little soldier here, but in reality, he was still a kid who wanted his mother. He was the one that Burnside and everyone else thought as going to be fine, but at this very moment, he wasn't so sure.

How was he going to tell his mom? How was he going to tell her that he'd done something so stupid and dangerous, and that she wasn't going to be able to fix this one for him? His well-to-do family usually got him out of the shit storms that he got himself into. He'd never seen this side of the fence. He had never had to deal with the consequences of his actions before.

He remembered back to the guy who had come to his school and who hadn't talked about this side of enlisting. He only told stories Ray would be able to tell his grand kids and when bullshitting with the guys at the bar about how cool it had been to see the world. Now, he was just pissed off about it all. He wanted to punch that guy in the face right about now. He wanted to put his fist down his throat and rip his heart out for bullshitting ignorant kids into giving up their lives for something they knew nothing about.

Patriotism, heroism, and seeing exotic lands was a load of crap, he thought. He had never been told about assholes like Burnside screaming in your face for hours on end. He hadn't been told about having to scrub the floors of bathrooms that a hundred guys had just pissed all over. He surely had never been told about this gut-wrenching stomach ache that he had had for the past two days.

Ray was mad at everything and everyone. *How dare they trick me into this bullshit*, he thought. He wondered how many of the other guys felt like the idiot that he did. He felt like the coyote on those cartoons.

He saw other guys on their bunks writing letters, which was no odd sight, but there seemed to be more writing in the past two days than before. Many guys helped pass the time by writing their parents or their girls or, for some, their congressman, asking them to get them the fuck out of there.

Ray pulled a pen and paper out from under his pillow. He too wrote a lot to help pass the time, but mostly just to stop the voices in his head telling him to run.

There was no sense in pretending anymore. He was big, and he was a great soldier, but that was all well and good there at camp where he was safe. Now that he knew where he was going, his mouth was dry and his shorts weren't. How low would he have to sink in order to ask his dad to make a few calls? Could he ever live with himself? Could his dad get him reassigned to somewhere like France, or England, or maybe Mexico? It had gone through his head, but how would he say it without asking?

He didn't know how to start the letter to tell his mom that he was going to Kabul. *"Hi, Mom, I'm going to Afghanistan?"* Or: *"Hi, Mom, I'm not going to be anywhere near home for Christmas?"* How about: *"Hi, Mom, I guess you heard about me being shipped to the Middle East?"*

He wondered whether, upon hearing the news, his parents would take it upon themselves to get him stationed somewhere in the States. He shrugged off the smart-ass comments running through his head, took his pad and flipped it open to the next blank page. He knew this letter was not going to be easy to write. He went over it in his head, but nothing sounded like it should be written down on paper.

Ray sat staring at the wall, the other guys, the windows. Nothing was inspiring him to write a beautiful letter letting his mom know that he loved her but that he wouldn't be back soon. He knew what he wanted to say, but how would he say it? He was so sorry. He was torn between the fear of getting killed and the fear of his siblings growing up without him.

Dear Mom and Dad,

I got my orders today, and I just wanted to let you know that I'm going to Kabul in a few weeks. That is, unless some miracle happens and I get stationed somewhere else. That isn't very likely, since God is about the only person who can get me out of this jam. I guess maybe it won't be too bad. I will help my country.

He had to stop there. He could give a shit less about this country, but he hoped that his father caught his hidden request. Then he decided to really throw down the gauntlet.

I will be able to show my kids that it might have been horrible to go through, but at least some good came out of it. I know you love me, and I know you both know I love you too. I wish I could be there with you, especially since Christmas is coming up soon. I'll write to you again soon, I promise. For now, just know that I love you and I hope I will see you soon.

Love, Raymond

He wanted to add more, but he didn't want to make his point too blunt. He figured that if they were going to step in, that would do it. If they didn't, he knew he was fucked.

He tore the paper from the pad and folded it neatly before placing it into the envelope.

Would his dad pick up the clues and get his buddies to do him a solid? Is his dad going to come through for him again? Just like he did the time he got arrested for spray-painting that bridge? Or the time he got a little too frisky with Penny Johnson after football practice? That stupid cow knew he was just playing around with her. He should have done a lot more than just grab her tit.

He knew his dad would come through this time, too. He just had to. He had thrown the dice, and instead of getting some cushy job in London, he had gotten thrown under the Baghdad bus. He felt so trapped. He'd alienated himself from most of the other guys there. Even the ones that he thought were his good buds got tired of being compared to him by Burnside. He knew that Burnside hadn't done him any favors by singling him out, but at the same time, it had made him a better soldier, and Burnside left him alone most days.

He had tried harder in the beginning to do more push-ups or pull-ups or whatever made him stand out as the best. But it wasn't doing him any favors now. It had just made him alone, very much alone. Recently, there had been times when he tried to understand how people lived a whole life of solitude, like monks. His thoughts would travel to some Shao Lin monk sitting by himself practicing some kung Fu. And then what? What do you do when even that finally becomes not enough? Ray had found himself at that point right now. He was the best soldier there, but the isolation and loneliness were deafening at times.

He watched as the guys wrote their letters, and the ones who didn't know yet were all huddled up in a corner over by Private Knox talking about their predictions about who, what, and where. Knox was a prick, Ray thought, but at least he was liked by most of the guys, even if he was a scrawny little broomstick. But as Ray would be happy to tell you, most of these guys were broomsticks compared to him.

He rolled over and punched his pillow a few times. Some nights it was Burnside's face in the pillow, and some nights it was Knox's. But most nights, it was his own.

DOUG HARRISON

Doug scanned the Barracks and saw what looked like a bunch of guys buried in pen and paper writing out what he figured was their last will and testaments. It was eerie, he thought to himself. Everything seemed to be moving in slow motion almost. It was as if they were in their own world, and no one else existed. He too was definitely not happy about going to Kabul, but he was happy to actually be doing something that meant a damn. His philosophy was that there was a huge difference between living and just existing. He knew that he may not come home, but he'd gladly die trying to do something that he thought was right, like fighting for his country, than sitting home and polishing his '52 Chevy that rarely left the driveway. He didn't want to just simply exist until someone said, "Hey, look at that old fart over there, I think he's dead."

He had seen it every day on the news with his dad when he was a kid. His dad thought there was something to be said to being honored for a day rather than simply surviving until some doctor pronounced you dead. Doug had a lot of his dad's ways about him. He had been reminded of that fact almost daily around his house when he was growing up. He ate the same as his dad, he crossed his legs like his father, and hell, Doug always figured they probably peed the same, too.

He had to write to his mom and tell her where he was going and when he was leaving. It wasn't going to be an easy letter to write, but just like everyone else was doing, it had to be written. Ever since his dad left a few years back, it was up to his mom to be the sole parent, and he knew that it wasn't easy for a woman with three kids to start over.

He wasn't hateful toward his dad. He didn't still love him the same way, but he was pretty much indifferent towards his memory. He thought of him as the garbage man. He knew he existed, but that didn't mean that Doug wanted to talk to him if he saw him walking down the street in front of the house. Doug remembered a lot about his father, but the emotion was gone. He saw his dad simply as a person who couldn't handle the pressure of being a dad anymore. His mother didn't speak ill of him after he left, either. Mostly she just cried. But for all the pain that his dad had caused, he'd still taught Doug one or two things about life. One of those things was that if you have the chance to be remembered, take it. He never forgot that about his father. He figured his dad was always regretful of missing his own chance. In some ways, he felt sorry for his dad, because that emptiness eventually swallowed him up.

Doug took out his piece of paper and wrote a bunch of things in the air, but the pen never reached the actual paper. The paper in front of him was still blank. *What should I write*? he thought. *How do I say it?*

He had sat down with his mom months before he enlisted and told her how he felt. He wanted to join and to learn everything he could. It was a great way to get an education, and possibly a security clearance so that he could eventually be making the big bucks. He knew his friend Jake's dad was rolling in the dough with his government job. He used the army to get where he was today, and Doug planned on doing the exact same thing. His mom and siblings would be able to sit back and not worry about anything. But what would they do until he got back, got educated, and got that cushy job?

He wasn't sure, but he knew that leaving them behind might have hurt them more than helped them. He figured he would send them what money he could until he got back. But he wasn't as sure about it all as he had been a few months ago, and he didn't know what laid in store for him, but he knew one thing: he would just die if anything happened to his family while he was gone. There were so many things that could happen, but if everything went according to plan, in five years he would be sitting on easy street, and so would his family. It wasn't a plan without risks, but it was a better plan than just hanging out watching television and scratching his balls for fifty years.

His mind wandered to one of his dad's favorites: "The Avon lady don't knock on doors anymore, boy. You have to make shit happen, and you might have to get fucked in the process of making it happen."

For a while now, he had felt that he had made a big mistake. His morale was in the toilet, and his attitude towards people was that of someone uncaring, unsympathetic, and callous towards his fellow man. He wasn't sure if that was the making of a sociopath or a psychopath. He always got those two mixed up. He knew that joining the army may have been a risky move, but for his own mental health, he knew he'd made the right decision. He hoped he had, anyway, and he hoped that his decision would someday make his mother proud of him. He wanted nothing more in life than that.

He was a good older sibling to his younger brother and sister, but he knew that most people would step on you and make you feel two inches tall before they would help you. He'd heard stories about how nice the South was, and he wasn't saying it wasn't true, but Virginia being in the South wasn't showing him much about that old myth being anything besides just a myth. All he saw were neighbors who pretended to be looking in the other direction as you drove by, or family who couldn't spare a few dollars when they needed rent money. In his opinion, the idea of family and neighbors coming through when you needed them was nothing more than a crock.

Maybe he would take his family down to Atlanta, or somewhere in that area. Maybe he had to go down where the mint juleps grew and where gentlemen still tipped their hats when a lady walked by. He wanted his mom to know that kind of life. Maybe not plowing the fields deep, but the deep South that had the nice parts that he always saw on television. That was what he wanted for his mom.

He didn't want to forget his brother and sister, either. He wanted Billy and Diane to see that life, too. Doug wanted a better life for them than cereal for dinner and holes in their socks. He could see it all in his head, but his head wasn't reality. He wanted to be their hero; he wanted to be someone that his brother and sister could look up to. He wanted to be someone who other people could go to as well. Hell, as far as he was concerned, his family wasn't something he was going to run out on. He wasn't going to be a dick that just up and left and then was never heard from again. That wasn't how he wanted to be remembered.

Doug started getting a bit misty-eyed. He tried not to think much about his dad and what he had done by leaving him and his siblings alone with their mother. At times he tried to forget that he had ever even existed, but then there were those times when he just wanted to see him on the street and bust him in the head with a pipe wrench. He wanted to stand over him and laugh as the blood poured from his skull. He was sane enough to know that it was crazy to feel that way, but he knew that most people would have similar fantasies in similar circumstances.

He rubbed the tears from his cheek and pulled himself together. He picked up his pen and grabbed his pad of paper off his footlocker. He wasn't completely sure of what he was going to say, but whatever he said, his mother was going to be a nervous wreck until he got home, so it didn't much matter. He and she both knew that this was a very real possibility, and whatever happened just happened. It was the gamble that he was willing to take, and he just prayed that he came back with all his fingers, toes, and eyeballs, and that his head was still screwed on straight.

He tapped the pen on his two front teeth, and then he began with.

Dear Mom,

I guess you know already that I love you and that I miss you. I mean, I guess that's a bit redundant, but I know you like hearing it anyway. I got my orders today, and I am going over to some place called Kabul, Afghanistan. I can't say exactly where that is on a map, but I'm sure it's sandy and hot. Probably hot enough to melt the tar on our roof. I just want you and Billy and Diane to know that I'll be thinking of you guys every single day, and when I get home, we are gonna have a big ol' feast, my treat. We're going to go to whatever restaurant you all want to go to. No matter where, Mom, I'll take you there and you can get whatever you want, I swear.

Let everyone know that I love them a lot, and if anyone messes with you while I'm gone, tell them that I'm going to come back and mess them up. You're going to be fine, Mom, but I wish I were home right now. Seeing your face and getting one of your home-cooked meals sounds pretty damn good right now. I know you're proud of me, and I just want to say thank you for raising me to be a good kid, and I will try and make you so proud while I'm gone.

You'll see when I see you again, you're going to hardly recognize me. I am a big galute now. I'm not as tiny as I was four months ago. I've probably done enough push-ups to count to a million. I bet I've done enough running to run around this whole state, too, maybe twice.

I have to go now, Mom, but you know I love you so much, and just saying that I miss you doesn't cover it. I see you everywhere, and this place is so cold, and no one loves anyone. It's just a meat packing plant. They didn't make me the man I am today-you did, Mom.

I love you so much,

Douglas

He read the letter over again and he thought it was about as good a letter as he was capable of writing. It said everything that he wanted to say, and he hadn't even cried on it. He did indeed miss his mom a lot, and every day without her made him wish he'd done more with her. He knew that if anything happened to her while he was gone—or to him, for that matter—that would be one of his biggest regrets.

He folded the letter and placed it in the envelope. He didn't want to think about it anymore, because thinking about it made him feel like such a loser for not staying home. Would it have been more courageous to stay home and make sure that his mom and siblings were taken care of? This was something that he wrestled with on a daily basis.

He flipped around and saw that most of the guys had turned in for the night. There were a lot of guys curled up in the fetal position, which meant that they were sleeping or sucking their thumbs and crying like little girls. He rubbed his hands over his face. He was barely out of high school, and now he was getting ready to go overseas and kill people he'd never seen before. Was it right, he thought? Was this something that a good and kind God would want from his children? He wasn't a particularly religious guy, but he figured that if there was a God, it didn't make much sense for God to be a five-year-old kid playing with army men.

Why would so many people worship an all-powerful being if He couldn't even stop kids from being killed by car bombs, or little children all over the world from starving in slow, painful deaths? He sure hadn't done Doug any favors throughout his life, that was for sure. The entire religion thing didn't make a whole lot of sense to him. He'd thought it over more than once, wondering why so many people believed in a God. The only rational reason he could ever come up with was that we were all just scared little kids, and He was the security blanket that helped us get to sleep at night.

Doug lay back with his hands intertwined behind his head. He thought about God a lot. Not that he believed in Him, because he kind of fell on the side of the non-believers. Why was it so right to believe in Jesus on a wooden cross, but not believe in a rock that some pygmy tribe in Africa swears is where their God resides? It didn't make sense, and lying here, it still made no sense. He figured that now would be a good time to want that blanket to help make him feel safe and secure, but he just felt more alone than ever. He felt total solitude, even with a bunch of jarheads not ten feet from him. He felt like the most alone guy on this planet. There was no God carrying him over a sandy beach, or a warm hug when he needed one most. He was on his own, and until he saw his family, he figured he would stay that way.

Doug sat there and thought about a million things at once. Everything still felt so surreal. He wouldn't have been one bit surprised if Rod Serling had walked out from behind his locker smoking a cigarette. But he looked over at the locker and saw nothing that resembled a shadow or a sliver of smoke rising up to the ceiling. He was completely alone, which pretty much summed up exactly how he had felt for most of his entire life.

DONNY

onny sat and watched as the other guys around him went through every emotion in the book. He could read it on their faces just as easily as reading a billboard alongside the highway. He saw courage, mostly fake, and total fear, which was not fake, and also elation on the faces of the ones getting cushy assignments. He saw them all, but he also saw everyone writing their moms, telling them the good or bad news. As far as he knew, he was the only one there not with a pen and paper in his hand. He had maybe one or two people he could write, but why bother?

He did have a friend or two before he had joined up, but truthfully, he was a loner. He preferred being by himself. He didn't do well with girlfriends; he didn't do well with friends, period. He knew he was a nice enough guy, but at the end of the day, he thought he was just better off being by himself. No one wanted the baggage that came along with hearing about his life. No one wanted to hear the horror stories from the orphanage where he'd heard kids crying themselves to sleep every night. He was totally sure that no one wanted to listen to the woe-is-me speech. Not that he had that many, but he was just better off not getting too close to people. To him, the difference between old friends and new were that the new friends just hadn't let him down yet.

This was the first time he had even considered letting someone into his life. But Andrew was already like a brother to him, and as much as he wanted to keep him at arm's length, he kept allowing him further inside. Donny wanted to push him away, but for some odd reason, Andrew was like the kid brother he'd always wished he had. Sure, there were lots of kids at the orphanage that he had considered friends, but none of them made him want to take a bullet for them. Andrew, on the other hand, was one of those rare people who you meet once or twice in a lifetime who doesn't want anything from you other than friendship. It was strange, in a way, because Donny had always thought that everyone wanted something. Some people seem to want to help the poor orphan so that they can feel better about themselves, but they were really doing it only for themselves. He had seen it a hundred times. Kids like him were like pet turtles that somebody took home and only played with for a few days before setting them aside.

Donny jumped back to the present. He looked around at Andrew, Raymond, Doug, and the whole gang that he knew who were going to Kabul. He wasn't overly fond of Raymond, even though Doug seemed to be okay, but he never got too close to either of them. He could tell that everyone, including himself, was scared shitless, but there was no turning back now. They just had to hold their heads up, walk through the fire, and hope that they didn't get burned too badly.

Deep down, Donny wanted to be friends with these guys, but he knew that if he became close to them, it would change him in some way. He didn't want to be the guy who enjoyed taking score of how many people he killed. He didn't want to be the guy who saw a terrorist in every person's face. He wanted what Andrew had given up. Donny wanted a Ma and Pa to come home to every day, and to wake up in a house where people really, truly loved him. He couldn't believe that Andrew was so stupid, but it was his life to be stupid with, he figured.

There was a time when he would get upset when he heard somebody talking about Mother's Day or Father's Day. Now it was just another day that came and went each year. He thought aloud, "The pity train has left, Donny boy." Then he grabbed his pen and paper from under his bunk. He didn't know what he was going to say, but he needed to tell the Sister that he had appreciated all that she did for him. He may never see her again, and she deserved to know. And more importantly, he wanted her to know. *What to say, what to say*, he thought, and then he began to write.

Dear Sister Agatha,

This is Donny, your favorite. I know you aren't allowed
to have favorites, but between me, you and God, I know
I was your favorite. I've been in the army the past few
months and am getting ready to finish basic training. I'm
going to then be shipped overseas to relieve some guy
so that he can come home to his family. I just wanted to
write you to tell you something that I should have said
a long time ago. Thanks so much for everything. I mean
that. In some of my worst days, I saw you try and pull
me from the muck of life and try your hardest to breathe
life back into me. Whether you were wasting your time
isn't relevant, I guess, but I just wanted you to know that
it was appreciated more than you know. I won't make this
too long and sappy. I just wanted you to know.

Thanks again.

Don

SO READ IT ALREADY

ndy sat on his bunk with all the peripheral movement and noise just white noise at this moment. The lights in the dorm had a haze today that kept him from focusing on anything in particular. Andy's face was blank. He was obviously a million miles away.

Don looked at him from across the room for a moment and then saw the letter he was holding in his right hand. *It's about damn time*, he thought to himself. *He got his orders, and it must not be good news*. He went over to find out from his friend where he was headed. He could read it on his face as if he were reading the letter himself. He walked over to his friend and said, "What's up?"

Andrew wasn't feeling too well. His stomach had been doing flip-flops ever since he read the letter. He was going to Kabul. He'd been hoping and praying that he'd be going to help count chopsticks in South Korea, but no such luck.

"Kabul." That was all that needed to be said.

Don knew there was no cheering up his friend in a moment like this. He knew that Andy's head was going to be screwed up for at least a day or two. "Dude, I'm sorry," he said, "but at least this means we should be together."

"Yeah, I guess," said Andy. He saw that as probably the only bright spot in this whole situation. It was just his luck that he would probably be in a different outfit.

"When are you leaving?" asked Don.

"I don't know. I read 'Kabul' and stopped there." He figured he was in shock.

"So, read it already. I mean, don't you want to know when?"

Don was hoping that Andy was leaving at the same time as he was. It was a big joke around here that Knox would be the first guy with a bullet in his head, but Don didn't take it as a joke. He was going to help Andy get back home if it killed him. Something Burnside had said to him stuck in his head: "The things you would die for often do just that." As much as he hated that tub of lard's face, he knew he also didn't want to prove him right.

"Hold on a second," he said. Andy unfolded the letter and looked at it again. The big letters saying "Kabul, Afghanistan" jumped out at him again. His stomach churned as he skimmed down to his departure date. "I leave December third," he said. "I leave on the transport at fifteen hundred. That's only a couple days from now. Holy shit."

"That's the transport that I'm on," said Don. "At least we can stay together for a while longer."

Then he saw Andy's face go white again. He knew he'd just realized the letter he had to write to his mom. "Come on, dude," said Don. "Let's go over to your bunk. You've got some writing to do."

"You read my mind, young Jedi."

How the fuck am I going to tell my mother that I'm going to the Middle East? Thought Andy. The knot in his stomach grew even larger. He almost lost it just thinking of the tears his mother was going to shed over this letter.

Don saw him to his bunk and then handed him his pad and paper, then gave him some space. He knew Andy was going to need some time alone to get his thoughts and emotions under control. Don could see the blank expressions not only on Andy's face, but on many others as well. It seemed that just about everybody there must be getting on that transport with him and Andy. Don walked away and went over to see Glen Jones, a black guy who now looked as white as the sheet he was sleeping on. He looked behind him one more time to see what seemed like an empty shell of a person sitting on his friend Andrew's bunk.

Andrew watched as Don walked across the barracks to Glen's bunk. He was happy that he didn't have to pretend anymore. He could see his mom's face in his head. She was crying. It wasn't something he enjoyed seeing. And now he couldn't hold it in anymore. He grabbed the bridge of his nose with his thumb and index finger. He couldn't hold back the tears any longer. He was so sorry. He was wracked with guilt. He wanted to scream that he was sorry, but he couldn't. He just turned his head away from everyone else and tried his best to hold everything in.

Don could see out of the corner of his eye that his friend wasn't doing too well. He was obviously crying, but this was one time when Andy would just have to deal with his feelings on his own in order to grow. Don figured that sounded so cheesy, but in a way, it was true.

Andy had to stop this. He wasn't a little kid anymore. He was a man, and men did not cry like he was crying, which was more like muffled sobbing. He could just imagine everyone behind him laughing at what a big baby he was being. He glanced around quickly, but no one was even paying any attention to him. He wanted to run out of there, steel a jeep and go give his mom the biggest hug he'd ever given her. He wanted to grab her and never let go—wanted to, but knew that he couldn't. What he did have to do, however, was man up, write his parents that letter, and tell his mother he would see her soon, and not to worry.

He grabbed his shirtsleeve and wiped the tears from his eyes and cheeks. His mother was going to be fine, and so was his father. They were both going to be fine, and when he did return, the pride would be beaming off of their faces like sunrays.

He grabbed his tablet that was sitting in the spot where Donny had thrown it, and he started writing. Short and simple. No mushy letter saying how much he missed them, and all that jazz. He clicked the pen.

Dear Mom and Dad,

I got my orders today, and they want me to go help the boys in Kabul, Afghanistan, leaving on December third. I know mom, you and me both, but you have to be brave just like me, and keep me in your prayers. I will be home before you know it, and I'll have so much to tell you. You know I love you both, and you know I always will.

Your loving son, Andrew

Writing the letter wasn't as hard as he'd expected it to be. He figured he would have teardrops smearing the ink, but to his surprise, there were no tears at all, which felt kind of strange. Was he growing up, he wondered? Was he wrong for coming to terms with it so quickly? He felt as if his mother were a million miles away. He couldn't exactly explain it, but he wasn't the same guy he'd been, or he saw his life totally differently than before. Something had changed in the past twenty minutes that made him feel very odd.

He sat there on his bunk raking his fingers through his hair. He had come to terms with everything. It was the only way he could explain it. There was no one coming in and yelling that they'd made a mistake and that he was needed in Philadelphia to help guard the Liberty Bell. He was going overseas. He was probably going to have to shoot someone in the head to save his own life, or maybe Don's. It was a fact, and it was clear that dealing with the truth was the only course of action he could see taking at the moment.

Andy just sat there with a calm washing over him that he hadn't ever experienced in his entire life, as far back as he could remember. He was going to be okay. He didn't want to leave with a feeling of impending doom, thinking that he would never come home. But he found that it wasn't there at all. It was more a sense of stillness in the air, as if everyone in the room had suddenly frozen in place. He just smiled to say that he was okay and that he was going to stay that way. It was eerie, but at that very moment, he didn't feel like joking around or being the life of the party. He had a mission. He was going to see it through, and honestly, no one was going to stand in the way of him accomplishing that mission. He couldn't explain it, but the hairs on the back of his neck were standing at attention. It was kind of freaking him out.

Don had been keeping an eye on his buddy. He saw him go from denial, anger, guilt, and now acceptance all in a span of thirty minutes. He got up from where he was talking with Glen and said, "Hey Glen, let's go over to Andy's bunk and see why he's smiling. I want to know what is so damn funny. I need a laugh, too. How about you?"

Glen looked over at Andy and saw him sitting on his bunk with a big grin on his face. He looked like he'd just gotten away with something. "Sure," he said. "I need a laugh, most definitely."

They both walked over to Andy. Don looked down at his buddy and said, "What the hell is so funny?"

"Nothing."

"Then why the hell do you look like you just ate a big old fat canary?"

"No, really," Andy said. "I'm just suddenly okay with everything. I have to go, so let's go and get it over with so that I can go home."

"Now I *know* you're crazy. When the hell did you get so mature?" Don wasn't buying the pretense. Not too long ago he'd thought his friend was about to throw up all over the floor.

Glen said, "Andy, you're so full of shit. You know damn well you ain't alright with it." He thought this had to be true, because he wasn't alright with his own news at all.

Andy looked up at the both of them staring down at him as if studying a bug on the sidewalk. "Look, I know it sounds crazy, but I think I'm okay with it. Not *okay* with it, but I can't explain it. I just feel like the only way I'm really going to be fine is to complete this part of my life and get it done and over with. I have to believe I'm here for a reason, and I don't think it's just to get over there and not do anything but die. I mean, I really do think that I'm going for a reason, and even if I do get killed, I want my life to mean something, you know? I want to help somebody besides myself."

Glen was envious of this attitude, even if he thought that Andy was full of crap. "Whatever, man," he said. "I have a wife and two kids, and I want to see them again. I would trade anything to be out of here and sitting in my living room eating Fritos with my two kids." He could feel himself getting a little choked up.

Don asked, "Then why did you join? I mean, I'm not being an asshole or anything, I'm just curious."

"I joined so that I could give my kids someone to look up to besides a janitor working sixty hours a week and still not having shit to show for it. I wanted them to have perks that a janitor could never give them. I wanted them to be proud of me instead of one day pitying me for being nothing but a shit-scrubbing janitor. That's why I joined."

"Well, you're a few years older than us, so try and look at the positive side." Andy sounded like some bullshit motivational speaker, and he knew it. He tried to stop, but the garbage just kept spewing out. "I mean, if you go, you come home and you're set for life, and your kids think you are frickin' Buzz Lightyear and shit."

Glen managed a grin. "Yeah, I guess, but I know that if it doesn't come true, my boys will never know their dad. And that keeps me up at night."

Don finally broke in. "Listen, Glen, you knew that this was a very real possibility. We all did, and now it's time to go over there and hope for the best. We may all die, but we may all come home, too."

Glen was not impressed with Don's profound insights. Ever since he'd been there, he'd heard all the horror stories about little kids walking up to soldiers, and after asking for a dollar, the soldier bends down and the kid explodes. Or some car crashes into a Humvee and blows everything in a two-block radius into itty-bitty pieces. The job was dangerous, and they all knew the odds were slim that they were coming home. Glen knew all too well what the chances were. But he only said, "I hear you, Donny. I hear you."

Don knew a blow off when he heard one. It didn't matter, though. Glen wasn't a close friend, so what he thought didn't mean much to Don. He was older, and the fact that he was acting like the scared little kid made him no more attractive. "Good. Now what we have to do is try to have each other's backs so that we all come home without a scratch."

Andy chimed in. "Yeah, we have to keep each from getting our heads blown off. Think of what we can tell everybody when we get home. We're going to be so cool when we get home to Haymarket."

Don didn't buy the Sylvester Stallone routine that Andy was pushing down their throats, but at the same time, who gave a shit? It didn't matter, anyway. It didn't matter how you got through or who you had to pretend to be in order to do it. The idea was just to get through it. Andy could have thought he was Mighty Mouse or Wonder Woman for all he cared.

Glen eased out of the conversation and went back to his own bunk. The others could pretend that everything was cool and that they were going to come home as conquering heroes, but he knew the real deal. The odds of him getting home were slim, and he knew it. He wished he'd never even seen that recruiting office six months ago. What he wouldn't give for a mop bucket right now.

Don sat down on the end of Andy's bunk. "Now that he's gone, you can tell me the truth," he said.

"The truth about what?"

"Don't bullshit me, dink. I know you're scared to death, and I know you're bullshitting me right now."

"I don't think so."

"This is really how you're going to play this?"

Andy just leaned over to Don and whispered, "It's okay, dude. Really."

"Fine," said Don. But Don knew shit when he smelled it, and Andy was slinging it.

"Dude, I'm being serious. I swear."

"Who was the guy less than an hour ago trying to hide the fact that he was crying into his hand?"

"That was me," Andy admitted, "but I also came to a realization at the same time. I can't change any of this, and if I go into it like a scared rabbit, I'm going to get slaughtered."

"You came up with a new philosophy in half an hour?"

"I don't know whether I can explain it, but I'm serious. It was like a calm came over me, sort of like saying that everything was going to be okay. Something just made me feel at ease. I can't explain it, so stop looking at me like I'm some freak or something."

Don stared at Andy for a good thirty seconds. He wasn't quite sure why, but he believed him. "So, you're okay with this now?"

"Fuck no," said Andy. "I would give my left nut to get out of this." They both busted out laughing at the same time. "The truth is, though, my left and right nut couldn't get me any closer to home, and I know it. Mine and yours together wouldn't get me home tonight."

"Hey, let's leave my nuts out of this please."

Don was glad that Andy was not sitting here sucking his thumb. Truthfully, that was exactly what he had imagined would happen if Andy got Kabul orders. He wasn't fully convinced yet, but he thought that Andy was trying to believe what he was saying, and that was good enough for now. "I'm glad to see you not curled up in the fetal position," he said finally.

"I was close, real close," said Andy, "but like I said, I got this warm wave of something that just made me feel like it was going to be okay. Don't get me wrong, Donny boy, I'm scared shitless and I bet I'll soil my shorts at least three or four times before we get there, but for now, I'm still not okay with it, but I'm handling it."

Don grabbed Andy's hand and shook it violently. "Good man," he said in a terrible British accent, which made both of them laugh. "Jolly good ol' bean."

"God, you're so retarded sometimes," said Andy. He paused for a second and then added, "Ol' bean."

They both roared with laughter. Don wasn't happy about going, but he felt that no matter what happened, he was going to come out of this a much better person than he'd been six months ago.

Don and Andy heard the other guys talking about being out at the rifle range, and that got them to thinking that they'd better get their shit together. The last thing they wanted was ballbuster Burnside to come in and grab them by the testicles and drag them outside. Don reached for his uniform jacket. "You better get ready, Andy. You know Burnside would love nothing better than to drag you out of here by your little dick."

"I think you're right," said Andy. "I've always gotten the feeling that he wanted to grab my dick. I'll tell him 'hands off, because that is Birch's dick, and no one grabs it but him. Sir!'"

"Shut up, you perv. You wish I would grab it, but the only way I could is if you got your own hand off of it first. You really don't think all that shaking you do down there goes unnoticed, do you? I mean, I don't think we get many aftershocks here."

Andy felt a bit embarrassed. There were a few times that he may have made just a bit too much motion in the ocean, as he would call it. "Yeah, right."

"If it wasn't you, then someone was giving you a handjob while you were sleeping."

"I bet it was Burnside, that old pervert," said Andy, trying to save face.

"It didn't sound like you were resisting too much," countered Don.

"Fuck you, man. Let's get out of here before you piss me off."

"Yeah, so pissed off that you say hurtful things to me and get your scrawny ass kicked," said Don. "You mean like that?"

Andy was beat this time around. But he would have his time later when Don was the butt of the joke. Unfortunately for Andy, that didn't happen often enough. "Come on, dink."

"After you, Madam."

GLEN JONES

Glen watched as the other guys did their own thing. Since he was a bit older than most of the others, he didn't fit in with their fifteen-year-old antics. He was only twenty-seven, but he was already much more mature than most of his bunkmates. He had to admit that some of the things said by Knox and Birch were pretty funny, but he still saw them as kids. They weren't buddies to hang out with. They were the guys you would ask to shovel your sidewalk after a heavy snow or to rake fifty bags of leaves in late fall.

This was one of the reasons he felt like an outsider. Just about every guy in there was just pulled out of high school. To him, some of these guys even looked like they could have been *starting* high school, not finishing it.

Glen remembered back to not long ago when he had this great idea to join the army. His life was not much better than a homeless man's at the time, in his opinion. He had a wife who loved him and two kids who were just getting old enough to be interesting. They could talk and they could do things like catch a ball or play in the playground. He loved taking his kids to the Heritage playground on his one day off from work. Jeremy, who had just turned five, was pretty cool. Tommy, who was four, tried to keep up with his older brother, but in that one year Jeremy's legs had experienced a growth spurt. He could outrun Tommy with very little effort. Glen could see them in his mind's eye running around the playground, and it brought a smile to his face.

His wife Sandy was a good woman, too. She made him feel good even on the days when he didn't feel too good about himself. She knew instinctively the days when he was low, and she tried to make him believe that things would get better. Most days, it worked, but he knew lately that it was getting harder and harder for him to believe that it would.

He was living off the scraps that he made by working as the school janitor and at the car wash and on construction when Smitty needed an extra hand if it didn't rain, or snow, or there wasn't enough work for a whole crew. He was always thinking that he had work for the next day to make extra cash, only to get a phone call late the night before saying that he wasn't needed. Everything had led him to this day and to this place. He didn't join to kill foreigners, or to protect his country, or for the honor. He joined to be able to have something that he could bring to the table for his family. And he wanted to make his family proud of him. A toilet scrubber, a sponge, and a bag of concrete wasn't doing it. He knew that his wife could have done much better, and in his heart, he recognized she would grow to resent him.

He sat there now wondering whether he had done the right thing. Had he just screwed himself and his family? Would they be okay if something happened to him? These are questions that he should have asked before signing on the dotted line, he thought. All the guys pretty much knew where they were going by now. Only a couple guys weren't going to Kabul. Glen would have given anything to change places with Tyler, who was going to some cushy job in Maryland hacking networks for the government.

His thoughts were interrupted by a big yelp across the room. He stood up and saw two guys fighting across the room. Flannery and what looked like Thomas. Obviously, everyone was tense. But Reynolds and Birch broke it up as quickly as it had started. Both men were bullied back to their bunks. Reynolds was too big to get away from, and Birch was no small guy, either.

After a few moments, it seemed like the fight was over, and Burnside wasn't rushing in yelling. Glen had never hated anyone as much as he hated Burnside, that sadistic bastard. He knew about tough love and all that, but it seemed as though Burnside took it to a whole other level. He seemed to really gain pleasure in making a kid cry, or in William's case, to piss himself. It didn't make sense to Glen, but he didn't rightly care, either.

Burnside could yell at him all day long and all he would think about was his boys. He never gave that bastard any inkling that it bothered him in the least.

I need to write Sandy and the boys a letter, he thought. *I need to let them know what is going on and tell them they will see me soon.*

He pulled out some paper and pen from his footlocker. But he had no clue about what to say. *Don't be screwing no other guys while I'm away? Keep my kids safe and make sure you keep those legs closed while I'm gone?* Nothing seemed to sound right in his head. He trusted her, but if the roles were reversed, he didn't know whether his eye wouldn't wander just a bit.

Screw it, he thought, *I'll keep it short and sweet.*

He sat back down on his bunk, then took a deep breath and exhaled slowly. He let his mind go clear. Then he started writing.

> **Hey babe,**
>
> *I got my orders yesterday, and it is not here in the U.S. It's some place in Afghanistan. I know we were hoping that I would stay here, but I thought about it a lot, and I think when I get back we're going to be set. I think that by the time I get home, I should be able to get all kinds of jobs, and won't have to hope and pray for a call from Smitty. When I get back, we're going to move into a nice place where we'll have a dining room and an eat-in kitchen, too. I think we're going to get a house in that Country Club Estates that you always talk about.*
>
> *I love you, babe, and I know you and the boys are going to miss me, but think of all the good stuff we're going to be able to get. I mean, my idiot cousin will eat his heart out after I get home. They will all wish they'd had the guts to do what I did. I mean, it takes a real man to look down the barrel of someone else's rifle and smile. I learned here that you can't call it a gun. According to Burns, a*

gun is something that holds caps and is given to little kids on their fifth birthday. There is a rifle and a pistol. But if you ask me, it's a fucking gun and he can kiss my ass.

Tell Jeremy and Tommy that I love them and that I will take them to the playground when I get home. Tell them, please. I'm going to get out of here. I'm going to be leaving on the third of December, and as far as I know, we will be hopping over to Osamaland.

P.S. Please call my parents and let them know that I will write them as soon as I can. I don't feel like writing right now.

Take care babe,

Love you all,

Glen

He read the letter and he could tell he was trying to convince his wife that he was okay with everything. But he knew that she wasn't that stupid. He wasn't okay with any of this. He was just the opposite of being okay. He wanted to shoot his way out of there and go home and just screw his wife and play ball with his boys.

He was not much on religion, but he figured that now would be a good time to get acquainted. He looked up and stared at the ceiling. Nothing spectacular was coming to him. He wasn't feeling like a divine power was reassuring him. *Well there, Jesus, I guess you and me have a few words to say to one another. It seems that I need your help here. It don't look like you're going to wake me up in the morning in my bed back in Crownsville, Maryland, now are you? I think we should get one thing straight. I will help you if you help me.*

But he thought that sounded like a bunch of horse crap. He started over.

Let me start over, Jesus. What I mean to say is that I need your help. I have a wife and two kids who need me to come back to them and take care of them. If you help me get home and help me get a job so that I can take care of my family, I will help others who need help, I swear. Please get me home with all my body parts.

But he figured the bullshit that he'd just emitted out was a waste of energy. Glen wished he could believe in a God, but if he believed in someone who would purposely screw someone over as royally as had been done to him, then Glen figured what kind of person would that make him? There were a lot of things Glen thought when it came to a higher power, but gratitude wasn't on the list.

SAYING GOODBYE

It was December third, and all of the guys in the barracks were nervous and jittery. Most of them were ready to kiss anyone's hindquarters just to get out of there. Then you had the ones who were all gung ho and couldn't wait to go out and catch the next Osama Bin Laden themselves.

Andy was somewhere in between the two positions. He wasn't as scared as he thought he would be, but a lot of that had to do with Don. He pulled strength from the other man. It wasn't a macho thing, more like a serenity thing. He still couldn't explain it fully, but he knew that it was one of those things that you feel. He was ready to go. He had said all the prayers that he was going to say, and he knew now that whatever happened was simply going to happen. It was his destiny to have this adventure. For good or bad, it was his.

He could see relief on the faces of those who weren't going, and dread and excitement on the other faces. Going over and taking his gun and bashing some guy's head in did not appeal to him. He had asked the Lord what to do, but he got no other answer than to "do what you feel you must to come home and take care of your parents." He wasn't quite sure who'd said it, but he thought it was good advice. He wasn't sure whether he could live with himself if he killed some ten-year-old kid waving a grenade in his face, but one of his prayers was that he would never have to find out.

All of the other guys were finishing packing up their gear. Most were going to see each other on the transport anyway, but it still seemed like they were leaving and would never see each other again. Andy wasn't the most beloved cadet, but he wasn't the most hated, either. He was the kid who had stayed a kid, and that was probably the worst thing that could have happened in this hellhole. He didn't take things seriously, or as seriously as some of the others did. Of the thirty or so guys in the platoon, he was the one who thought everything was an exercise rather than not real life. That is what most of the men thought of good old Andy.

Andrew and Don were all set with their gear and were waiting for the word to get their asses outside and get in the transport truck. Andy was on pins and needles. He wanted to get it over with. He acted like he was at the dentist and was about to get a root canal.

Don looked around at the rest of the guys. He was indifferent to most of what was happening around him. He was scared, of course, but he also had feelings of achievement. He had achieved the one thing that he never had as a kid. He had found a purpose, a reason why he was on this dirtball of a planet. One of his favorite quotes was from Hemingway: "The two best days in anyone's life, the day you are born and the day you figure out why." It was sort of the code by which he lived. He didn't really have anyone to write to or anyone to let know that he was going off to war. He had no idea whether anyone was sitting home watching television and wondering if he was okay.

Don had been here for four months, and he could honestly say that the people he had met were more like family than anyone he had ever known. Not in a mushy after-school special kind of way, but in a way that he could see himself helping them if they called him up in need. He was fond of a few guys there, but he and Andy seemed to have been twins separated at birth. He couldn't understand it, but he figured the two of them were where they were supposed to be. He could say that it was some divine power at work, but he figured it was more like dumb luck on both their parts.

Don and Andy had talked about doing something when they got out, but what if he didn't make it back? Andrew wasn't smart enough to do anything besides castrate hogs without him there. Without him, Andrew would go from millionaire to broke-ass farmer. Don knew it, too. He would go home and help his parents out until he himself became an old farmer just like his dad.

He looked over at Andrew who was just checking his bag for what must have been the ninth time, and he saw hayseed written all over him. Don knew that it was up to him to get them both home safely and save them both from the lives that they would have led if they hadn't met one another.

He pushed Andy onto the bunk. "Are you ready, dink?"

"Uh, yeah, I guess so," said Andy. "I got my toothbrush, I got my undies, and I got my toilet paper. I think I'm ready. Oh yeah, I got my sunscreen too. I think it's like SPF ten million. Did I forget anything? Did I forget to hug you or something? Why are you looking at me like you are getting ready to break up with me?"

"Now just what the hell would your virgin ass know about anyone breaking up with your skinny ass?" Don said with a smile.

"So, you are saying that you're the girl for me? That's what it sounds like to me."

"Don't flatter yourself, little man," said Don. "And I do use the 'little' in describing anything south of your belly button."

"How would you know what's south of my belly button?"

"I've lived on top of you for four months." Don stopped, cleared his throat, and composed himself. "Let's just say I was talking about those chicken legs you're hopping around on. You know, if you and your legs ever get a divorce, you could sue them for non-support."

"Bite me, dick." But Andy had the biggest smile smeared across his face.

"Did you just say you wanted to bite my dick?"

"Why are you always talking about that little thing like it's something anyone would want to look at, suck, or just touch in general?" asked Andy.

"You're absolutely right there, but just in case you *are* thinking about it, I think you have to get those teeth fixed before you can suck on it. Your mouth looks like an old barbed wire fence."

"Let me say this again," said Andy. "Bite me." He said the last two words slowly. He wanted Don to understand him through his grill. "Can you understand me through this barbed wire face of mine?"

"Most of it."

Don loved messing with Andrew. And he got the better exchange on most occasions, which made it all the better, as far as he was concerned.

"Good," said Don. "Grab your shit and shut up, and let that cut underneath your nose heal." He was going to say more, but he was interrupted by the words, "Sargent on deck." He dropped his bag and ran to the front of his bunk.

What the hell does he want? thought Andy. *Does he just want someone to pee his pants as a send-off present? Whatever it is, it can't be good, that's for sure.* He kept his eyes to the front and didn't give that bastard any reason to come over and hassle him. *Isn't it bad enough that we're going a million miles away from home and maybe getting killed? Do you have to be a prick one last time before we leave?* Andrew wished he had the balls to punch Burnside square in his jaw. He knew one thing, though, and that was that he didn't have the guts. It may keep him here, but his life would be totally screwed. He just kept his face forward and listened.

Don was wondering why Burnside was showing up ten minutes before they had to leave. He figured that he wanted to get his jollies off one more time. Don wasn't crazy about going thousands of miles away from there, but it had to be better than being where he was. He had no family, so what difference did it make what bunk he slept in and where it was geographically located?

But Andrew and Don were both surprised not to hear any screaming or demeaning comments coming out of Burnside's mouth. He didn't even say anything, really. He looked like shit, Andy thought. He looked like he'd just gotten home from three tours in Vietnam. He was definitely not himself at all. He walked slower, he wasn't looking directly at the men. He was just off, Andy thought to himself. And it was disconcerting, to say the least. *Could he really be showing a heart this late in our relationship?* But Andrew couldn't believe that something so farfetched would be his reason for being there.

He watched as Burnside walked up and down looking at the recruits but not saying a word. He wasn't worried about their bunks or their hair or how they were dressed. It was almost as if he just wanted one last look at them. He walked past Andy and didn't say a word. He just kept going. Andy felt creeped out, like he was in some kind of horror movie.

Don wanted to believe that the guy was showing his softer side, but up until now, Don hadn't thought that he even had one. He looked rough this morning. Something was wrong with him. He looked like someone had taken him to the back room and worked him over. Don figured maybe he'd just gotten beat up by a fifth of bourbon.

Burnside walked up and down and looked at his men for the last time. These men would have to make it on their own now. He had taught them everything that he knew. He taught them how to survive. He taught them how to kill. The rest was up to them, and them alone.

He stopped midway and said softly, because he did not want to yell, "Look, girls, I tell this to all my guys who come through here. If you use what I taught you, you're going to be fine. Remember to have each other's backs, and to stay alert." He looked over at Knox when he said, "Take your jobs seriously, and you'll come home to eat another one of your mommy's apple pies. The transport truck is outside, and you should get your gear together and get outside. I know each and every one of you will make me proud. Now get the fuck out of here and do what I trained you to do."

Everyone saluted him, and he saluted in return.

Andrew ran past Burnside on his way out. He gave the sergeant a look. Not a look of hatred, but one that said, *I'll show you*. He didn't get anything in return. He knew that Burnside hated him, so it was no big surprise that he didn't get any encouragement from the man. It did flabbergast Andy nonetheless that Burnside had said anything that even resembled kindness and pride in his men.

Don stopped and grabbed the sergeant's hand, as did some of the other men. No matter whether he wanted it or not, he would accept the gratitude. It was true that Don hated his guts, but as he had said in the beginning, he knew that this was the only way to properly train them for what might happen. But he got no reply from the sergeant; he just shook his hand and ran out.

Burnside hated every single one of them men. He hated knowing that most of them were already dead and just didn't know it yet. More than anything, he hated himself for giving such a putrid, morale-boosting speech, as if any one of these guys had any chance against what they were going to come up against. He knew personally what war was like, and these kids knew nothing about it. The scared ones were scared for a good reason. The ones who were all gung ho and wanted to go slit someone's throat should have their own throats cut. His hand was grabbed by his men, but he showed no emotion at all. He didn't want their gratitude or appreciation. He wanted them to disappear. And as they all piled out the door, he took one more look around the barracks. He was sure that he wasn't going to be there ever again. He knew it was time to just disappear along with the men he'd trained.

Don filed in next to Andy outside the hut. He was still a bit shocked at the show of emotion, but at the same time he was ready to move on to the next thing. He saw the huge transport truck. He thought that it probably could've housed the whole orphanage in the back. He looked straight ahead, but it did not keep his mind from wandering all over the map to think about the kids he left at the orphanage. He thought about his teachers. He thought about what they would think if they could see him now.

Burnside walked outside and ambled slowly over to the truck. "This truck will take you to another base where some of you will be going to Ft. Meade in Maryland, and the rest of you will be going to another transport at Mayo Airbase a few miles away from Meade," he said. "Good luck. Okay, girls, let's see some hustle. Move it, move it. I want to see everyone in this transport in the next sixty seconds."

He saluted the corporal driving the truck and then walked back to his office. He had some retirement paperwork to fill out and sign.

Andrew hopped up in the back of the truck. His stomach fluttered with butterflies the size of B-52s. He thought it wouldn't take much for his insides to be seen on his outsides. He tried to compose himself. Now was not the time for crying.

Don sat across from Andrew, and he didn't think his friend looked too hot. He thought that Andy could've barfed right there. "You okay there, buddy?" he asked.

Andrew took in a deep breath and swallowed. "Yeah, I'm fine, how about you?"

"Just *fine?*" But then Don looked around and noticed that Andy wasn't the only one a little green around the gills.

"Good," said Andy, and stopped there. He really didn't want to talk too much. He felt better with his mouth shut and his mind somewhere far away from there.

He laid his head back against the tarp and let his mind drift. He could see his mom folding clothes in the kitchen. He could see his dad out on the tractor tilling up the area in the back of the barn. That was where they had the little area just for his mom. They had all kinds of things there, but none of that stuff was for sale; it was all for them, and no one else. The corn was always as sweet as if it had been planted with a few tablespoons of sugar. Mom always made the string beans just right, and she never had any complaints from anyone, especially him. He loved his mother's cooking, no matter what she made.

Don sat there and watched Andy float away into another world. He could only imagine that he was probably somewhere on his parents' farm. It wasn't the first time Don had seen Andy just lay his head back and disappear somewhere else.

Don did his own version of Andy's daydreaming. He saw himself coming home and finding some hot little woman who thought he was the only man in the world. He wanted to find someone who thought he was enough to make her happy. He wanted kids, maybe twenty of them, he thought with a smile. He wanted so many kids that he would have to build a house so big that it would take three whole days to clean it. When he was imagining his future, he saw a young woman, very pretty, about five-foot-four, and the most beautiful red hair, just like his.

Don laid back and imagined everything he was going to do with her. He was going to take her to all the places he'd wanted to see as a kid. He wanted to go out to Hollywood and Las Vegas and Texas, and other places like Boston. He saw them laughing all the time and sipping wine together at little French bistros, he'd see that look in her eyes that told him that she was satisfied with him and that no other man was as good as he was. He couldn't wait to find her, fall in love with her, and have those little red-headed children with her.

A big smile came over his face. His eyes were closed, but his lips were smiling from ear to ear. Now all he had to do was come home alive.

Andy was jarred out of his daydream. The truck had begun moving. They had a few hours of travel to get to Fort Meade, and he was trying not to be scared, but in al truth, he was petrified. Everything he had told Don a few nights ago had just flown out the window. He wanted to jump out of the truck and go A.W.O.L. He figured he could live on the farm for a while, and then the army would forget all about him. But he knew they'd track his ass down and throw him in a deep hole where no one would ever think of looking for him. He'd heard all the stories.

Don and the rest of the guys just sat there in the truck. They didn't say anything at all. They seemed to be in a trance, but it was more accurate that no one wanted to talk. Everyone was dealing with his own demons. The ones who were going were scared to death, and the ones who were staying were relieved, but with a slight hint of guilt in their eyes. Don knew, because he knew that that was how he would feel in the same situation.

No one said a word. The whole ordeal was unexplainable. Andrew didn't necessarily want to talk, but it was spooky how he knew that everyone was thinking the same exact thing at the same time.

Please Lord, let me come home.

WHAT'S IT SAY?

It wasn't a minute after the mail was dropped in Marie's hand that she scurried across the yard and into the kitchen entrance, the door slamming shut behind her. This was something that she never normally did, but when she had one of Andy's letters in hand, she could be in the middle of a hurricane and not even know it. This time, it seemed that there were two letters from Andy, and she was almost ready to pass out from excitement. She knew it would be soon that one of these letters would be telling her where and when he would be going, and she prayed that it would be *here* and *now*, even though she knew that was impossible.

Mike saw his wife running across the yard like her butt was on fire. That could only mean one thing—a letter from Andy. He dropped his rake and ran into the house not far behind his wife. He opened the door and saw Marie holding two letters in her hands. He knew that this could be great news or the news they had feared from the beginning.

Marie ripped the letter from the envelope.

"So, what does it say?" Mike asked impatiently.

"Hold your horses, mister." She checked the front of the envelope. "Yeah, this is the oldest one."

"Well?" he asked again. He didn't like waiting, and something this important made him even more impatient than usual.

Her heart sank as she scanned the beginning of the letter. "He's going to Afghanistan." She didn't say anything else. She was stunned, in shock. Nothing else seemed to even matter.

"When is he going?" Mike was suddenly sick to his stomach. He felt as if a horse had just kicked him in his balls.

Marie tried not to break down completely. She could barely see the letter behind the tears welling up in her eyes. She continued reading after choking down the tears. "He left yesterday, on the third. He's probably sitting on some sand dune right now."

Mike's eyes were stinging with the tears he was holding back. It was no use; he wasn't going to succeed in keeping his composure. He sat down at the table next to his wife, wrapped his big burly arm around her, and they both cried together. He looked away, but his tears fell nonetheless. He wanted to be strong for his wife, but at that moment, he was in no shape to do so. He sat there for what seemed like hours, but was probably more like five minutes. They both purged the fear and guilt and anguish from their hearts as best as they could.

Mike pulled his wife's head up from the tabletop and away from her folded arms. After composing himself, he shook her just a little by the shoulders. "Listen, this is not doing Andy any good, do you hear me?" He wasn't sure whether it was too soon to take the tough love approach, but it may have been more for himself than for his wife.

"What does the other one say?" he asked. He waited for Marie to get herself together. She wiped the tears from her eyes and cheeks with her shirtsleeve, then she wiped the small puddle from the kitchen table where she had laid her head a moment ago. She opened up the other letter more slowly than any other. She was afraid of what it might say. She figured it was doubtful that it would say that it was all a big mistake and they were sending Andy home due to an arched foot or bad eyesight. But she wouldn't even let her mind go there.

"Go ahead, babe, it's alright," said Mike. "Everything that happens, we'll deal with together. You hear me?"

She wanted to tell him to go jump off a bridge, but she knew that he was just trying to help in his own way. "I hear you, Mike. I do, really." She started crying again. "Why did we let him do this? It's all our fault."

Mike took her by the shoulders again. "Andrew had to do this or else he would've been miserable his whole life. He would have resented us if we'd tried to stop him, and you know it. You have to accept that. We did not have a choice in this. It was his decision, and he's old enough to make his own decisions."

Marie knew exactly what he meant, because she felt the same way, but she couldn't help think that they should have locked him in his room until he got over the notion of joining up. And Mike continued, "If you let this eat you alive, you'll be no good to him or yourself."

She did appreciate his attempt to make her feel better, but nothing was going to make her actually feel any better until this whole mess was over and her son was home safe in his bed where he belonged. It was just that simple.

"Let's read the letter," said Mike, and Marie ripped open the second letter like she was opening up a package that might contain a bomb. As she pulled out the single piece of paper, she wiped her eyes once more. Then she started reading.

> **Dear Mom and Dad,**
>
> **I just wanted to tell you both again that I love you so much. I guess you got my letter that I sent yesterday about me leaving to Afghanistan. I was not happy about it, but the sooner I get this done and over with, the sooner I will be home.**

Marie stopped there for a second. "You know that boy had to probably change his shorts when they told him where he was going."

Mike cracked a slight smile. "I think he probably did, too. I know I would've definitely dropped a load."

"Damn, Mike, do you have to be so… *unsophisticated*?" It took her a moment to get the last word out. She had to think of just the right verbiage.

"Unsophisticated? When did I become a caveman?"

"When you started saying things like 'dropping loads.'"

"What does the rest of the letter say? Do you want me to read the rest of it for you?"

Mike was glad to see Marie smile, and if he had to be a caveman to get her to stop crying, then so be it. She continued again.

I'm not happy about going over there, but me and Don are going over together, and we will take care of each other. I know I told you about him before, but is it okay if he lives with us when we get home? I know he'll help us around the farm, and Pop can stop working himself so hard. I will send you my new address when I know where I'll be. Is Peanut being good? Tell everyone that I love them and I'll be home before you know it.

Your loving son, Andrew

Marie looked up at Mike and could see that he was using all of his will to keep from crying, but it was obvious that the corners of his eyes were full. She felt so bad for him. A million things were going through her mind. *What can I say to him to make him feel better? You don't see a man of Mike's size crying every day, but it just goes to prove how much he loved his son, and how deeply scared he is for him.* She blurted out, "I'm going to write him a letter. Is there anything you want to say?"

Marie knew that Mike wanted to go out to his barn where he could be alone with his feelings.

"Just tell him that I love him, too," he said, "and of course his friend can come stay with us. Just tell him that he's responsible for him if he wets on the rug."

"I'm not saying that. That's disgusting."

"You asked me what I wanted to say."

"Fine, if that is what you want to say to your son, then so be it. You're still a disgusting human being, though."

"Yeah, I know," said Mike, "and that was one big reason why you fell in love with me."

"I was a very stupid kid," she replied. She did love him, but his gross sense of humor usually only went over well with kids under twenty, or adults who acted like kids.

"Are you saying you wouldn't love me if you met me today?"

"Of course I would, dear."

Mike turned and walked out the door, and before leaving the house, he turned to his wife. "Are you okay? Do you want me to stay?"

"No, go on and do your manly things. I'm going to write Andy a quick letter and then make you some lunch. I will give a shout when it's ready."

"What are you making?"

"You will eat whatever I make," she said, "and you will love it."

HELLO BOY

It had been four days since Andy left Aberdeen and Burnside, and he was wondering how in the hell he was sitting in the middle of Afghanistan panting like a greyhound after a six-furlong race. It was a hundred and nine degrees in this desolate, godforsaken place. The sun was high in the sky, and he figured it was just around noon. He smacked his lips, making sure that his tongue hadn't melted. It was still there, but it felt like it had fuzz growing on it and was stuck to the roof of his mouth. He figured he probably had some weird desert dweller disease. He scanned the area and saw nothing but sand. Just sand dunes, mountains of sand dunes, and of course the American soldiers all standing guard, wondering what the hell they were even doing here.

He had his rifle. He had his sidearm. But what he didn't have was one of his mom's ice-cold glasses of lemonade washing down the sand in the back of his throat. He had been here for only a short period of time, but he could already testify that this was the absolute weirdest place on earth. All the people were different. He got the feeling that every citizen he came in contact with hated his guts. He knew that that wasn't actually the case, but they greatly outnumbered the ones who seemed to love his being there. He could honestly say while attached to a polygraph machine that he had no clue whether his presence was doing any of these people a bit of good.

Andrew sat and listened to the soldiers who had been there for a while. They were sick and tired and extremely misinformed as to why they were actually there. They didn't seem to think they were saving anyone from nuclear attacks or some massive covert uprising. They seemed to see it for what it really was. Afghanistan seemed to be a humongous gas station where everyone in the world was coming over and filling up their tanks.

Andy looked over and spotted a young boy in his mid-teens, he figured, running outside the compound. No citizens were allowed inside the perimeter, and it was Andrew's job to make sure that they stayed on their own side, even though both sides were technically their property. He wasn't going to pretend that he understood it all. He just wanted to do his tour, get the hell out, and go home and beg his mother to make him a homemade potpie. He could almost smell the pie in the oven.

He smiled and thought back to his first day there, and his first encounter with Sergeant Brey. He wasn't the sadistic son of a bitch that Burnside was, but he had his moments. On Andy's first day, he wasn't much the class clown kind of soldier, but more like the little boy who had just wet his pants kind of soldier. The whole attitude in the air there was that of *you are going to die, so deal with it.* The sergeant got in Andy's face and started screaming just like Burnside had used to, but with a huge difference—Burnside never actually threatened to kill him. Not like Brey did, anyway.

Even though his surroundings reminded him daily that he was only a fraction away from death at every turn, Andrew was happy as hell that at least he got to stay with some of his buddies from boot camp, especially Don. He knew that it would've been ten times harder for him if Don were not in his platoon. He knew instinctively when he was about to crack and go off screaming in the night with his junk flapping in the wind. It was as if they had known one another all their lives. It was great, as Andrew saw it, but at the same time it was a bit eerie. However, Andy just took it as something that was meant to be. Don was meant to be here at this time and this place in order to make sure that Andy made it home okay.

Andrew marched up the fence perimeter, and then back down. He had been doing the same thing almost nonstop since he'd gotten there. Mind you, he wasn't complaining. He figured it was probably the safest place in all of Afghanistan. Sergeant Brey told him over and over to watch out for cars racing up the road, or suspicious people who were trying to get friendly with him. He told Andy that the friendliest people were the ones that wanted to slit his throat.

Andrew thought, *God forbid I tell my mother how Brey really talked with me and the troops.* Sergeant Brey was a no-nonsense kind of sergeant. But Andrew didn't mind, because he knew Brey was trying to keep him and everyone else alive, but between the spittle flying off his lips onto Andy's forehead and nose, and the ringing in his ears, he figured that every enemy within twenty miles could hear him screaming. How could he tell his mom that a five-foot-six, two-hundred-pound gorilla threatened to rip his heart out, squirt bug spray on it, and then put it back in his chest? He was told specifically that if he needed to pull the trigger and didn't, that he would take Andrew and ring him out like a wet towel, hang him on a line, and put holes in him. Andy thought back and tried to remember his exact words: "If you jeopardize any of my men because you can't pull the trigger, then I will kill you as sure as you stand."

Andrew suddenly stopped in his tracks. He peered across the fence where he was posted and he saw a young kid of about ten just staring at him. He looked a mess, from his shoes to the top of his head. The boy didn't stop staring. He was studying Andy, and for what reason, he didn't know. Was he curious about skinny pale Americans? The boy was drilling a hole in Andy's head with those mournful eyes of his, and he wished that the young boy would just stop staring. He was obviously a peasant boy. Rags were his pants and shirt, and his feet looked to be wrapped in some sort of cheap rubber shoes that Andy assumed had many holes in their soles. He'd been told that they used old tires and formed shoes out of them. It took skill to carve a useable shoe from a Bridgestone tire, he figured.

He was starting to get paranoid by the look of this kid. Was he wearing a bomb or something? Was he getting ready to jump over and blow Andy into little pieces? He wanted to believe that the kid was just a curious little kid who wondered what all of this was all about. He wanted to believe it, but after the stories he'd heard in the past few days, he was definitely skeptical about the boy's intentions. Shit, he was distrustful about the goddamned camel spiders that walked past him every day. He could only imagine what one of those crawling on his back would feel like. It made the hair on his neck stand at attention just thinking about it.

The two of them just stood there and stared at each other for what seemed like hours, but Andrew knew that in this case, time was practically standing still. Andrew flinched when the boy broke his gaze. He was looked over at someone coming in the boy's direction. Andy figured it was probably his mother. She was acting like a mother protecting her cub. She grabbed him by the arm, practically jerking it out of its socket, and pulled him away from the fence.

Andrew met the stare of the mother. She gave him the most hateful look that he thought he'd ever seen or probably would ever see in his lifetime. She looked as though she could have stuck an ice pick in his brain without thinking twice about it.

As the two walked off into the hazy distance, Andy wondered what the hell he had done to that woman to make her hate him so much. He had never even met her before. Why would anyone hate a person they'd never met? He knew about racism and stuff like that, but this seemed to be way more than that. It was so personal to her. That was the piece of the puzzle that he didn't get at first. This was not the kind of hate that you reserve for friends who had screwed you over. This was reserved for strangers who came and took your land. Andy had never even come close to looking at a person as he had just been looked at. The closest thing was probably when Bobby Parker had pushed him outside school and stole his lunch money.

Someone grabbed his arm and swung his whole body around, abruptly breaking Andrew's stare. Andrew heard someone say, "What the fuck are you doing, man?"

He got his bearings and saw that it was Karl Tesler standing in front of him. He was the guard who had been standing about thirty yards away. "What?" he asked.

"Look, man, if the sergeant sees you staring at some woman on the other side of the fence, he's going to rip your head off. They're on that side for a reason. Some love us, but most would spit in our faces in a second if they got the chance, and they would blow us up just as quickly. So stop staring, jackass."

"Okay, I got it," said Andrew. He didn't quite understand, but he didn't want his head ripped off, either.

Karl stared at Private Knox, and he heard the words coming out of his mouth, but what he was really hearing was, "I'm a total fuckup. I'm going to get myself and everyone around me killed." Karl wanted to jump his shit, but he knew it wasn't his place. He didn't want Brey in a bad mood. No one wanted that. He liked everyone, for the most part, but he just wanted them to do their job and go the hell home, and take him along with them.

"Good, and don't do that dumb shit again," said Karl. "Watch your post, and that's it. You're standing here to make sure they stay on their side, you got it?" Then Karl hustled back to his post. He too was doing something that could get his head ripped off.

Andrew watched as Private Tesler made his way back to his watch and started walking up one side and back down the other just like a good soldier should. He watched the scrawny private taking his job incredibly seriously. He couldn't see himself being so gung ho about it. He knew in his heart that he should, but at the same time, he knew that he could never be a Tesler or a Brey, or even a Burnside. It just wasn't in him. He was the guy who would have trusted that boy completely, and then gotten his head blown off. But he would have preferred that to being an automaton in a very tacky uniform.

He peered out into the haze and spotted the boy again. He didn't want Tesler to run over and make a scene again, so he walked back and forth as if he were not at all interested in the boy. He wondered to himself, *Would you kill me, you little bastard? Would you be the one to put a bullet in my chest?* He wasn't saying the little peasant boy wouldn't do that, but he had to think about why would someone ten years old or even fifty years old would hate him so much. He couldn't wrap his head around the concept. He didn't see the woman anywhere anymore, which he was grateful for, but he saw the kid's face pop up between passersby going about their daily lives. He was curious, Andy thought, and he wasn't quite sure he himself would have been behaving any differently if their roles were reversed.

Andy repositioned his rifle to take some of the weight off his already burdened left arm. After a few hours, that rifle felt more like a howitzer that he was trying to carry around. He was not fond of this duty, but if he had to choose this or field reconnaissance, the choice would be easy. Most of the new guys started off right there, walking up and down a hundred-foot section of fence until their shoes wore a rut in the dirt. Could he walk this post for another seventeen months and twenty-six days? He doubted it, but he was willing to give it a try.

He peered over his shoulder and saw Tesler marching like a first-rate private, and then he looked back at the kid. The kid didn't flinch. It was as if the boy was just looking for a weak spot or something, and Knox was the first to admit that you wouldn't have to look long to find one. He turned again and Tesler was marching in the other direction with his back turned. He then looked back at the kid and waved. Not a smart move, but he thought he should let the kid know that he wasn't the enemy, and then maybe one more kid wouldn't grow up to hate the American flag.

The kid still did not flinch. He didn't move a muscle. He knew exactly what the soldier was trying to do, but he knew all too well from his parents that they say hello and then take everything you have in this world. He'd heard it from every adult, and he wasn't going to fall into the American's trap. He just stared, and he watched, and he too wondered why they hated his people so much that they would come in and think that they could take everything he'd once known. It wasn't fair. According to his mother, American's were just big bullies who thought that their shit didn't stink. And he couldn't argue with her, after what he'd seen.

Andy paced back and forth while watching the kid. He would not have been a good soldier if he hadn't kept an eye out for suspicious behavior. He was just doing what he'd been told to do. In his heart, he knew that the boy was doing nothing more than showing some boyish curiosity, but according to Brey and Tesler, he may have a whole army right behind him ready to strike on his command. Andy didn't think that was the case, but he wasn't sure.

The boy sat and watched as the American walked up and walked back. *Why did he wave unless he wanted to lure me into his trap?* he thought. But after what seemed like an eternity, he waved back. He wasn't quite sure why his hand went up in the air, but it did. This soldier didn't seem to be like the other Americans. The others looked mean and they stared at him with suspicion. This one didn't, though, and he wondered why. What was so different about this one? Was he one of the few good ones, as his Uncle Saheed said on occasion?

Andy's mouth almost dropped. The boy waved. *Why?* Andy sat almost frozen in his tracks. He looked over at Tesler and saw him doing his rendition of a good old Nazi Gestapo soldier, or one of those wind-up soldiers he had let walk across the tabletop when he was a kid. He had only known Tesler a few days, but he could tell that he was suspicious of everyone and everything that didn't say "made in the USA" on it. Andy figured he had probably interrogated a few lizards since he'd been there, too. It wouldn't have surprised Andy in the least.

He looked back to the little kid. *What do I do? Am I going to get my ass kicked if I say hi to him?* Andy knew the answers to those questions, but his whole being told him that the only way to make it better was to address the situation. His dad would have asked him what his gut was telling him. He felt so conflicted.

The boy moved a bit closer. He was just as conflicted, but his gut also told him that America had to have some men who were okay. They could not all be monsters like his mom said. He listened to the adults as he ran through the streets. He heard so many conflicting stories that sometimes it hurt his head to try and decipher what was real and what wasn't. How could one person he really respected think that they were monsters while one equally respected person felt like they were God's gift? It made no sense. Where was the truth? He figured the only way to find out was to meet one of them face to face. He knew his mother would strip the skin from his hide if she'd seen him, but he had to know the truth.

Andrew gripped his rifle a bit tighter. The boy seemed to be getting awfully close to the fence. *But why?* Was he just a curious boy, or was he walking with ten pounds of C-4 down his shorts? Andrew was unsure of what to do. He knew that Brey would kill him, and probably rightfully so, but his gut kept telling him that it was so unmistakably wrong to just go around feeling like everyone was out to get you. *We were told that we were here to help these people. If we are, shouldn't we actually meet one or two of them?*

He nonchalantly met the kid halfway. Before he could get too close to the fence, he put up his hand for the boy to stop. "Can I help you, kid?" he said hesitantly.

The boy had no clue what had just been said to him. He knew bits and pieces of English, but nothing with which to hold any kind of a conversation with an American. The soldier might as well just be mumbling to himself, and it would have made just as much sense. But he waved again, hoping to convey the message that he meant no harm.

Andrew was kind of scared at this point. He knew he didn't want to shoot some little kid dead in the street. He put up his hand again and emphasized that the boy should stop. He was relieved when the kid stopped advancing.

"What do you want?" he asked again. They were both only a few feet from each other, gazing at one another as if to say, *What are you?*

Andrew spun around quickly. He was half-expecting the whole platoon to be coming down on his heels. But he saw no one out of place. Everyone was either marching or walking around without a care in the world.

In a very thick accent, the boy said, "Hello. I am Sanjay." And then he just waited to see what the American would do. He knew in the pit of his stomach that he may be shot.

Andrew said, "Hi, I'm Andy. Hello." He spun around again, but no one was coming. He was responsible for his own actions. A thought flashed through his mind that nothing could ever get accomplished if everyone had their backs turned to one another.

Sanjay couldn't believe his eyes and his ears. He was talking with an American, a real life American! For what he had done, he knew his mother would kill him for sure. The Americans would not even have the chance, he thought, a sly grin on his face. He could see his mother's face in his mind, and he saw red in her eyes and a hand coming up in the air and then down on his little head. He said nothing else; he did know a few more English words, but what else was there to say? Sanjay felt that the two were thinking the same thing: *What now?*

Andrew's mind was racing, but no words came out of his mouth. He did not know how to speak in Persian, and it was obvious that the boy knew very little English. He wanted to ask so many questions, but he didn't know where to start. He wanted to let the boy know that he was not an enemy. He wanted him to know that he wasn't there to hurt him or anyone else. But the words just did not formulate on his tongue.

The boy finally turned and ran like a scared rabbit. At first, Andy didn't understand why, but then he heard the footsteps behind him. He turned around quickly and saw that this time it wasn't Tesler, it was Brey himself.

Andy stood rigid as a board and waited until the grown, snarling man was in his face. He knew for sure that Burnside's punishments were going to be nothing compared to Brey's.

Sergeant Brey wanted to break the boy's neck, but he wasn't the first recruit to want to make friends with the people outside the compound. Instead of bending him over and snapping his spine, he just said softly, "Knox, what were you doing, boy?"

Andrew started to answer. "Sir! I was—" and then he was abruptly cut off.

"I will tell you exactly what you were doing, Knox! You were not following my orders! That was what you were doing. That boy is not a puppy that you can go up to and try and pet. These sneaky bastards will use a boy like him to blow your face off, and if you don't believe me, I'll get a few parents on the phone that you can talk to. If this task seems to be too hard for you, Knox, I'm sure I can find you some potatoes to peel or an officer's ass to wipe."

Brey stepped back to see whether the boy was listening to him. He wanted to see the understanding in his eyes. And he saw it. "Do we understand one another, Knox?"

Andrew took a deep breath and then answered. "Yes, Sir!" He was sure that his knees were shaking, but he tried not to let anyone see. "I understand, Sir!"

"Good, Knox, very good," said Brey, who disappeared as fast as he had appeared.

Andrew watched as the Sergeant disappeared around the corner. He let out his breath in one big gulp. *I'm still alive,* he thought giddily. He'd been certain that Brey was going to rip his spine out through his ass. He looked over, and even though he couldn't see Tesler's face clearly, he knew that it wore a disapproving look. It didn't matter, though. Andrew knew what he knew, and going around mistrusting everyone he met just because they didn't look like him or believe in the same rock that he did was not a reason to feel paranoid. That was something that neither the Breys nor the Teslers in this world were ever going to get him to believe.

He looked around again, but there was no sign of the kid. There was a whole slew of kids on the street, but not the one that went by the name of Sanjay.

He couldn't wait to get done his shift so that he could tell Don about what had happened. He laughed aloud for a split second at the thought, *He's not a unicorn, Andy, damn.* He tried not to think about it in those terms, but then he couldn't get the image of a unicorn in a turban out of his head.

He repositioned his helmet and checked his rifle just to feel like a good soldier. He didn't peer out into the crowd anymore. There was no use in trying to find someone he was never meant to know in the first place. One thing did occur to him, though, and that was that none of these people would ever trust him or any other American as long as they saw the American officers reprimanding the peons simply for greeting these people.

He wasn't sure whether he was trapped in there, or if these people were being kept out for his safety. He figured it was probably a little of both. His fundamental belief was *do unto others as you would have them do unto you*, and the way he was acting and the way he was being told to act were going against those core beliefs. He didn't understand how anyone could accomplish anything other than killing by pointing a gun at something and telling it to buckle. It didn't make any sense to him. He saw the American flag go up wherever the oppressed were in need, and he saw that Americans prided themselves on rescuing those who couldn't save themselves. It just made him feel that maybe, just maybe, Americans weren't as right as they thought they were, and maybe the Americans just had a good public relations representative.

Andy walked back and forth, back and forth, reciting things that his dad had said to him when he was up against something that he wasn't quite sure about. There were so many times when Andy had come home from school with a look of *I hate my life*, and his father would take him out to the barn and they would have a chat. His father would always start off by saying, "What do you think you should do, boy?' And he wasn't always sure what the right answer was, but his dad seemed to always walk him step by step toward the right answer. His dad was in his head, and he couldn't shake the thoughts that came to his mind: *What kind of man are you going to feel like if you do nothing but hate these people? How are you going to feel about someone else when you get home that doesn't fit the pattern? How are you going to be able to help an old lady across the street if all you see is a foreigner?*

Andy stopped and peered out at the hazy air shimmering in the sunlight. It was so hot that the air looked like it was melting. He just wanted to go home.

WHAT DO I SAY?

Andrew sat on his bunk staring down at his boots, and he found himself thinking again about the kid he'd seen on his watch. Every little detail of the kid's face was ever so clear. He couldn't put his finger on what was bugging him, but he felt like such a hypocrite, for some reason. He felt an enormous amount of guilt. He hated himself for having stuff that this kid never would. The whole ordeal with Brey and Tesler was about imagining he was wrong for thinking that these were human beings worth talking to. He respected his elders for the most part, but this was leaving a mighty bad feeling in his gut and a nasty taste in his mouth.

He'd spoken with Don about it, and even though Don seemed to not care one way or the other, he did help Andy realize that everyone there was an automaton, and that they just followed orders and didn't think for themselves. Andy figured that if the captain told Brey to piss while standing on his head, he would flip himself over without thinking. He could tell that Don wanted nothing to do with these people, but they were a means to an end for Don. Andy wanted to separate himself just as his buddy had done, but he didn't quite know how. He had feelings and emotions that told him that it was wrong. He wanted to yell out that the Americans were wrong, but how and who would listen, anyway? Talking with Don about it was a waste of time, and most of the other jarheads here were the same way. They would probably go out and just start shooting people, rationalizing it by saying, "He ordered me to," or "We're saving these people from cutting each other's peters off."

He looked around the barracks and didn't see anyone who he would even consider talking to about this. He knew it would get right back to Brey that he was a sympathizer or something, and they would probably go out and shoot his ass and bury him in some sand dune outside the compound. It sounded odd to him that something like that could really happen, but he knew in his heart that it wasn't too far off the mark.

Andy wished his dad were here. He always knew what to say. He would explain that stepping on bugs was wrong, but in a way that put him in the bug's shoes. His dad was the greatest, as far as Andy was concerned. He was smart, but not arrogant, smart in that way that got Andy to see beyond the black and white world. He got Andy to see things in a way that made him think how things *could* be, the way things ought to be. He thought, *What would dad say here?* And he realized that he would say something wise like, "If your gut is hollering at you, it might be wise to listen to it."

Don plopped down on his bunk and interrupted Andy's daydream. They didn't bunk next to each other, but they were still in the same barracks. Don was always over at Andy's bunk, or vice versa. They didn't hang with too many of these other guys on a friendly basis. They were a team, but truthfully, Don didn't care for the *kill kill kill* mentality that plagued his barracks.

"What's up, Don?" asked Andy.

Don had seen from across the room how Andy had this look about him as though he was deep in thought. Either deep thought, or constipation. Since he'd that near death experience with the sergeant, Don figured Andy was thinking about what had transpired that day.

Don knew that these philosophical musings meant that Andy was still thinking about the kid from earlier that day. It wasn't healthy to do that kind of thinking around there, though, especially with these guys. These guys wanted heads to be chopped off, stuffed, and mounted over their fireplaces. The last thing you wanted to be labelled around here was a sympathizer. It was a simple gesture like shaking hands with some seemingly innocent local citizen, a mistake that changed your life forever, and never for the better. Don knew some of the guys felt bad for the locals who went home in body bags. He also knew a few guys who went home wishing they'd been lucky enough to go home in body bags themselves. It was easier on them, as well as on their families.

"Just thought I'd stop by and see what was going on in that head of yours?" said Don.

"I guess you heard about me getting my ass chewed out today?" said Andy. "I don't have a lot of ass to spare." He had always told people, "If Olive oil had a twin brother, he would have probably looked a lot like me."

But Andy could see from the look on Don's face that he wasn't on his side. He had the right to his own opinion, but he knew that Don wasn't happy about treating the locals like they had some terrible disease that you would catch if you got near them. "Looks like you agree with dickhead Brey, then?" Andy added.

Don didn't answer right away. He wanted to choose his words carefully. He knew that both men were right, but it was hard to say who was more right, which was something that Don struggled with as well. "Look, jackass," he began. "You are right, but so is Brey. He has a responsibility to every guy here, and to every guy's mom, dad, sister, and second cousin, too. You can't fault the man for that."

Don knew exactly how hard it was to stare a man in the face and act like he was just a piece of shit, because he had to do it every single day. He knew all too well how easy it would be to let his guard down, but the truth was that he saw firsthand how some of the locals would gladly give their own lives to kill just one American. The saddest part about it was that most of those idealistic locals were young kids with big puppy dog faces and sad eyes. Knowing these things about who you were dealing with made it very hard to trust any of the locals. Man, woman, and child, all with sad stories, and they all have the same ability to push a little button and ruin other people's lives forever.

"I know, I know," said Andy. "But it's not easy to look at a kid who appears to be starving and say to yourself that he's not worthy of my help. What the fuck are we doing over here if not to help? How do you help someone you mistrust so much? How do you look at yourself in the mirror every morning and call yourself the good guys?"

Andy was starting to get on his soapbox, which meant he needed to zip his lip, and he did so right then and there. "Whatever," he concluded.

"It's not a whatever moment," said Don. "It's something that you just need to deal with. You need to come to terms with it, and soon."

Don's gut had the same questions as Andy's, but he just didn't ask them out loud. "I don't understand how Indians can call an ugly ass cow sacred, but they do. It's just their culture, and it's these people's culture to live forever in song for killing an American."

"Not you too, Don?" Andy couldn't believe what he was hearing. "I thought you were better than these yahoos. Not all of them hate our guts. Some of them want us here to help them get a better life."

"You're right, and I'm sure a few of those Indians eat hamburgers, too. But can you tell me which ones just by looking at them?"

Andy suddenly wanted to punch Don in the face and break his jaw, but he knew that had nothing to do with his friend and all to do with the frustration he felt about his situation. He was there to help, and so far all he had accomplished was feeling like a heel ten times over.

"I hate you, do you know that?" He didn't really hate Don, but he wanted to hate somebody besides Brey, or whoever the hell had put him here.

"You loved me last night," said Don, grabbing and tweaking one of Andy's nipples through his shirt.

"Get off me, you sick bastard," said Andy, shoving Don away.

Andrew could understand why some guys came home all screwed up in the head. It was a no-win situation here. The Nazis were evil, but he knew there had to be millions of Germans who hated the Hitler. But Don was right; how do you tell which ones were which? He needed to write a letter to his dad to get this crap out of his head so that someone knew how hard it was to just survive here. To survive and not hate yourself in the process was more like it, he thought.

After Don left for his own bunk, Andy grabbed his paper and pen and turned over to start his letter to his Pop. He never liked the feeling that he let his dad down, ever. He put pen on paper and started to write, but then stopped. *How do I say this honestly without making the Army, the soldiers, and the whole country not sound like raving hypocrites?* He had to think for a moment. Then he just told himself to start writing, and the rest would take care of itself.

> *Dear Dad,*
>
> *I wrote this letter to you, Dad, because there might be a bad word or two. I need your advice, because I need someone to tell me what the hell I'm doing here. I feel like such a jerk. I can't talk to the locals, and I don't feel like I'm doing anything other than pointing my gun at ten-year-old kids.*
>
> *I got yelled at today for showing affection to a young boy who looked like he hadn't eaten in days. I felt so sorry for him. Every fiber in me said to help him, because that's why we're here, but every other soldier is saying I'm an idiot and I could have killed myself. It's true that some locals do get close so they can use themselves as a bomb. It's very sad how some guys leave here. Guys have left here with half a body, half a face, and sometimes as half the man they were when they got here. But if we can't help the starving people who come to us with their hands outreached, then why are we here? Dad, I'm so confused.*
>
> *I feel so damn guilty. I can't shake it. I can't hate everyone I meet. And I can't turn into one of those guys that you and mom tell me not to be like. One of those "brown menace" kind of people. They don't hate us because we're white. They hate us because we think we know what's good for them and are willing to shove a rifle in their face to make it happen. How do you be that guy and at the same time not turn into that guy? I think the way these guys here think is wrong, but I'm outvoted*

a thousand to one. So, can I be wrong? Are they just brainwashed into believing this crap? I guess you can tell I need a barn chat with you, but I hear you in my head, and between you and Don, I know you'll keep me safe.

I know I've spoken about Don a few times in my letters and we are still together, but even he thinks I should just do what they ask and get home safe. But when I do, I hate myself for turning my back on starving kids. What do I do? I feel like I'm sowing a field, knowing there's not gonna be any rain. It just doesn't make any sense to me.

I don't mean to vent to you, because I know you have your own things to worry about, but I'm so ready to get the hell out of here. There is no winning in this. If we help them, we could get blown up, and if we don't, then what good did the great United States do over here? We might as well go home and let them work out their own problems amongst themselves. Don't get me started on that topic, because if they're going as far as to blow their own kids up to get us out, maybe we should take that as a hint that we don't belong here.

Okay, enough of that... Tell Mom I love her, as always. I love you too, Dad, and I can't wait til October; fifteen months, twelve days, and about fifteen or so hours, and I should be on a transport back to the States. Me and Don are going to start a business together when we get back. Maybe a hardware store. And you can be the guy that talks with all the locals, like Eddie does at the barber shop. Yeah, people will come in just to bullcrap, not even wanting anything, but then leaving with a wheelbarrow or a box of screws.

Thanks for letting me get this out, Pop. I feel better knowing that you're on the other end telling me to be safe and come home to you and Mom. I will be home before you know it.

Your Loving Son, Andrew

KEEP YOUR HEAD DOWN, ANDY

Marie as always at this time of day was sitting in the kitchen getting dinner prepared. She was cooking Mike a nice pot roast with potatoes and biscuits. This was one of Mike's favorite meals. He loved to slop up the juice with a good 'ol biscuit.

Marie peeled her potatoes and peered over at the crock pot with the roast cooking slowly and permeating the whole house with the delicious smell. She used her knife to push the curtains aside so that she could check on her husband. He was right where she expected him to be, down on one knee tinkering with the tractor. He was always in the same position—it was just the device he was tinkering with that changed. She wasn't one to bother him while he was outside. She wished once in a while that he would come in and converse with her, but she knew that Mike would never be the same person again until Andy was by his side handing him tools as needed.

She allowed her gaze to wander from her husband over to the mailbox and to the road. There was no activity at either site.

Marie let the curtain fall and went back to peeling her spuds. She silently cursed the mail lady for being late. She was usually putt-putting up the road around this time. She was anxious to check the mail, as she was every day. Ever since Mike got that letter addressed to him and not to the two of them, he had been acting a little weird. He wouldn't read the letter to her, but she knew that it was something Andy just wanted to share with his Dad, and she was okay with that. Andrew and Mike had always had a special bond that made Marie proud.

The older Andrew got, the more he was interested in doing things with his dad and hanging out with the guys talking about how big the fish was or the size of the antlers on that buck that just got away. Andrew got to hear so many stories about when his dad was a bit of a wild child. Marie remembered when Mike told her some of those stories, and she'd wondered if this was really the guy for her. But his bar-fighting days and running around days all came to a screeching halt when he met Marie, or that is the way she hopes he tells the story.

She perked her head up like a hound dog and tuned her ears to listen to what was going on outside. It sounded faintly like a motor. With her paring knife, she opened the curtain once more to see good old Gladys putt-putting up the road. She wasn't going to get all excited, though. She didn't want to act like a school kid waiting for the ice cream man. If there was a letter, then great, and if there wasn't, then that was okay too.

Oh, who was she kidding? She was wishing with all her heart that there were a couple if not more letters from Andy in that pile of bills.

She noticed Mike's head pop up like meerkat. He honed in on the noise and got stiffly to his feet. Marie was nowhere near him, but she could hear and feel the creaking in his knees as he stood up. He acted like he wasn't in a hurry, but just like the creaking knees, she could feel his excitement about getting down to the mailbox before Gladys got there. She knew that if he sat and talked with her for a few seconds, there was nothing from Andy, but if he excused himself quickly, that meant there was a letter. She watched hopefully.

She saw Gladys finally pull up to their house. Marie thought, *A turtle could have beaten her up that hill.* She watched as Gladys handed the mail to her husband. He thumbed through the envelopes and then excused himself. Gladys waved and moved on towards the next mailbox on her route.

Marie hoped that this meant that Mike had a big fat letter in his hand. Hopefully it was one of Andy's three- or four-page letters. Some letters were much longer than others, and it was easy to know the ones when Andy was bored and the ones where he felt obligated to write to them.

Mike walked through the door with the mail.

"Well?" she asked.

Mike did this to her almost every time he had a letter in hand. "Well, what?"

"Don't make me kick you in your bad knee, Mike. You know I will. Is this one addressed to just you and only you?"

"Nope. This one is addressed to Peanut, but since he's a dog and can't read, I guess we'll have to read it to him."

"Seems logical. So, what does he say?" she asked anxiously.

"Damn, woman, let me get it opened up," he said. "Okay, let's see now. It feels like a good one. Seems like at least two pages."

Marie felt like snatching the letter from Mike's old, feeble hands. He wasn't normally feeble in any way, but to her, he was acting like an old fart right now. "Well?" she said. "Just open it before I stick this knife in your leg."

Mike cleared his throat and opened up the letter, then began to read.

Dear Mom and Dad,

I am okay, as always. I just wanted to let you know that we are down to fourteen months, and it can't go too fast for me. Just got off guard duty, and as always, it's boring as heck. I sat there for six hours counting rocks in front of where I was standing. I like the border patrol better, because at least then you get to move and walk around. Guarding a shack is like having your feet planted in one spot. After a while, you feel like you're growing roots.

Well, I don't want to give away any military secrets, so I won't tell you any more about the shack I was guarding. I'll tell you about what we're going to do when I get home.

I talked with Don, and if it's still okay with you that he can stay with us for a while, he said he will help around the farm in exchange for three hot's and a cot.

I personally think that we should make him do all of my
chores and his, because I told him that mom's cooking
don't come cheap. We can make him up a nice hay bed in
the barn and make him beg for food.

Just kidding, Mom. I wouldn't do that to anyone, but your
food is amazing. I miss your food so much that I have
dreams about it sometimes. I can't wait for one of your
homemade pot pies or your roasts with baby potatoes.
Oh my god, I have to stop, because I'm making myself
hungry. The grub they feed us here is one step above
what we feed Peanut. Maybe half a step.

I think we're going to help you out, use the GI Bill to
get our college education in business, and then start
a business somewhere near home. We said a hardware
store, but I don't want to limit myself until we find out
what is needed in our area. Whatever it is, we're going to
make a boatload of money and pay off the farm. Donny
agrees that this should be our first goal, and then maybe
open up a second and third and fourth store and become
millionaires. I can get you a new tractor and a new truck
to just ride around in and let everyone know that your
son is the man. What do you think of that?

There is so much that we can do when we get back. I want
to take you all out to your favorite restaurant, I want to
invite all our friends over so they can meet Donny, and
I want to make sure that everything around the farm is
sowed, fixed, or reaped. Whatever needs doing, Donny
and I will do. When I get home, Dad, you will be able to
delegate everything to us. You take it easy and rest those
knees for a week or two. You won't recognize me. I have
muscles now. They aren't huge, but they are there. Don't

worry; I could probably still hide behind a one-year-old oak tree.

Well, my wrist is getting tired, so I will slow my roll, as Mom would say. It's hard to believe that it's been almost eight months since I left, and it's almost like time is going super slow just to make me crazy. I can't wait to see you guys and Peanut, and even the old curmudgeon down the street who never has a good word to say about anyone.

Love you guys so much, and will see you soon.

Your Loving Son, Andrew

"It seems that our kid Andy is still a kid, Marie," said Mike. "Chasing big dreams and running at top speed. I really hope he makes it as high as he wants to go."

Marie had to stop him there. She could tell by his facial expression that he had something on his mind, something on the tip of his tongue. "What is it, babe?" she asked. "You're acting like something is wrong. He will be home soon."

"No, that's not what's got my belly aching," said Mike. "It's just, what does he know about this guy Don? I mean, I bet he's a nice guy, but what if he's just one of those guys who is taking advantage of some stupid kid?"

"But what if he's everything Andy says he is?" countered Marie. "What if he's a nice guy, a great friend, but just a lonely guy who has no family?"

Marie was always the optimist. *Why not*, she thought? She figured that the more positive energy you released out into the universe, the more that bounced back onto you.

"I just have this feeling like he's getting his lunch money taken away from him every day," said Mike.

Marie had to stop him once more. She cleared her throat before speaking, and that meant that she was getting ready to let him have it. "Michael!" she began. "I cannot believe you're sitting here telling me that you think our boy is getting taken advantage of. That's how much you think of your son?"

Mike tried to interrupt, but she spoke over him. "Here I thought you were out there being proud of your son and his choices," she said, "when you were out there this whole time thinking our son was a punk."

"Marie, get off your high horse. You know damn well that I'm proud of Andy, and you know damn well that I don't think he's anyone's punk."

"Well, I'll pretend this conversation never happened, because if Andy ever got wind of it, he would be crushed."

She turned to walk back to the kitchen window but then spun around like she had one more thing on her mind that needed to be said. "And let's just say that this guy is everything you accuse him of," she said. "Let's just say our boy is giving this Don his lunch money. Andy is going to have to learn who this guy is on his own, and us giving him advice is only going to make him think that he's that much greater. Believe me, I know. That's how I ended up with you. My family was full of good advice about who not to hang out with."

Mike sat there with a dumb look on his face like he had never known about what Marie was saying to him, when in reality he knew all too well. "What?" he asked.

"A bus boy at Denny's, Mike? Really? A bus boy? Who would advise me to go out with someone who obviously appeared to not have his life on the fast track to being a millionaire?"

She stopped before she got to sounding too much like her family. She could still hear the pings of advice telling her how she was going to regret everything, but truth be told, through the good times and the bad, she wouldn't change a thing.

"I was a bus boy because that's what people do when they're getting started and have college books to buy," Mike said defensively.

"Babe, I know all this, but I'm just telling you what they saw, because you're doing the same thing with Andy. You don't know this Don from apple butter. I think it's better if we meet the kid, then make our decision if he is a lunch money thief or not."

Marie puffed her chest out a bit like a proud peacock, because she knew she was right—and even better was that she knew that Mike knew it, too.

Mike hung his head in submission. "You got a lot smarter hanging around bus boys, didn't you?"

"No, I was always this smart," said Marie. "I just didn't show off to make you aware of how unwise you were, foolish, and a whole bunch of other words that I don't want to say. I don't know which ones you will know the definitions to."

She got a big smile on her face as she finished speaking, and Mike reached out his hands as if to say, *come here so I can choke you.*

"Nice one there, Marie," he said. "How smart could you really be if you married me?"

"According to my family, I'm right up there with monkeys who use rocks to break open coconuts, but I would rather be a monkey here with you than a genius anywhere else."

"I feel so privileged," Mike said. "And what's that word that I can't think of? Oh yeah, honored. Sometimes I still have dish washing suds in my brain."

They hugged, and then Marie pushed him away. "Listen, Mike, seriously," she said. "Andy has found a brother, a best friend, and possibly a business partner, and if you say anything, anything at all negative about this guy before you meet him, you're not going to like the outcome. Okay?"

"Yeah, I got you. Meet him then dislike him?"

He put his finger to his lips as if to tell her to be quiet. "You know I'm just kidding," he said. "He's probably the greatest guy since well, me, I guess."

"Let's just be okay with him being half the man you are. I just want our boy home, and that to me is all I care about."

"I can agree with that."

Mike turned to go back outside and fiddle with something or other, but when he turned back, he said almost shyly, "I know you're going to write the boy tonight, so tell him I'm very happy that he has a guy looking out for him, and that I can't wait to meet his new business partner. Also, tell him that I miss and love him."

Mike paused for a few seconds, as though he had another thought. And then it occurred to him to ask, "Oh, yeah, and when's dinner?"

"When I ring your bell is when dinner is."

She scooted Mike out the door and watched him take a few steps. She loved him so much, and she wished with all her heart that she could help him with his fear, his anxiety, and his panic. He was where Andy was right now. He saw the enemy staring him in the face. He knew exactly what Andy was going through, and it was eating him alive that there wasn't a thing in the world he could do about it. The only thing that was going to make that old farmer feel better was to have Andy wrapped up in those big, burly arms of his.

She went back to cooking and started thinking about what she was going to say in her next letter to Andy. *How can you I say I miss you, I love you, or please keep your head down any more ways than I've already said it?* She wasn't sure at that moment, but she knew the words would come to her when she needed them.

AGAIN, REALLY?

On one of the rare occasions when they weren't being yelled at while standing motionless for hours on end, the soldiers got to enjoy one of their bunkmates telling a story about his adventures on duty earlier that morning. Andy, Don, and every other guy there had their stories of weird occurrences while on post. Some saw a jackal or a camel in the distance, and some saw local guys trying to sneak in on post. Those were the ones that were the scariest, because you never knew what they wanted. Did they want to blow you to a thousand pieces and have you rain down on your comrades, or were they just hungry? The most common reason was that they were trying to steal medicine to sell on the black market.

Andrew watched his bunkmate, Tommy Carter, as he did the facial expressions showing how he wanted to squeal like an eight-year-old who'd just found out that her favorite boy crush was coming to her birthday party. All the guys loved Tommy's stories because he was so good at being animated while telling them.

Don was also watching Tommy, and out of the corner of his eye he could see Andy busting out laughing. It was good to see Andy doing something besides reading and writing letters. It was almost to the point where he wanted to walk up to him and slap him silly. Everybody had their own way of dealing with this hellhole. Andy wrote, Tommy told stories, and Don, well, Don thought about having something real in his life for once.

Don didn't show it, but he was very excited about living on a farm and going to school and making something of himself. He knew that Andy meant well, and he knew that his parents did as well, but he knew the truth of the matter was that they didn't know him from Adam, and Andy was not the most mature in terms of making choices like going into business and bringing in strays from the street. It didn't take a rocket scientist to figure out that Andy's parents likely had reservations, but were willing to overlook them and trust their son. To Don, that spoke volumes about what kind of people they were.

Don watched as Tommy made a swooshing motion, almost as if he were pretending to be an airplane. The next thing he knew, there was a roar of laughter from his audience. Don figured he would get the story again from Andy later on.

Don let his mind wander to what Andy and he had been talking about a few nights before. After what had seemed like an eternity in this place, Don was ready to go home, too. No one was more ready than Andy, though. Just nine more months and he would be home, and maybe just maybe he'd be living with Andy. Don understood that nothing was set in stone, though, and nothing was definite when it came to the army. He was expecting an announcement any day now telling the short-timers that things had changed and they were staying another year, or maybe even more. It was a real possibility. He knew how things worked. If you didn't have enough people, you just stalled the ones who were there until more came to replace them.

He scanned the room and saw a few empty bunks, and empty bunks meant that either guys had gone home because they had enough points, got wounded, or sometimes worse. They were just a set of dog tags that got shipped home. It was dangerous there, and Don knew it, but if he kept your head down and stayed sharp, and of course stayed lucky, you were usually okay.

Andy broke Don out of his daydream. "What are you thinking about so damn hard?" he asked. "Or are you just constipated?"

"I'm only constipated when I have to listen to your crap," said Don. A broad smile spread across his face. Andy could always make him laugh.

"What's up, home slice?"

"Just thinking, is all." Don's face told the whole story.

"I thought we already discussed this. You don't have to come and stay with me, but do you have a better offer? I mean, other than signing up again and staying in this shit hole."

Don was definitely appreciative of the offer, but what did he really want to do? The question plagued him all the time. He knew for sure that the army was not the life for him. He didn't want to become one of those jerks who got their rocks off by yelling at little kids until their shorts turned yellow. He couldn't see his life following that path.

"Listen," said Andy, "I don't know how many times I have to say this. After one day at the farm, my parents are going to love you just like they love me. But I just want it to be clear that I'm the only one in their inheritance. If you work hard for me, I might give you my dad's lawnmower."

"You know where you can stick that mower, right?" Don held his hand up as if to say *let's be serious for just one damn second.* "You know and I know that your family is a bit leery, to say the least, about some man coming to live with them who they know nothing about, and who they figure you barely know. I don't need a damn crystal ball to know that. It's okay that they do, because that only means they care and you should not fault them for thinking it."

He had to be honest with himself. Part of him was based in daydream and was excited about the prospect of the farm, and the other part of him was based in reality and knew that the rug could be pulled out from beneath him on a whim.

"My mom and dad aren't spring chickens," said Andy. "They don't do adventurous things. They don't play with the stock market, or worry about the latest cell phone, or worry about who won on *Dancing With the Stars.* What they do worry about is me." He paused and put his hands up. "Am I saying this slowly enough?"

"Yes, dipshit."

"Okay. I was enjoying a good story about a camel spider crawling up Tommy's leg, and I have to miss that so I can tell you something I have already said a dozen times? Thank you for that, by the way. As I was saying, they worry about me, from what I put in my mouth to eat to who I bring home and let play with my Transformers. It has nothing to do with you.

It's all about me, and that's how I like it, so let's stop worrying about how you feel and concentrate back on me, okay? Let's just call it the Andy hour, and the show runs all day, every day."

"Wow! Are you finished?" Don had to admit that Andy had a way of making him laugh that no one else ever had before. "I'm going to say this once and once only. I hear you, but I want you to hear me, too."

"I do hear you," said Andy. But Don just waved his hand at him.

"No, you don't. You hear me saying that I don't want to stay with you, and that's not the case at all. I would love to do all the things we've talked about. Living on a big farm sounds great, going to school and making something of myself sounds great, and starting my own company and selling it someday for two hundred and ninety million dollars sounds great, too."

"Where did you come up with that number?"

"I don't know," said Don. "It just sounded like a good number. Enough to live like a king."

"Uh, excuse me," Andy interjected. "I would be getting half of that. I mean, we're partners in this made-up company of yours, aren't we?"

"I fired you because you were sleeping with my secretary, and there's a strict policy about dating or screwing co-workers. Especially ones that I'm screwing," Don added.

"You bastard! You fired me?" Andy punched Don in his chest. "She'd better have been hot, is all I've got to say."

"She was hot as anything, but soon after you got fired, you found out she gave you herpes. I tried not to laugh, but I told you she was a whore."

They both busted out laughing and a few guys turned towards them with looks of wonderment. The other guys seemed to be envious, or maybe they just thought the two of them were weird. Andy knew he was not the most-liked guy in the barracks, but he seemed to be okay as long as he had Don to talk with. They didn't agree on everything, but he figured it would be awfully boring if they did.

Andy shouted to the onlookers, "What? You can laugh, but we can't?"

Don chimed in, "Yeah, John, I'm sure Tommy's story was no funnier." The few guys who had turned around were now back in their original positions listening to Tommy go on and on about how he'd almost crapped his pants when he saw the spider on his pants leg. Don agreed that it was a good story, but it was time to give someone else the floor.

Andy gave them a flick of his hand as if to dismiss them from his presence. "They act like no one can talk while Tommy has the floor."

"I don't think that's it. I think it's more the fact that they look for any reason to give you crap, since most of the guys here don't like you."

"That was brutally honest."

"Yeah, and? A lot of guys think you are on the wrong side." Don Purposely did not clarify that he was not one of them.

"I guess and that was not a nice thing to say to your so-called best friend."

"The not nice thing to say to you would have been a lie," said Don. "But I don't lie to you, and I hope you don't lie to me. That's the relationship I hope we always have with one another."

"Okay, well in that case, I do have something to tell you that you might not want to hear," said Andy. "But I think you need to hear it anyway."

"Okay, smartass. Get it out of your system. "

"You are one ugly, no fugly, someone." Andy cracked himself up. "I'm sorry about that, dude, but wouldn't you rather hear the truth from a friend rather than from some girl who's only after your money?"

"Are you finished, Jerry?"

"Jerry?" Andy was confused.

"Jerry Lewis, dumbass."

"Oh my God, you couldn't think of a comedian from this century?"

"Sorry, but he was the first really bad comedian that popped into my head," said Don. "I mean, to be honest, most of your jokes are only funny to you."

"Damn, Don, I thought you were my friend. I thought you cared about my feelings?"

"I do care," said Don, "and that's why I'm telling you to your face. You aren't that funny." Don liked pushing Andy's buttons just a bit.

"Okay, enough Andy bashing. Let's talk about something else. Something like, what kind of company do you want to start?"

Don had actually been doing a lot of thinking about this. According to Andrew, everything that his dad needed to buy, he would always have to drive a good distance to get it.

"How about some kind of a store that has everything that anyone would ever need?" Don began. "How about a store that sells everything from groceries, to car repair, to cell phones, and maybe even a restaurant where your mom can sell her potpies and pot roasts? I mean, think of it as a store like a Super Walmart, but not a Walmart. We can start small, but our ultimate goal would be to bring something like that to your backwoods area."

"That sounds like a lot of money. I mean, *a lot* of money." It would be expensive, but Andy liked the idea a whole lot.

"I'm not talking about opening a store right off the bat that does all this. I'm talking about a store that starts off small, and as we get bigger and add an addition or two or five, we bring in more people who want to start their own thing, and we just keep building on until it's huge. I've read about this going on all over the place. Rural areas that pop out with this strip mall so that people don't have to drive eighty miles to find a K-Mart or a Walmart. I've actually been thinking a lot about it, and if we could get the right investors and the right contractors interested, we could offer them a piece of your momma's pie and we make it rich. Then, after a while, we won't need anyone else's money, because we'll have so much of our own."

"Slow down, cowboy. Sounds like you see us as millionaires before we turn twenty."

"Why can't we be millionaires at twenty?" asked Don. "I mean, look at all these other guys building pet rocks or whatever, and bam, they're multi-millionaires. Or people inventing a light bulb that runs on the rays of the sun, and bam, you're on television selling your crap for nineteen ninety-five."

Don had been very interested in this idea ever since Andy had begun talking about it. He made it sound like it was going to be just that easy.

Andy was excited to have a partner who was this ambitious and wanted to make it all happen, and he made it sound like all they had to do was connect the dots and then there was the whole picture. "I guess it can be done if the right things happen and we get lucky," he said.

"That's where you're wrong. It has nothing to do with luck. You get what you work for, not what you wish for. You come up with an idea that sounds profitable, and then you let the people who already have the money pay for it. You sell your idea, and if that idea is a good one, I mean a *really* good one, one that makes people pull out their checkbooks and say *how much*, that's what you sell."

"Okay mister genius, what's our idea? I heard you spout off some stuff, but thousands of people have had that idea in my neighborhood. How is your idea different from every other yahoo in Haymarket?"

Don still had to work out the kinks, but he figured that if he could just get the people behind them, it would all work out. "You've heard of an employee-owned company, haven't you?" he asked.

"Yeah, so?" Andrew felt like he was back in school listening to the teacher give a lesson about how to become a millionaire.

"Why can't we have a city-owned company, then? We get everyone, and I do mean everyone, to chip in money, or labor, or materials, and then we just start building. We have so many pies out there, and owning a very small percentage of a shit load of pies is a lot better than owning half of one. It'll keep everyone in town buying from their own stores. Everyone in Manassas will want to buy from the stores in town, because every loaf of bread you buy and every time you eat at Joe's Diner, your monthly royalty check gets bigger. I mean, if you think about it, it has limitless possibilities."

Andrew was impressed. He really was. It sounded like Don had put a lot of thought into what he'd just rambled out.

"You're saying that two kids barely out of high school are going to go around like Amway salesman telling people that they have the opportunity of a lifetime? Sounds to me like a great idea, but convincing guys like my dad, you'd need a wooden club to make him give up his hard-earned money on a maybe."

"We're not kids anymore," said Don. "By the time we get home, I'll be twenty and you'll be pushing twenty. You'll never be able to do anything if you keep thinking inside the box about everything. You have to say that your idea is the best idea that's ever been conceived, and that everyone would be stupid idiots to miss out on the opportunity."

"First of all," Andy began, "I don't think I can call my dad a stupid idiot. Secondly, I don't think you're going to find many people who will follow twenty-year-old men who don't have any business experience at all."

Don heard him, but not really. He'd read too many articles about guys who made it rich on stupid things that anyone could have thought of, but the difference was that they'd had the guts to put their balls on the chopping block and go for it. The other thing they had was a good idea that no one else had ever put down on paper. He'd read that there were so many people out there with a few thousand in the bank who wanted to invest it, but were waiting for that one perfect goldmine to drop in their lap. To Don, he believed he had that goldmine, and he couldn't wait to convince everyone else.

"I will put it to you like this," said Don. "If I can convince your dad, then you think I can convince anyone, right?"

"I think if you can convince my dad to part with anything out of his piggy bank, you're a miracle worker," said Andy. "My dad came from that era when you were taught to save your money, pinch those pennies, and don't lend money to family. You're asking him to part with his three most prized philosophies."

Don understood, but it was just a feeling he had. It was a great idea, and no one was going to tell him any differently. In his heart, he knew it, and he also knew there would be a lot more people on board once they got it all rolling.

He looked up to see that Tommy Carter was gone, and so were most of his bunkmates. He'd been so wrapped up in conversation that he didn't even notice thirty or so people leaving the barracks.

"Where did everyone go?" he asked.

Andy took a look around and he too was a bit shocked to see just a handful of people still inside with them. Most of these guys were just sitting on their bunks reading, or huddled in small groups bullshitting with one another.

"I guess we were too loud, and ran everyone out," said Andy. "Tommy probably went out to find some mortar fire to have a backdrop for his next story. You and I both know that it makes the story a bit more dramatic."

"You might be right." Don stopped mid-thought and looked at his watch. "Oh, damn, I thought we were late, but we've still got a bit of time."

"Yeah, I know, we got guard duty this evening at eighteen hundred." Andy was no different than anyone else. Everyone hated guard duty, but guarding the armory was the worst job for Andy. You had to just stand there like a statue until you were relieved.

"Don't make me late, dipshit," said Don, "because I will kick your ass."

"Me? You were the one running your lips like Jesse Owens. I think it's time for you to let that cut underneath your nose heal."

"Good one."

"You liked that?"

"Yeah, not bad for a tard." Don knew who Jesse Owens was, but he wouldn't bet that these other guys would have had even the slightest clue. "Don't forget to be on time, because I'm not covering for you next time."

"You just worry about yourself," said Andy.

HE IS NOT YOUR FRIEND

It had been a few days since Andy's last ass-chewing by Brey. He didn't know for sure whether that meant he was getting better, or whether Brey was just tired of trying to make him a better soldier. He thought that he was being a good soldier, but truthfully, all he could think about was going home. Nothing else mattered to him anymore, and he was getting more and more desperate with each passing day.

Andrew could feel the heat permeating up through his boots. It was so hot in this hellhole that he could smell it. It was like the temperature had a scent to it, and it wasn't a pleasing one. He couldn't figure out if it was the sand or the smell of starvation, depression, and death wafting through the air, but he would certainly never forget it, and he knew it. *Ten times worse than a dead skunk on the highway*, he thought to himself. *It would follow you no matter where you drove.*

He looked down to see the sand lit up by the few lampposts he was standing near. There was nothing special about it, but to him, the sand was soaked through and through with death, sadness, and countless tears.

He was having short-timer's disease. Only a few more months and he would be going home to his mom and dad, to hot apple pie and home-cooked meals. He would be going home to real dirt and not just a massive sandbox in the middle of nowhere. On that thought, he brought out his mom's last letter. *She is such a sweetheart*, he thought. He looked over about fifty feet or so to his side and saw Don peering over at him. If he could read Don's mind, he would hear him screaming at him to pay attention and stop daydreaming about mounds of hay to roll around in and squirrel pot pies and other shit like that. Andy had a big grin on his face at the thought of a squirrel sticking out of his mom's potpie.

Don saw Andy sitting over there with his stupid hillbilly grin. God, sometimes he just wanted to hit that guy right in the face with a crowbar, or take a baseball bat to the back of his head and just beat it to a pulp. It wasn't a good thing to think about doing to your best friend, but he was such a kid sometimes. Don knew that Brey was close to waterboarding him, and so was everyone else there. He hated Andy's way of not taking shit seriously. It was Andy's way of fighting the nightmares that haunted him every night, but he was being self-centered, and that was never good in an environment like this. He had lots of baggage that he'd be taking home from this place, and the last thing he needed was to get someone hurt from having his finger up his nose and acting like an eight-year-old.

For the most part, Don knew that sending them to fight this war was about as shitty a thing as you could ever do to someone. To make them come over and then say to them, "Shoot this guy if he gets too close, or blow this guy's face off if he looks at you funny." Those orders were drilled into each of their heads. On a daily basis, usually. Don knew that some of these people were bad, but he knew that some had to be good, and just as many had to be scared and just wanting a good life for themselves and their children. He kind of figured that thinking they were all bad was like them thinking that everyone in the United States was a member of the Klu Klux Klan or something. Or that every American loved Brittany Spears and the Kardashians. But he knew that Americans were spoiled rich people who thought for the rest of the world, and that arrogance alone warranted the hatred that they received. And as much as Don hated to admit it in the end, they were right.

Of course that dipshit Andy was reading that letter again. If he were closer to him, he would've kicked him square in his nuts. If someone else caught him reading that, he'd get his ears bopped up smart, as Brey liked to say. He had no idea where that term came from, but he assumed it was in the hills of somewhere. Or maybe in the woods of somewhere.

Don thought that maybe putting Andy into solitary confinement might be the best for the whole squad. Everyone here knew that not paying attention to what was going on outside the fence was the difference between making it to the end of your shift, and not. It was very annoying to see Andy in Lala land half the time, and not doing what he was here to do. Don made a few *psst* noises over in Andy's direction that sounded as though he had just sprung a leak, but nothing was getting Andy's attention. He was off, way off, in dreamland again, and despite what he thought, Andy didn't want to put himself in any situation that would cause him to shoot someone. But unfortunately Andy was only seeing the picture from one angle. *Yep*, thought Don, *this boy definitely deserved a good ass whooping.*

Just then, Don thought he heard something down the line, like a chain link fence was being rattled. He didn't want to move out of the comfort of the light, but he knew that the sound needed to be checked out. He said, "Andy, I heard something. Put that fucking letter away and pay attention. I just heard the fence rattle. Stay sharp."

Don was scared. It was dark past the lights hanging above his head. All the light was being swallowed up like a black hole, and now he had to walk straight into the darkness.

Andrew was only a few paces away and began moving stealthily towards Don's position. He stopped sharp when his friend put his hand up to stop. He stood with one ear to the wind. In an almost inaudible sound, Andy whispered, "What did you hear?"

"I don't know, but I'm going to check it out. Stay here and pay fucking attention!"

Don was nervous. He felt like he had sand in his boots. His feet were sweaty, and his brow, cheeks, and neck were soaked with perspiration. He could feel the nervousness running up and down his spine like tiny little needles jabbing him from all directions.

He whispered, "Be right back, and motherfucker, stay sharp."

Andrew did not say a word. He just nodded his head and watched as Don disappeared and was engulfed by the darkness. Most of the compound was lit up, but there were definitely some pockets of extreme blackness.

Don watched as the light on his rifle scanned left, then right. He couldn't find any signs that a human was there at all. He kept walking, and the further down he walked, the more he convinced himself that it must have just been an animal that he heard. There were no footprints, no holes in the fence where someone had tried to get through. He finished walking the perimeter, which was about thirty yards or so, in a hurried pace.

He didn't like leaving Andy alone for more than a few seconds, because God knows what kind of trouble he would get himself into. He took a few short glances around again, but he found nothing. He then looked down and saw what looked like a single drop of blood.

Don knelt down to get a closer look. He shone his light on the barbed wire, and after close examination, he did indeed see some red splotches on one of the barbs. His mind went to Andy. *Oh shit*, he thought. And as he came into the light, he saw what looked to be a small boy, and Andy had knelt down about five feet in front of him.

Andrew didn't want Don to get any closer. With a stern voice, he said, "Don, stop now! Don't say anything! Please don't come any closer." Andy knew that this wasn't a joke, and this wasn't a situation that he was going to be able to talk his way out of with jokes and sarcasm.

"I can take him down," said Don.

"Please shut up, Don. This kid seems to have something strapped to him, and I have no clue what it is, but we both know exactly what it might be. I have to assume it will go boom if you put a bullet hole in it."

Andrew looked at Don with a quick glance, and then turned his head back to the boy. He smiled and tried to convey that he was a friend, and not that he was about to piss his pants. It was definitely not the same boy that had said hello to him a few times in the past. This boy was a few years older. If he had to guess, he would say fifteen, maybe sixteen. *Why is he here? Why did he hone in on me? Why tonight?* There were a thousand questions racing through his brain, and they all started with *why*.

Don couldn't believe his eyes. Was this actually happening? Why did everyone know that this was the outcome that Andy was destined for? *Why, dammit? Why?* He'd found himself in a situation that never ended well. His life, Andy's life, and who knows how many other lives were going to be affected by this kid, and he knew for sure that this day, this moment, would haunt him for the rest of his days.

Andy looked at the kid, but didn't want to believe that any of this was happening. He was going home soon. He couldn't die here, now, like this. He couldn't let them be right, that he'd gotten himself and God knows who else killed because of his naïve, uneducated little brain. He put his rifle down on the ground next to him and put his hands up in the air on either side of his head, as to say, "I come in peace, and we are friends." As he tried to move closer, the boy stepped back a step. He obviously didn't want to be approached.

The boy looked at the American and couldn't quite understand why he was supposed to hate this person, and he wasn't sure why, but he knew that he was doing a good thing. He was doing something that he knew his family would love him for. He was fighting for his country. He showed the American his thumb on a thin black tube, and his shiny new Primacore vest. He wanted him to understand, and judging by his reaction, he understood very well.

Don clenched his fist around his rifle and started shining the light on his scope over to the barracks. It was the only thing he could think of to get someone's attention aside from screaming his bloody head off. After ten seconds or so, he saw a solitary soldier step out of the hut. In an instant, he was back in the barracks. Don knew that he knew exactly what was going on and had gone for help. They had all trained over and over for this. They had listened to Brey preach this protocol in every one of the pow-wows.

He turned his attention back to Andy. "Andy, you have to let me take him out, or someone else will."

"No! Damn it! Sit still and let me talk with him."

Andy looked back at the kid with heartfelt eyes. He knew that the boy couldn't understand him, and it didn't really matter. With his rifle down, he sat cross-legged in front of the young boy. "Please don't do this," he said. "I can see in your eyes that you're not a killer. Please don't do this."

"He doesn't understand you, Andy. He doesn't want to." But Don was hushed with a wave of Andy's hand.

Then all hell broke loose as soldiers seemed to come at them from every direction. The light post turned into a pimple-faced private, and the trashcan a trigger-happy corporal. Four or five military police had arrived within seconds of Don's S.O.S. They were all stopped in their tracks with Don's hand motion to back off, which they did.

The young boy didn't like what he was seeing. There were too many people, and he knew that every single one of them wanted to put a bullet in his brain—all of them except for the man sitting in front of him. Why did he have to be here? He was supposed to sneak in and put the vest on the weapons' shed and then run away and disappear in the subsequent confusion. His instructions were to not get caught, and definitely not to give up the vest. Now he didn't know what to do. He was confused, and he wanted to go home and feed his sister, who would need breakfast in a few hours. He stared at the man sitting in front of him, then stared at the man behind the friendly one, and he glanced over at the four larger Americans with patches on their arms. He understood that his sister was not going to be fed by him on that day.

Andrew watched the boy look back and forth, side to side. He tried to talk to the boy. He tried to get him to calm down, but with guns being pointed at his face, Andy knew that wouldn't be an easy thing to accomplish. He could see now that the boy had tears streaming down his cheeks. Why would a killer be crying? It was because this boy was no killer, and Andy knew it. He couldn't explain why he was there, but he did know a terrified kid when he saw one.

After all, he saw one in the mirror every day.

Andrew watched on as everyone on his side of the fence just acted like zombies. Some wanted to run, most wanted to blow the boy's head off into tiny little pieces, but he could tell that none cared a rat's ass about this young boy's life. They wanted to make a trophy out of the kid's skull and draw straws to see whose mantle it would go on first. No one cared, and that was the saddest thing about the soldiers over there. This whole exercise in futility was a means to an end for fat cats back home, and kids like these were being used on both sides to sell a belief. His heart ached at how far humanity had fallen.

Don saw the lieutenant walk up behind him and the MPs. Don was ordered to give a status of the situation, to which he softly said, "Sir, the young boy snuck over the barbed wire about twenty yards down, and when

I went to investigate the commotion, I saw drops of blood, I ran back here to see Andy trying to talk to the boy. He appears to know no English, but Andy's calm voice seems to be helping. The boy seems to have a Primacore vest on with his thumb on some sort of push button trigger."

Brey just stood there, seeming to gather intel while he could. And then without another word, Brey just turned to Andy and said, "Knox!" But he got no response. He tried again, but not with such a hushed voice. "Knox!"

"What, dammit?"

Andy stopped in his tracks when he realized that it wasn't Don whispering in his ear. "Sir," he began, "with all due respect, I'm trying to keep everyone within fifty feet of this boy in one piece, and this kid is scared enough without people yelling."

The lieutenant took a second before replying, "Can you get close enough to him to grab him? Can you get him to surrender?"

Oh my God, what an idiot, he thought.

"Sir, I don't know how to talk to this kid except to keep calm, talk softly, and hope like hell that he doesn't blow me up, Sir."

Andy tried to see the good in everyone and everything, but this guy took the cake. You could hear it plainly in his voice that the lieutenant was way more worried about what his commanding officers were going to say than what he or the kid or anyone else was going through at the moment. Andy just wanted that man to go hide under a bed and leave him the hell alone. Could he just do that, please?

Andrew was glad to see Brey walk calmly back over to where he'd come from with one of the military policemen. He could only assume what the lieutenant had told him. He probably asked the MP to go get a flamethrower or something, since his idea of not overreacting was killing a fly with a panzer tank. But he couldn't worry about his dumb ass at the moment. It seemed that all of the commotion was bringing people to both sides of the fence. As soon as they saw what was going on, the locals started to run in the opposite direction.

So much for finding a local who spoke English, Andy thought to himself. The thought ran through his head that he was thousands of miles from home, but gawkers were no different anywhere in the world. They all wanted to see what was going on, but in this case from a safe distance. Everyone wanted to see the carnage. They wanted to see the blood all over the road.

Andy put his hand up so that the young boy would turn his gaze back on him. The boy was looking around at everyone again, and Andy couldn't get him to focus. He was obviously listening to the people yelling from down the street. He saw frustration and fear on his face.

Brey knew what was coming next, and he had no way to help Andy stop it. Brey ordered his men back. "Get back, dammit," he barked.

Knox couldn't speak the boy's language, so he couldn't tell him that everything was going to be fine. He couldn't tell him how wrong this was. He couldn't tell him that everyone here had a kid, a mom, a dad, or a cousin that they really wanted to see again.

The boy watched the conversation between the two men and realized that they didn't like one another at all. He looked down at his hand holding onto the button. He was pressing on it so hard that his thumb was starting to go numb. He didn't want to let go, but how could he tell this guy he was sorry? That he didn't want to hurt anyone? Would his mother be proud of him for this? He remembered hearing his mother and uncle arguing constantly about the soldiers that were taking over their land. Someone needed to do something. His mother would always say that not all Americans were bad, and his uncle would reply with, "Show me a good one."

Andy couldn't understand the concept of someone throwing their life away to kill other people. He couldn't understand the concept of killing people just because they didn't believe in your god, but this was a whole different can of worms to him. He'd heard the stories, he'd seen the results of these actions, but he always wondered *why*. Why would someone want to blow themselves up just to kill a handful of people who were so far down on the American totem pole that no one would even bat an eye at their destruction? Were they the bravest people in the world, or were they the most evil?

He knew that this was nothing new. Kamikaze pilots had done this eighty years ago in Japan, and they were revered as heroes. But wasn't that the government's way of brainwashing dipshit kids into throwing their lives away? *Have you ever seen a high-ranking official in one of those planes? Probably not,* he figured. Since he'd been there, he had learned that cultural beliefs were a huge influence on how you carried yourself. Unlike America, where the Kardashians were CNN-worthy and whoever had gotten a boob job made the eleven o' clock news. Sometimes he could honestly understand why his country was hated so much. He stood for the most arrogant and pompous nation in the world by far. How can you like a single person who thinks that they are so much better than you just because of their house or their car or even their bank account? *How could you not hate that country's guts?* he thought.

The young boy was getting overwhelmed. It wasn't supposed to be like this. His uncle had promised him that he would be done in ten minutes and then his sister would think him a hero. Then all of the lights came on, and he could see the people staring at him. He could see soldiers on rooftops. He saw people he knew outside the gate staring at him. He saw his neighbors, his cousins, and the parents of the kids he played with. They all kept their distance, but they were all watching him. In a matter of a few minutes, all hell had broken loose in his head, and he just wanted it to stop. What would they think of him?

He turned his gaze to the one man on this side of the fence that had shown him any kindness. He began rattling off apologies to Andy, his entire family, and most of all to his little sister. He didn't want to let her down, but he knew he'd done the one thing he swore to the heavens that he would never do—let her down—and he was so ashamed.

He didn't want to kill anyone. He didn't want to be a hero anymore. He just wanted to go home, but in his gut, he knew that that wasn't going to happen. He'd heard the stories of how the Americans would rather shoot you dead like a dog rather than help you. He could see in their eyes that he was never going home again, and nothing would ever be the same. He was never going to see Bita, his little sister, again. The only thing he prayed was that he would see his mother in the afterlife. He didn't want everyone to see him cry, but there was nothing he could do to stop the tears from coming.

Andrew saw the kid getting more and more upset. Tears were streaming down his face. He then shushed everyone in English and tried in the universal language of gesture to tell the boy that everything was going to be okay. He wasn't a master negotiator by any means, but he knew a lot of lives were on the line and it was up to him to get this boy to calm down. He said in a calm, soft, and friendly voice, "Hey buddy, it doesn't have to go down like this. It can be alright if you just calm down."

The boy had no idea of what Andy was saying, and for that matter, neither did Andy himself. He felt like a bunch of meaningless words were just falling out of his mouth like water out of a bucket. In the middle of everything, without turning around and without losing eye contact with the boy, he yelled, "Don, get me a fucking interpreter!"

The boy started spouting off more gibberish. He was trying to tell Andrew that he was repentant. That he didn't want to do this. That he knew that Andrew was a good person, and that he knew not all Americans were like his uncle had said they were. He tried to get Andrew to understand that he was so sorry. He wanted someone to know that he didn't want to kill anyone. He had just wanted to come in and sneak out without any good people getting hurt. He knew that the guy in charge was a bad man because he saw how he treated his people. He saw how he screamed his orders at them. The boy wanted to make sure that only the bad people got hurt. But the more he talked and rambled, the more clearly he understood that he could not be a hero this day. He was going to be known as the kid who had died for no reason. Or even worse, the kid who had disappeared into the Americans' clutches.

The boy thought that his mother was the sun and the moon. She was everything to him, but like everything in his country, she had a short life span. His uncle had told him about how the Americans had brought all of this death with them, and they'd brought about his mother's death as well. Now he just gazed down at his hand and wondered how he'd come to be in this situation. Did God want him to kill these people? It wasn't making sense. When his uncle had explained it, it had sounded so logical, but now it just felt so wrong. The soldier in front of him was scared, and he knew it, but he also knew that it was too late. There was only one way to fix it.

He let go of the button.

Andrew's heart felt like it was about to burst as screamed, "No!" He clamped eyes tightly shut, but now he slowly opened them. How was it that he was still alive? Nothing had happened. The boy was still in front of him. The boy too seemed shocked and amazed. And it was obvious from the look on his face that he'd thought he too was supposed to blow up.

The young boy stared at the American in front of him, and even though he knew not one word that he'd just said, he was different somehow. He had kind eyes, and he'd known that he didn't belong there with the rest of those bloodthirsty guys. This man wanted to be a friend, he wanted to help, and he meant what he said. He was a genuine person, the boy believed it. Unfortunately, though, there was going to be no happy ending for him.

He gazed out at the sea of people. Would he be a hero now? Would he be someone that his parents would have been proud of?

Then he felt a sharp pain in his gut like a hot knife burning his skin. He dropped to his knees.

Andrew was desperately pleading with the young boy to help himself, and to help everyone there, but before he could get his next word out, he heard the sharp pop of a pistol firing. He saw that it was the young boy who had taken the hit. The boy was rocking back and forth as if he didn't know which way to fall, and before he could think, Don was screaming at him, "Move, dammit, move!"

He got to his feet, wiping the splatter of the boy's blood from his cheeks, and before he could get ten feet away, a thunderclap suddenly went off in his ears. He felt himself fly forward in a hurricane of hot air. He heard a familiar voice screaming, "Medic!" He heard many other people just screaming. And then he heard and saw nothing.

GOOD TO SEE YOU AWAKE

Doctor Adam Hill watched as Andy's eyes fluttered open like a newborn butterfly. He was dazed and confused, but at least he was alive. He watched as Andy focused in on his gruff exterior. A scraggly beard that showed that he was closer to the end than the beginning of his life, naked ladies tattooed on his arms, and a scratchy voice that would scare most kids more than a Freddy Krueger movie.

Doctor Hill was an old warhorse surgeon. He had seen battle after battle and patched more kids up in his military career than a hundred doctors back in the States. He wasn't the one that you'd come to and tell him that your willy wouldn't rise, but if it got ripped off by mortar fire, then he would be the man to sew it back on. "How you doing there, my boy?" he said. He gave Andy a smile, but not a comforting one. It was either that or bark at him to get his ass up and stop wasting everyone's time.

"Where the hell am I?" asked Andy. His skull felt like someone had just hit him in the head with a sledgehammer. He tried to look around, but all he saw was light. He got the idea that he was nowhere near where he last remembered being.

The doctor watched with a big smile on his face. This was a good sign. Sarcasm was usually a confirmation that a soldier's brain didn't now resemble scrambled eggs.

The doctor pulled his light pen out of his pocket and shined the light into Andrew's eyes. "Please follow the light without turning your head," he said.

Hill was glad to see Andy respond positively. He followed his light perfectly. "Please look up," he continued, and Andy did so. "Now look down, please."

Hill didn't see any signs of neurological stress. *Good*, he thought, *one less thing I have to fix.* "Andrew, you're in a hospital just outside Kabul, and I just want you to relax for now."

Andrew blurted in a panicked voice, "Donny. Where's Donny?" He didn't have all his faculties back yet, but he did remember what had happened. "Where is Don?" he demanded.

The doctor put his hand on Andy's shoulder, keeping him from rising. "Don is fine. Mister Birch is on this ward as well, a few beds down from you, Andy."

"I need to see him. I need to see him now."

"No," said Hill, "what you need to do is lay your ass back down and relax. If you can't do that, I will have the nurse give you a shot in the butt that will relax you into a coma. Okay?"

"Okay," Andy said grudgingly. He had never heard a doctor speak to him like that back in the States, but he could tell by this guy's presence that he wasn't someone who took too much crap from anyone. He lay back on his bunk and folded his arms over his chest in a sign of reluctant submission, a promise that he would follow orders.

"Is he okay?"

"Mister Donny will be just fine. You both will. Now just relax and let the pretty nurses give you some TLC, and maybe a boner or two, okay?"

The doctor had too many people to examine to concentrate on this one patient. He'd seen this kind of patient before. The second he turned his back, he was going to be dragging himself with his elbows over to see his long-lost love.

The doctor looked up and scanned the room. "Maggie," he said to the first nurse who caught his eye, "can you come here a moment?"

Maggie set her clipboard down. "Yes, sir?"

"Can you do me a favor and put Mister Birch over next to our latest patient here?" Then he said to Andy, "Now, if you two don't play nice, I will put you at opposite ends of the room. Do you get me, Mister Knox?"

Andy nodded his head. "What's wrong with him? I mean, is he okay?"

"Any day above ground is a good day, my boy. Don't you know that?"

Hill meant what he said, but it was also his signature answer when he didn't want or have the time to go into a long, drawn-out explanation to someone. "You're both alive, and I can't fathom how that happened, but right now, both of you have some physical therapy, some counseling, and some hard looks at what just happened to you. Don't take this lightly, my boy, because if you do, it will seriously fuck with your head. I hope we are on the same page on this, Mister Knox?"

Andy figured that this was just a blow-off, but he didn't feel like arguing about it, because for some reason he was getting really sleepy. Before losing consciousness, his last thought was, *That bitch just gave me something to shut me up.*

The doctor turned to Maggie and gave further instructions. "Have him on watch, please. I see him as a little rabbit ready to hop, and I don't feel like chasing some kid around this room, so get his buddy over here as soon as you can and let me know if he gives you any shit."

"Yes, Doctor."

The nurse checked Andy's IV bottle levels, as well as his oxygen and blood pressure, and after feeling it was okay to leave, she looked down to see just a sleeping little kid.

Later, Andy's crusty eyes opened up once again to lights and noise all around him. It took him a moment to remember where he was, but then it hit him all at once. He remembered the boy. He remembered the bomb. He remembered Donny screaming at him to get the fuck out of there. Without moving his body, he looked over his right shoulder, and he was glad to see his friend in the bed next to him. He was reading what looked like a comic strip.

Andy said in a low, guttural voice, "What's up, jerkface?"

Don looked over and saw that his friend finally awake. "Good to see you awake, jerk wad," he said, matching Andy's tone. Don hadn't been sure that they would ever hold a conversation again. "About damn time. You scared the fucking shit out of me, dude."

Andy tried to sit up, but was still too weak. He let his body crumple back into the mattress. "God, I feel like I've been out for days, or years, even."

"Try days. You've been out ever since I've been here. You were in a coma for three days, at least."

Andy shook the cobwebs from his baffled, drugged brain. The last thing he remembered was some cute brunette nurse slipping him a mickey to go to sleep so that they wouldn't have to take care of him. "Days?" he asked. "Wait a minute. I was awake a few hours ago, talking with the doctor." He needed some answers, but everything seemed so foggy, and it seemed like everyone knew what was going on but him.

"I don't know about that, little man, but since they moved my bed over here, you've been zonked out like a lil' baby who just got fed."

Donny had already had a few days to get used to everything, so he figured he would show the same courtesy to Andy. "I think you should talk with the doctor, and he can fill you in on what's been going on."

"What happened, Donny? Are you okay? Don't give me that any day above ground shit either. I remember we were on post, a kid, a bomb, and Brey acting like a complete dick. So, what have I forgotten?"

Andy didn't like feeling woozy; he didn't like the feeling of helplessness sweeping over him in that moment. "Spill, damnit!"

"Okay there, guy, hold onto your panties," said Don. "Don't make me call the nurse to stick a needle in your ass again." He put his hand up to tell Andy to calm down. "I'll tell you what I know, and what I've heard. I was told by one of the guards who was here for a day that the whole thing turned into a complete shit storm. Eighteen dead and twice as many injured, from what I was told. It was a huge explosion that could be seen for miles, the way he told it." He sprang back up onto one elbow. "Oh my God, I forgot, seems Burnside blew his fucking head off in a bar a few months ago."

"What the fuck?" said Andy, shocked.

"Yeah, I know. Who knew that that dick would do something to actually help mankind for a change. Seems he was in a bar and just pulled a gun out and blew his fucking head off right then and there. Hate to say it, but I'm glad."

"Dude!"

"Well, I'm sorry, but I am. He didn't give a shit about anyone but himself. He probably got fired or something and then just couldn't handle it."

"He didn't say anything?"

"One guy told me he pointed to everyone at the bar and said 'toe tags' like five times, and then, *pow*."

"What the hell does that mean?"

"Don't know, and I don't care."

"What about the kid with the bomb?"

"He turned out to be some kind of diversion," Don continued. "A nobody that no one wanted to claim. No one knows his name, and no one ever came to claim the body. No one came forward about it at all, but they damn sure used him to tell the whole world about how the American bullies shot him down before he had a chance to surrender."

"That is so much bullshit. He was—"

"Are you going to let me finish or do you want to tell this story?" said Don, interrupting him.

Andy gave him the sign that his lips were sealed.

"Everyone knows that was crap. Everyone knows that our rifles don't make a popping sound like we heard out there. More than anything, everyone knows that the minute he started rambling, he had to be shut up, and quick. I can't tell you who shot him, and I can't even tell you whether the boy had a name, but I can tell you with certainty that whatever went down out there, there won't be a damn thing done about it."

While Don had to pause to take a breath of air, Andy took the opportunity to slip in his own thoughts. "That kid was not a murderer, and it's so fucked up that this shit had to happen. So now it's all swept up and forgotten already?"

"The dirt is all under the rug and patted down, and a file cabinet was set on top of it so that the dirt would never get out," said Don. "No one cares even a little bit about that boy, and no one cares two shits about anyone over here except the people raping the women and taking the resources of the land and squeezing every dollar they can squeeze out of this place. We came over here naïve little shits thinking that we were coming over to save these poor people. But that's not what we're here for, Andy. We're here to stand guard while our government robs these people blind. I hate to admit it, but all the evidence points to just that conclusion. You were right."

Don leaned back on his left arm and let out a sigh that indicated that he knew he was part of the problem, not the solution.

Andy totally agreed with everything Don had just said. He knew that he too was just a pawn, and that no one gave a crap about these people even a tiny bit. Watching the news, you would think that America had run over there like the Red Cross to give aid to Afghanistan, but the ugly truth was that if there was an opal, a diamond, or a drop of oil, some congressman was making sure it was on a boat headed back to his house.

"Enough about this shit," said Andy. "How are you feeling?"

"I feel like someone ran over me with a Hummer, but it's not as bad as it looks," said Don. "I just had a third surgery on my hand, and I have another grueling therapy session in an hour or so, but when all is said and done, I think we're both lucky to be alive. I wonder sometimes what could have happened, but I try to just concentrate on getting better, going home, and hopefully forgetting about these dickheads all together. In a nutshell, that's how I feel. How about you?"

"I feel okay, I guess. It may be the pain killers talking though. I feel like two Hummers ran over my chest, and I itch all over, especially my back, but I guess I'm doing as well as can be, since I could just as easily be playing a harp right now."

"Your chest hurts because you had two broken ribs. I heard the nurse and doctor talking about your injuries a few days ago, and it seemed like the doc said you had broken your leg or something, and I did hear him say something about two ribs that he splinted. So, you better sit still, or they'll put you back to sleep again, and the shit they give ain't like the Tylenol PM that you get back home. This stuff knocks you out for days."

Don didn't want to think about any of this too much. He just wanted the doctor to make his hand better so that he could just go home and forget about everything.

Andy peeked under the covers and saw that his chest was bandaged. He tried to take a deep breath, but had to stop as a sharp shooting pain stopped him in his tracks. He wondered how badly his leg had been broken. He couldn't tell with it all bandaged up from groin to toenail. His frustration was written all over his face.

"How long are we going to be here?" he asked finally.

Don knew the look on Andy's face all too well. He felt the same way. No one liked hospitals, but every day he looked at his hand, and every day he couldn't feel his fingers, and every day he had to look at the other guys who were all royally messed up, and he was reminded every time of that night. He just wanted to be someplace where there weren't constant reminders everywhere he looked. He didn't want to see friends of his crying in their pillows because they knew what the rest of their life was going to be like. A good number of them crying not because of their injuries, but because they hadn't died.

"I don't know about you," Don began, "but they're giving me therapy almost every day and trying to rehabilitate my injury, and I'm hoping they send my ass home afterwards. Either way, I think I'm going to be here for a while."

Andy could see how worried Don was about his hand. "How does it feel?" he asked.

Don wasn't one to say *boo hoo* or the *why me?*; he was more the *get it done and don't stand in my way* kind of guy. "How it feels is sucky," he began, "but shit happens, and we just have to deal."

Andy had never seen Donny like this before. He was always the cool cucumber of the bunch, never letting anything bother him. For him to be snapping his head off like this, he must have been told that he might lose his hand or something. "I'm so sorry, Don," said Andy. "I hope everything will be okay."

"Yeah, it's going be fine," Don agreed, "but it's going to take some physical therapy is all." Even as he said the words, though, he didn't feel like he was doing a good job of convincing anyone that he was fine with his uncertain future, including himself. In his mind he had already lost his hand. He knew his luck and it was never good. His mind kept going back to how his hand was burnt and unrecognizable when he'd passed out a few days ago. He knew about skin grafts and other procedures like that, but he was definitely worried about not ever being able to use his hand again.

Andy wanted to believe him, but he knew better. If Andy had to guess, he figured the doctor said something to Donny along the lines of, "If we don't see some vast improvement, we may have to consider more drastic measures." Andy wished he could do something, but he knew in his gut that it was all his fault.

He turned away and tried to catch the nurse's attention. "Nurse, can you ask the doctor to come over here please?" He paused for a moment and then asked, "Could I also get a pad and paper so that I can write my folks a letter?"

The nurse shook her head. "I will ask Doctor Hill to come over when he has a moment, and I'll see what I can get you for writing your folks." She then disappeared around the corner.

Andy could see Don out of the corner of his eye. He could tell Don wasn't in the mood to talk any longer. He just wanted to be left alone. He had to get ready for therapy and probably had to psyche himself up for the agony that he was sure he had to withstand.

Andy scanned the room and noticed the others lying around. He didn't know the majority of the people in the room. There was one guy who he may have seen once before, but he had no clue as to his name or where he'd seen him.

He interlaced his hands behind his head and let his thoughts wander back to that night. He knew he'd been getting through to that kid. *Why did they have to kill him?* Andrew knew that the kid was just a stupid pawn in some asshole's master plan to bring down the Big Bad Wolf. There was absolutely no reason for that kid to be there except stupidity. And the thing that got him the most riled up was the fact that not one soul cared about that boy or anyone who'd gotten hurt because of what he'd done. It made him sick.

As he was lost in deep thought, a reassuring hand landed on his shoulder. Doctor Adam Hill liked Andrew, but the majority of the guys there were also great guys who life had just taken a great big crap on. Most of them left there broken both physically and spiritually. It broke his heart some days, but if he wasn't more like a drill sergeant than Marcus Welby, he would have a ward full of sad sack, useless soldiers, and it would drain him until he was no help to any of them. It was no good to feed that thought process. He had to make them believe that they weren't broken, just different.

He didn't mince words with Andy, "Why are you just lying there?" he said. "You should be up and about by now."

Andy was confused, but he played along. He could banter, if that was what the doctor wanted. "If your nurse over there hadn't shot me full of a tranquilizer that could've knocked out a bull elephant, I guess I could've started therapy days ago."

Adam wasn't shy about barking orders, but he loved it when the guys tried to match wits with him. "Look, Mister Knox," he began. "What I do know is that it's time to stop lying here eating ice cream and playing with your peter when Maggie walks by."

He saw Maggie's eyes pop up from her clipboard long enough to give a slight chuckle.

"I can understand why," he said, "but it's not going to get you better. It's just going to make you dehydrated. How do you feel today?"

Andy was red in the face after the comment about the nurse. All he saw was Maggie walking by now and figuring he always had his hand on his peter. Andrew tried to sit up, but winced in pain for his efforts. He felt like someone was inside his chest and trying to pry his ribs apart to get out.

"I feel like shit," Andy said, "but I want to do whatever it takes to get me out of here so that I can go home. I only have a few months left in this army of ours."

"Well, I have good news and bad news. Which would you like to hear first?"

Andrew thought for a moment. "Give me the good news first. Tell me that there's a plane outside ready to take me home, and that my mother's chicken noodle soup is all the medicine I need."

"Well, I can tell you that after you spend a few weeks here doing therapy and getting your head screwed back on straight, you'll be on the next transport back to the States where your mommy can stuff you with all the chicken noodle soup you can eat. How does that sound?" The doctor cleared his throat and then continued. "The bad news is that until we get you up and walking around, you'll have more of a chance to get pneumonia and all kinds of other shit that you don't want. " Doctor Hill ran his pen up Andy's toes and asked, "Do you feel that?"

Andrew looked at his leg in a cast, looked down at his ribs, then looked back at Adam. "I didn't feel anything. Am I okay?"

"You took a pretty big chuck of concrete to your spine, and a temporary loss of function is quite common in situations like this. You will get your feeling back, and we'll work with you every day until you're chasing these nurses around." He bent down and whispered, "For the good-looking soldiers, the nurses run a bit slower, so you might have a better chance."

The doctor stood back up. He didn't believe in sugar-coating stuff, but he didn't want them obsessing about shit either.

"Sit back and relax," he said finally, "and if you feel good tomorrow, we 'll start a very light therapy session to get you out of that bed and dust off those bed sores."

"Do I really have a choice?" Andy didn't like it one bit, but in reality, a few weeks there versus a few months with Brey—to him, it was a no brainer. He joked, "I think therapy includes nice long sponge baths, doesn't it?"

"Sounds like a plan. I'll send Johnny over to get right on that."

Andrew took a big gulp. The thought of some guy bathing him didn't sit well in his gut. "I think I'm okay for now," he said. "Let's just worry about getting me home. I think I can go home a little smelly if need be."

"Your choice, my boy, but I hear Johnny knows how to give a great sponge bath," the doctor continued. "Some guys ask for him by name. He makes you feel like a million bucks, especially when he gets that undercarriage all clean and shiny."

He was just messing with Andy, who finally smiled and leaned back on his bed. Adam turned away from Andrew and started speaking with Donny.

"And how are you doing, Mr. Birch?" he asked.

Andy waved his hand until he got Maggie's attention. "Can I get that pen and paper, please?" He wanted to write his mom so she wouldn't worry. She'd probably be wondering why she hadn't gotten anything in the mail by now.

"Sure thing, hon," said Maggie. She grabbed a pad of paper and pen off the table and walked it over to the young man. "Here you go, Andy. I'm sorry, I totally forgot."

"That's okay, Maggie. I know you have a bunch of other stuff to do."

"Thanks. Tell your mom that you'll be home soon, and to have that chicken noodle soup ready when you get there."

Maggie tried to be a friend to the wounded soldiers, but on some occasions she just had to go into the other room and cry, because anyone an ounce of empathy couldn't help but feel for these guys. Most of them were either so messed up in the head that they could barely function, or else they wallowed in self-pity so badly that they isolated themselves from everything and everyone. It was the ones who got themselves together and dealt quickly with the hands that life dealt them who were the ones she tried to help the most. She wasn't sure which way Andrew fell just yet, but for his sake, she hoped that everything could be put behind him and that he could have some semblance of a real life.

"Anytime, Maggie," he said, "and I will."

Andy could see that even when her head was down as she wrote something in her pad, Maggie had heard everything that the old doctor had said. As old as he was, the doctor was either a great practitioner of medicine or an old senile man who left his wristwatch inside people's bellies. Andy just had to hope that the latter was not the case.

Andy took it slow and tried to pull himself up in the bed. Maggie instinctively went behind him and braced him under his arms so that he could pull himself up into a more upright position. Once he got himself situated, she adjusted the bed to meet his torso and slid a pillow down to his lower back for support. "How is that, young man?" she asked.

"Perfect, thanks."

He found himself liking her more and more. She was about fifteen years his senior, but he bet a lot of guys fell hard for her. She was so sweet, and had the smile of an angel. There was no other description he could think of. She was certainly in the right profession. He could tell that she truly cared about people, and in the very short time that he'd been awake and alert, he could already see that every guy that yelled out her name was met with nothing but a huge smile that lit up the room.

He watched as she walked back to the station, and he could tell she had a nice figure. *That nurse's outfit makes her look awfully cute*, he thought. Then he took to writing his letter to his parents.

Dear Mom and Dad,

There is so much to be said. First, I got wounded, but I'm okay. Secondly and most importantly, I'm coming home soon. I don't know when, but I just want this whole thing to be over. I thought I was going to help people, but I've determined that nobody is being helped over here. They are being pillaged just like we're accusing them of doing to us. I always thought that we were the good guys and that we came to everyone's rescue, but I don't see it that way anymore. My world, so to speak, has been turned upside down. And I don't know whether to thank them for it or hate them for it. I'm not the brightest candle on the chandelier, but I've figured out that if you oppress people, they will rise up, but if you get them to believe the Big Bad Wolf is out there and you're the only one that can protect them, then people will follow you anywhere and do anything.

I need to tell you this and get it off my chest. I'm not telling you this to scare you, but I'm telling you this to get you to understand that the world is not what we think it is. Don and I were sitting at our post and guarding our compound. It was routine stuff, or so I thought. A kid came in with a bomb on his chest, and to make a very long night into a very short story, the kid was just standing there in front of me crying, the bomb wasn't real, and someone used the kid as a distraction so that they could sneak in and blow up the thing that we thought the kid was trying to blow up, if that makes any sense. That kid wanted to be home playing stickball or whatever they play here. I wouldn't know, because none of the soldiers are let out of their cages unless it's to go kill something. We don't have any contact with these people to show them that we're here to help. We're here as pit bulls ready to bite if they get too close. It makes me sick, but anyway, I was trying to calm him down when a gunshot rang out and the kid fell to his knees, and a few seconds later a bomb at the munitions shack went off. I don't know anything after that except that I woke up in the hospital with a cast on my leg and my ribs bandaged up. I think I have a broken leg and a few ribs that are hurting like hell right now.

I feel so bad for the boy, but I got Don in this situation, too, and I feel like I can't fix it. He won't tell me, but I know he may lose his hand. I know how he thinks, and when he shuts down, he's scared. I know that you and I talked about this, but I want him to come live with us. I know you said it was okay, but I want him to know that he has a family when he gets out of here. I can't fix his hand, but I want him to know that I can at least help him not be alone. I hope this letter finds you still in a generous mood, because I need this as much as he does.

The doctor here says that I have a few weeks of therapy and then I'll be able to come home. This is my first day awake, so I'm still a little bit out of it. The stuff they give you here could knock out a rhino. I've never had a

*three-day drunk before, but I imagine it's something like
the way I feel now. I have such a headache, and my chest
feels like Pop's tractor is sitting on it. Pop, can you please
park your tractor in the barn where it belongs?*

*I'm going to let you go now, but I just wanted to say that
I love you both, and the good news is that I will be home
soon, and Maggie the nurse here told me to tell you to
have some chicken noodle soup ready for me when I get
there. I may have to be coddled for a while, but I should
be back to normal in a few months.*

*Don't cry, Mom, I'm fine. Could I be writing this letter if
I weren't fine? Just count the days off on the calendar
next to the fridge and figure that in six weeks or so I
should be back home helping Dad with the mowing and
helping you with the dishes.*

*And oh, by the way, the next time I get a big idea to go
see the world, hit me with a rolling pin, okay? I love you
guys.*

Your Loving Son, Andrew

Andy didn't realize at first that his cheeks were wet with tears. He
placed the pen on the blanket and hurriedly took his hand to wipe the
visible emotions from his face. He missed his parents so much, and he just
wanted to be home so badly. He wanted to forget about little kids who run
up to you with explosives strapped to their bodies. He wanted to forget
about people starving in the streets. He wanted to forget about dickheads
like Brey barking orders at you so that they can feel important. And he
mostly wanted to forget how he'd gotten his best friend blown up, and then
possibly having to deal with the guilt if he lost the hand.

He saw the face of that boy so clearly in his mind's eye. Why was the world so screwed up? He shook his head and broke himself out of the daydream. He could tell right away that this kind of thinking wasn't going to be healthy for anyone.

He tried to get the thoughts out of his head before they became overpowering. He looked over and saw an empty bed where his friend had been just a short time ago. He figured that Don must be in therapy somewhere. He sat and watched the happenings of the clinic. Nurses were running back and forth down the hallway. He watched as other guys walked around with canes, walkers, crutches, some of them with plastic legs and arms, and he wondered how many of them were there because of that kid.

Andy saw someone who he thought he recognized, but he didn't look like he wanted company. His face screamed, *leave me the hell alone.* He just sat there in his chair and barely moved a muscle. Andy wondered how people like Maggie could deal with this every single day. He didn't think he could deal with being around this kind of depression on a daily basis. It was too hard to be in a good mood and help someone wipe their ass or feed someone just because some jackass kid with a bomb strapped to his chest had ripped off their arms.

It's such a shame, Andy thought. He bet that the guy across from him was at one time a decent guy who thought more about baseball than killing people over in this godforsaken place. He wanted to get up and go help him, talk to him, and tell him that everything was going to be okay, but he knew that it wasn't. He was going to be like this for a long, long time, and when he did eventually snap out of it, he would be nothing like the boy his parents had known. Unfortunately, that was just the way things were over there.

Andrew watched as Maggie went from bed to bed. She beamed her big smile at each of the guys, and they couldn't help but smile back. She had one of those smiles that was infectious. Andy was even guilty of it himself. She made him feel like it was going to be okay. He knew that most of what these guys were dealing with couldn't be fixed with a smile, but it was better than the alternative. Andy wondered how many lives she'd saved with that smile of hers.

He leaned on his elbows and tried to prop himself up, but the pain in his side was excruciating, so he fell back into place. He let out a loud sigh. He just wanted to go to his old, broken-down house and see his parents and Peanut, and seeing the guy across from him and hearing another guy's cries on the other side of the room just made him want to go home even more. He wanted to leave before he became one of those guys lost to the war that no one was going to think twice about a month from now.

He took a deep breath, wishing that Don would get back from therapy. He didn't like being there by himself. He was in a ward full of people, but he couldn't think of a time when he'd felt this alone. He crossed his forearm over his brow and allowed himself to drift deeply into thought. In a place like this, he figured a man's mind was about the only place where he dwelled, and was probably also the most dangerous place to go.

He tried to think about what his mom was going to look like when he got home. Was his dad going to hug him, salute him, shake his hand? He was sure that his mom would cry, but would he be able to control his own emotions? He got choked up just thinking about it. What would the other guys that he'd known be like? Would they even be there, or would they have been blown up at some other stupid base?

The thought brought him back to thinking about the young boy. He couldn't get his face out of his head. He'd been so young. Not much younger than Andy, but he looked like a little kid to him.

How would you hate someone to the degree of throwing your life away? The questions plagued him. Andrew couldn't understand that level of hatred. He'd thought about coming over as some kind of ambassador of peace and having everyone holding hands by the time he left, but he knew now that he'd been a fool. Brey was right. Don was right. Why couldn't he just be more like what Brey and everyone else wanted him to be? More soldier and less stand-up comic. The boy, though, hadn't looked like someone who wanted to kill him. He looked scared. He looked like he'd just stepped into a cow pie and didn't know what a cow pie was.

It dawned on Andy that the kid had to be put down like a dog before he could change sides. It was all clear. He didn't want to kill anyone. Someone had made him do it. Every enlisted man had figured out

Andrew's epiphany already, unbeknownst to him. He was happy about the realization, but even more saddened at the thought of the boy being used. But then again, he knew all too well about how easy it was to do, because he'd duped as well.

He was startled from his daydream by a squeaky bed being wheeled up next to him. It was Don coming back from therapy. *Finally*, he thought, *someone to talk to*. He wanted the thoughts of little kids blowing themselves up, and thoughts of missing limbs and eyes and ears and fingers, to get the hell out of his head.

"Andy?" Don could see that Andy was a million miles away, and from the look on his face, he wasn't daydreaming about eating a potpie. "Andrew!"

"I'm right here," said Andy. "You don't have to yell."

He was glad to be shaken from the road he was heading down. "How was therapy?"

"It was fine," said Don. "My fingers still don't want to do what I'm telling them to do, but the doc says I just have to give it time which is bull. I know what road this shit leads down. I know when someone is looking at me thinking how can I tell this kid I can't save his hand. This time next week I know it will be gone. There is a time for self-pity, but now isn't the time. There's no real good time for self-pity, actually, but this is about the worst place you can indulge in it."

Don really didn't want to talk about it, because then he would contemplate all the ways he could have held his hand out or not been so close. He wanted to be away from this place. He wanted to be away from Andy. He wanted to be away from anything that reminded him he was never going to be normal again

"I'm so sorry, Don, Please don't give up." said Andy. And he wanted to say more, but was immediately cut off before he could utter another word.

"Stop it, now!" Don exclaimed. "Shit happens, and that's all that needs to be said. I could blame Brey for being such a pussy, I could blame myself for being so close to the bomb. Hell, I could blame the President for making me come over here. There are a million people I could blame, but neither one of us is getting any satisfaction from taking that road."

Don did blame Andrew for what had happened to him, though. He blamed him for not taking this shit seriously, blamed him for reading letters when he should have had his eyes peeled on real danger. But he could never let Andy know about these feelings.

"I hear you, Don, but I don't care what you say," said Andy. "It was my fault, and we both know it. So, we will agree to disagree?"

Andy laid back on his bed and stared up at the ceiling.

Don really wanted to yell out, "Damn right it was your fault, you stupid motherfucker!" But what came out of his mouth was, "Stop being such a drama queen. We're here because shit happens, and whether you did it, or I did it, or that kid did it, or the guy pulling the strings did it, it's irrelevant right now. We're here, and one day we won't be. It's that simple."

He figured he'd said his peace. He wished he could believe his own advice, though. It would make it so much easier. He loved Andy, but he really wondered whether he or Andy could get past this, and if they didn't, then what would that mean as far as their friendship beyond these walls? He wished he knew.

Andrew did not reply. He didn't want to hear it. He said a silent prayer for Don's hand, because if he didn't get better, how could he look at him every day and not feel guilty? How could they stay friends with that kind of cloud hanging over them? At the moment, it didn't seem possible.

BACK AT THE RANCH

For the last few months, Mike and Marie had been nervous wrecks worrying about Andy. They knew their boy, and they knew that killing anyone or anything was not in his makeup. He wanted to be the leader of a pack of do-gooders and make a difference. It was a shame that he'd gone over with one expectation, and that the real reason he was over there was nothing like what he had imagined.

Learning that Andrew had been wounded had made them ten times more anxious than before. After reading Andy's letter, Marie couldn't sit still; she was either cooking, cleaning, or crying. She wanted her son home, safe and sound. She didn't want to talk about any of it. She didn't want to hear about the things he'd seen. The cool vehicles he'd driven, or most importantly, the cool things that the other guys did. She'd heard so many stories from other mothers, and she didn't want Andy telling those stories anywhere near earshot of her. More than anything, she was afraid that she and Mike were going to get back a kid who looked like their Andy, but was really just a traumatized version of what their boy had been. It scared her to death that she might not ever see the real Andy again.

As Marie read Andy's letter for the hundred millionth time, she was startled by her husband's hands pressing down on her shoulders. "Hey, babe," said Mike.

Mike did his crying in the barn. He did his worrying behind the veil of a horse's mane. He fixed, oiled, lubed, and brushed anything and everything that he could get his hands on. He knew exactly what Marie was thinking, because he thought the same thoughts. "He's fine, Marie," he said. "He'll be home as soon as the doctor releases him. He's okay."

Mike wasn't a great liar, but he tried his best to put on his convincing face—for her and for himself. "Just think about how he'll be home soon and you can smother him in hugs and kisses and hot apple pies."

"Thanks, Mike, but I'm sorry, I won't be any good until he is here and I can make sure that he is really our Andy. I don't want a broken Andy that your army has turned into a mindless robot."

"I hear you, I hear you," said Mike. "He will be home soon, I swear."

Mike didn't even know what he was saying anymore. He just wanted her to stop crying, but he didn't think anything would get her to stop until Andy was home.

"Stop it, please," said Marie. "Just stop it."

"Exactly what does that mean?"

"You know exactly what that means. Who exactly is coming home? Who are we going to meet at the bus stop? Are we going to see Andy, or some kid fucked up in the head?"

Mike heard her, but he was still astonished at the fact that she had cursed. She usually only brought those kinds of words out for special occasions.

"I know, Marie. I know exactly. I've seen it."

Mike sighed and tried to change the subject. "How is Donna's son doing?"

His weak attempt to end the current line of discussion did not go unnoticed. Marie appreciated the attempt, but she wasn't done with the pity party just yet. With an agitated and perturbed tone, she said, "I have to go over there today, as a matter of fact. Jerry is in his own little world still. He rarely talks, and when he does, it's just about bullshit."

Another curse. Mike wasn't used to this side of Marie. She was scared, really scared, and unfortunately there wasn't a damn thing he could do but squeeze her shoulders and tell her that everything was going to be fine.

"It's not bullshit, babe. He's messed up because of the stuff he saw. He needs time to be surrounded by his mom and his family, and bring him around to the way Jerry used to be."

Marie didn't believe that for a second. Jerry had been home for four months, and he was still upset about everything. He got mad when Donna didn't have his dinner ready yet, or that the cable went out, or that the dog barked too loud. What if Andy came back like that? She didn't know if she could deal with that. She saw what it had done to Donna; the grey hair that had popped up on her head overnight. The way Donna seemed tense and frustrated all the time. The way she seemed to becoming a hermit. It had done a real number on her, and Marie prayed to God every day that Andy would not come home like Jerry.

"I know, Mike," she said, "but what if our little boy comes home stuck in that fucking place? What if he comes home and can't get that place out of his head? What do we do then?"

Mike was starting to get choked up. He knew all too well that Andy could come home even worse than Jerry. He could be the one that snaps and kills his whole family. He didn't really believe that Andy could do anything like that, but the news was full of stories.

"We hug him, and we don't let him go," said Mike. "We tell him we love him, and we tell him that he is the best thing that ever happened to us. We keep saying it until we have Andy back."

Mike wiped his cheek and turned so that all Marie could see was his silhouette. He stared out the window toward the weather-beaten barn. "We may be getting upset about nothing," he concluded. "According to his letter, he's okay. He's banged up, but he'll be home soon. He'll be home and then I can finally let out this breath that I've been holding."

"Do you really think that he'll be okay? Do you really think that he'll still be our son? I mean, do you really think he will be our Andy?"

Marie wanted Mike to convince her, because until she held him and talked with him, she could only see Jerry, or maybe even a worse version of her own son sitting at the table, throwing his food up against the wall.

Mike sincerely wanted to believe that Andy would still be Andy, but because of his own experiences, he knew that that was next to impossible. He himself had seen the carnage and inhumanity that he'd endured in the jungles of Vietnam. He remembered the crying and the moans from the guy lying next to him at the medivac. To this day, his dreams were sometimes filled with the faces of his youth. He missed Tommy, Johnny, and James. They were inseparable in boot camp and then over in Saigon. They were only eighteen, but they were the truest of friends, and it wrenched his gut when he saw them in his dreams get slaughtered by mortar shells. It was like a bad record that kept skipping, and he wished that it would just stop.

He chalked it up as penance for the sins he'd committed over there. He wondered if they would have still been friends if they had all lived. He liked to think that they would have kept in touch, but the reality was that those guys would have just reminded him of a time that he would have preferred to forget. It made him feel so guilty that he'd made it back and they hadn't, and truthfully, it had taken him decades to learn how to deal with that guilt. It wasn't until Andy was born that he could finally start living for the boy and not his friends. He was saddened to think that the burden had been passed down to the next generation.

He answered Marie's question as honestly as he knew how. "The day he left, Andy changed. He took one step closer to becoming a real man. He is never going to be the little baby that you want him to be forever. Whether he has issues or not because of his injuries, he is still never going to be that Andrew again."

"What about his friend that he plans on bringing here?" asked Marie. "What if *he* is all messed up? What if he's violent like Jerry?"

"I don't know about his friend. I can't tell you whether it's a good idea or a bad one. I guess we will have to meet him in order to make that decision. But if Andy sees a friend in him, then I guess we should, too."

Marie was usually the empathetic one in the family, but when it came to Andrew, her maternal instincts kicked into high gear and she became an overprotective lioness. "What are we going to do if this guy has a lot of physical problems that we can't help him with? Neither one of us are in any shape to help this guy to the bathroom."

She felt bad even saying it, but her main concern was her son, not some guy who she had never met. When Andy came home, it was going to be him that needed her attention, not some stranger.

It was odd for Mike to hear Marie talk about casting someone out, especially with all the work she had volunteered with Donna and Jerry. In his opinion, Jerry was a complete mess. He couldn't let it go. The war had done something in his head that his mother couldn't fix, nor could Auntie Marie's chicken soup. His paranoia and self-pity were eating him up, and as much as Mike wanted him to miraculously get better, he doubted very seriously that it would ever happen. That type of behavior usually turned self-destructive, ending most times in suicide, or at least a trip to an insane asylum. He prayed that Andy would not have the same grim future.

Mike looked at his wife with tears brimming in his eyes. He couldn't hold them back any more than he could hold back the ocean.

"I don't know what we'll do," he began, "but we'll do something. I won't know anything until he's here and we make up our own minds. If he's more than we can handle, or if I think he is anything like Jerry, then he will just have to leave. I don't know what else to say."

What Mike wasn't saying was, "What if Andy is more like Jerry than Donny?" It scared him to death to think of Andy's mind being all messed up because of the war. From his letter that he'd sent, he had been standing in front of a kid trying to talk him out of blowing everyone up, and before he could succeed, someone shot the boy and made sure that the bomb went off. Mike couldn't fathom the guilt and sadness that his son must be enduring at that moment. It broke his heart.

Marie wanted to wipe his tears away and take all of his heartache from him, but that wasn't something that anyone could do. What she could do was stand up, wrap her little arms around his forty-inch waist, and just hold him.

Mike draped his arms around her neck and just pulled her close. He was so fortunate to have someone who truly cared about him. He knew he without a doubt that he was blessed with having found her. He let the tears flow, some of them falling onto the top of his wife's head as they rolled off his cheek. He didn't like to admit it, but it felt good to let all of those emotions out. Being afraid, frightened, or terrified didn't even start to scratch the surface of the fear that was in his heart for both his boy and his wife.

Marie finally pulled herself away from him. "I told Donna that I would be over by ten, so I'd better get going. Do you need me to do anything before I head over?"

"I'm okay," said Mike. "I think I'll just sit here for a few minutes and then head back out to the barn."

"If you need me, just give Donna a call, but I should be home by noon to fix your lunch, okay?"

Mike just wanted to be alone. "That sounds great. I will see you later. Go help Donna."

Mike put her hand on his cheek to wipe the moisture from it, and then she walked over to the countertop, grabbed her purse, and went to the kitchen door leading out to the driveway in the rear of the house. She blew Mike a kiss and shut the door behind her before she started crying once more.

Mike took a deep breath and then let out an even bigger exhale. It was as if he was trying to rid himself of all the bad mojo that seemed to be unshakeable in his mind. He walked over to the counter and grabbed the pen and paper that Marie normally used. It was time he wrote his own letter. It was time that he had a man-to-man talk with his son. He needed to get some things off his chest.

He returned to the table and put his writing utensils down. He took a moment to think of everything he wanted to say and how to say it without the letter becoming some kind of great American novel.

Dear Andrew,

Where do I start, son? I'm sitting here alone writing this. You know I'm not the best writer or speller, so don't hold that against me please. Mom is over Donna's house helping out with Jerry. He is a handful, to say the least. Mom goes over and reads to him, helps out with laundry, or is just an ear for Donna to bend. I know that there's no person in the world more equipped to help than your mom, but that's not what I want to talk about in this letter. This letter is one between you and me, and this is not a letter I want your mother to ever see.

I want you to know first of all that we love you so much, and that nothing will ever change that. I want you to know how proud we are of what you've done. I want you to know that whatever you have to do to get home, you do it boy, and get your butt back here. Get back here and forget about all the crap that you've gone through.

I'm not the best one for reassuring words or comforting hugs, but I need you to know how we feel. How I feel. Once, I thought the worst thing in the world was to end up alone, but I found out being surrounded by people who made me feel alone was even worse. That is what the army did to me, and I believe that you now feel the same. I realized I had nothing in common with those people, even though we did fight a war together. I want you to know that I've been there, son, and what you're feeling will have to be dealt with. I want you to know that I'm going to help you with just that. I know the pain you're feeling. I know, believe me. I've never told anyone this, but the things I've seen used to make me sick to my stomach. It used to make me want to just hide away. I wanted everyone to just leave me alone. I wanted the pain to stop, but truthfully, it doesn't. It becomes a part of who you are, and it takes a lot of work and a lot of time. It gets easier, but it never leaves, so don't expect it to. That's my boy, is something you're going to have to come to terms with, the sooner the better. I'm so sorry that you have to feel this kind of pain, but you will find a good woman just like I did, have a great kid just like I did, and you'll learn that being there for them becomes more important than drinking the pain away. Or should I say, attempting to wash the pain away with a bottle. Trust me, son, it doesn't work.

*When you get back, I'll help you find the right people
that can help you with just how to deal with this. Your
letter was not that detailed, but the little we do know,
I'm sure is not easily forgotten. Use it to make yourself
better, more understanding. Don't let it make your heart
hard. For every guy who doesn't care, there are ten who
do. Make them the guys you hang out with, and you will
be just fine. I could sit here and write a hundred pages
about what you need to do, but the reality is that you'll
need to find your own way. But I will be there in any
way I can, so don't ever think you are going through this
alone.*

*I know you don't know what I mean today, but you will
eventually. Don't let that agony and darkness be who you
are. If you ever need anything, you just pull me aside
and tell me that you need me. Whatever you need to say
or do or deal with, I will try my best to help you.*

*Your friend Donny, how is he doing? Is he okay? Can he
use his hand? I know in your last letter you said that his
hand wasn't doing well, and the guys were calling him
Donny Crabclaw. First, guys can be such idiots. Second,
they're going through their own thing, and you should pity
them more than hate them for teasing your friend. I hope
he is doing better since your last letter. I look forward
to meeting your friend, and your mom and me will do
anything we can to help him.*

*Always know how much your mom and I love you. You are
the world to both of us.*

Your Loving Dad

TIME FOR THERAPY, ANDY

Andrew lay in his bunk listening to the moans and the sobs of the other guys around him, and he sometimes thought that he would prefer to take his chances out in the desert than to listen to this racket for one more day. His injuries seemed to be taking forever to heal, and it appeared that the doctors were keeping him there forever. It had already been weeks, and every time he thought he was getting better, they told him of another tear or a nerve malfunction or some other nonsense, and then he'd start a whole new round of treatment.

Andy tried to have a positive outlook on things, but without Donny around, it seemed harder and harder. Don was so wrapped up in self-pity and anger that he couldn't keep himself together. Every time he tried to do anything meticulous with his hands, he exploded. He was trying his best, but training his left hand to be his dominant hand was not coming easy to him. Every time he came back from therapy, he looked more and more distressed and distraught. Andy could see the anger in his eyes. He could see that it was directed at him at times, too. Don could say whatever he wanted, but Andy could tell that the anger he had toward him just on the surface was ready to explode. Andy didn't know how to help, and the guilt was eating him up.

Andrew saw the hate in his friend's eyes that a man has for an enemy, not a friend. He wore his emotions on his sleeve, and Andy could tell with each passing day that their friendship was in dire emergency of becoming something that only existed in the past. He didn't know how to fix it. He wanted to cut his own hand off and hand it to Donny, and he would have gladly done so if he thought it would have fixed Donny's problem. But he also had his own issues to deal with. His muscles were becoming fatigued. He wanted to be done with this place, but each time he took a step forward, it seemed something slapped him back ten steps in the other direction. It was annoying, frustrating, and maddening to feel like he was making headway only to hear some quack tell him that he needed more time, to be patient and let the body do what it needed to do. He didn't want to hear that he needed more time. He didn't want to hear some psychiatrist tell him that he had issues he needed to deal with. He knew that shit all too well.

He recognized easily that the kid would never have been there if Andy hadn't tried to become friends with the first one he'd seen, or that maybe no one would have gotten hurt if he'd let Don put a bullet in that kid's brain from the beginning. He understood how it was his actions that had gotten Donny hurt. It wasn't the war. It wasn't the kid. It wasn't even command. It was him, and he knew it. He'd thought being the comedian was more fun. The thought of his mother saying, "It's all fun and games until someone loses an eye," came to his mind. In this case, though, it was until someone lost a hand, or a leg, or even their whole face.

Andy threw his head back onto his pillow in frustration. He hated the fact there was nothing he could do except apologize, and neither Donny nor the other guys there cared a rat's ass about his apology. They probably wanted to string him up—of that he was sure.

"Are you ready for therapy, Andy?" the nurse said quite pleasantly, as she did with all of her patients.

Andrew focused back into the here and now. "Therapy? What therapy?"

Nurse Linda gave him a big smile that lit up the room. "You have an appointment with Doctor Larry."

"The head shrinker? Doesn't he have anything better to do than ask me about how my mom beat me as a young boy?" Andrew didn't dislike Doctor Larry Jackson, but the whole concept of talking to a psychiatrist just gave him the willies.

"You and I know that Doctor Larry is the nicest man on this side of the Mississippi River," said Linda. "He only wants to help, and if you let him, I know he can help you with all the crap going on inside that noggin of yours."

Nurse Linda was very aware of the signs of someone living the past. She wasn't a doctor, but she knew when someone was hurting inside. To Linda, there were a lot of guys that needed their brains adjusted. A quick lube here and there was healthy for anybody.

Andrew liked Linda. She was an older lady, very nice to everyone. She didn't take a lot of guff from these guys, but they all knew that if help were needed, they could count on her.

"He might be nice," said Andrew, "but he is still a shrinker of heads, and in my book, that makes him someone I want to avoid at all costs." He was just kidding, but he liked to see her smile.

"Well, I guess I can send over a not-nice doctor to come and sit with you, and maybe take your temperature the old-fashioned way if you'd like?" Linda also liked the little banter between the two of them. She felt very bad for Andrew, because he showed all the signs of someone who was definitely in need of Doctor Larry. "Now get your butt up, and let's go."

"Okay, geesh. I thought you were here to help us through our broken bones and give us sponge baths, not boss us around?" Andrew worked his way up through the pain and sat on the side of the bed. He still hurt from Adam's apple on down. All he kept hearing from the doctors and the physical therapists was how amazed they were that he was still alive after the injuries he'd suffered. He was tired of hearing it. He didn't feel lucky at all. He felt the opposite of lucky, and no Doctor Larry or Doctor Hill was going to wave a magic wand and make that go away.

Linda put her hand under his arm to help him upright. She pulled the wheelchair within arm's reach with her leg. With a swift lift and plop technique that she had perfected, Andy was in the wheelchair snug as a bug in a rug, as she would say. She helped him get his feet situated on the foot pedals, so as to not lose a toe going down that hallway. "Ready?" she asked finally.

Andrew was never happy going to see any doctor. He wasn't going to be happy until he was home helping his dad with mowing the grass or petting his dog or eating one of his mother's meals.

He was pushed to the point of reaching Doctor Larry's door. Linda opened the door so that the wheelchair could be pulled into the room. She walked over to the receptionist and said, "I have Andy here to see Doctor Larry. He's so excited."

But Andrew was anything but excited. He was more miffed, dissatisfied, or even peeved. "Excited isn't the word I would use," he said. "I can think of a few others, though. If you want, I can give them to you in alphabetical order?"

"Don't listen to him, Barb," said Linda. "He *is* excited, I can tell. It's all in the eyes, and his eyes say *excitement* through and through."

The doctor came out from an adjoining room to hear two ladies gabbing and a young kid sitting in a wheelchair with a sour look on his face. He wasn't the worst case he'd seen since he had been here, but he was definitely in need of help. He would classify Knox as a classic case of someone using sarcasm to hide depression, fear, and mostly guilt.

"Are you ready, my boy?" he said. He walked over to Andy and proceeded to push Andy past the nurses and into his office.

As much as Andy hated this place, he couldn't hate Doctor Larry Jackson. He actually reminded him a lot of his dad. He was kind, he was warm, and he was to the point, all of which were things he classified his dad as being. He didn't know the guy very well, but Andrew saw him as someone who came through for people. They had only had one session together, but it was actually nice to get some things off his chest.

"Ready, Doc," he said. "Let's get me all better so that I can get the hell out of here."

"Sounds good, my boy," said Dr. Larry. "Let's talk about the beginning, shall we?"

The doctor wheeled the chair over so that it was about five feet from where he was about to plop his butt down.

"Shouldn't I be on a couch, and shouldn't you have a pad and paper taking down all the pearls of wisdom spewing from my lips?" said Andy.

"Uh, no, and uh, no," the doctor replied. "That's what you get when you watch too much cable television."

Larry appreciated Andy's sense of humor, but he had to help the boy overcome using it as a defense mechanism.

"Fine then, Doc, I'll sit here all uncomfortable and hunched over like a loser, and you can make my mind beautiful, please."

"Andy, time to get serious, okay?"

Andrew sat upright and put on the most serious face he could muster. "Okay, Doc. I hear you. I want to get this shit out of my brain. I want to keep this whole experience from ruining the rest of my life. I really do."

That is what Larry wanted to hear. "Sounds good, it really does." He paused, clicked his pen, and flipped to an empty page on his pad. "So, when we left off, I think you were telling me that you were afraid that Donny wasn't doing well, and that it was your fault. Did I leave anything out?"

"It's not a matter of debate," Andy began. "It *was* my fault. I know it was, and there ain't a damn thing I can do to fix it. What I need from you is to help me figure out a way to deal with it without ending up like Jerry."

"Jerry?" Larry wrote a few things down in his pad and then said, "Why are you so sure you might end up like this guy Jerry?"

Andrew had it figured out to a T. It was he who Donny was always saving, and the one time Donny had needed him, he wasn't there for him. "Jerry is the guy who lives near us back home. My mom has been sending me letters constantly about things going on back home. Sometimes I get multiple letters, and sometimes she is talking about him."

"Why is his situation so bad?"

"I know his mom and my mom try to help him by reading to him, doing his laundry, and pretty much anything they can to keep him calm. It's your job to make sure that I don't end up just sitting there staring at a TV that ain't even on."

Larry felt bad for the kid, he really did. Here was a kid who didn't know how to control the rollercoaster of emotions that he was riding, and on top of everything else, the roller coaster was on fire. He was going to be a special case. He realized that this kid should never have been allowed into combat to begin with. He was nothing at all what a platoon sergeant wanted in a soldier. He was sarcastic, he didn't respect his superiors, and he didn't believe in the reasons his superiors gave him about why he was over in this bloodbath. He questioned everything, if he remembered correctly. He should have been left at home. This was no man yet, and yet he'd found himself in a group of men not knowing how to fit in.

Andy wiggled in the chair to get comfortable. "So, what I can I tell you that I haven't already told you?"

"Well, I think that is up to you, son. I think we still have a lot to work through before I can feel like you have a handle on the horrendous shit that you just went through. Until I feel like you have a handle on it, I can keep you here until you have whiskers as grey as mine. Are we clear on that?"

Larry didn't like getting tough, but being a patient's friend could only take him so far.

"Yes, sir," said Andy with a bit of disdain. "I'll tell you whatever you want to hear to get me back home. I'll tell you that you are beautiful and lovely, if that's what you want to hear."

"As flattering as that sounds, we can save that as a last resort, thank you very much. What I do want to talk about, though, is where we left off." Larry flipped his page back one sheet and read, "I know it's my fault. Whose fault can it be, if not mine?"

"I still say that's a true statement. It is my fault, Doc."

"Why?"

Andrew gave a sigh of annoyance. "I should have been a real soldier. I should have let them shoot the kid in the head and run for cover. I should have made everyone get away from me before risking my own life and everyone else's."

"I think what you mean is that you were put in an impossible situation and you were asked to find an impossible solution. You had no idea that that kid was holding a bomb, or what turned out to be just a good facsimile of one. Did you have any idea when he walked up to you that he was just a diversion to get you all looking one way while a couple guys tiptoed right past everyone?"

"No," Andy began, "but if I'd been paying more attention, he would never have snuck up on me. He would have never got that close. I let him get that close because I was reading a letter from my mother."

"I hear what you're saying, and if you want to hold the weight of the world on your shoulders, I can't stop you, but the truth is that every single guy over here knows that today might be their last. They know that everything may come to a screeching halt one day, and they have to deal with the idea of their world going to shit. That's this life that's been chosen."

Doctor Larry had a Doctor Phil mentality. He didn't think holding their hands was going to make these soldiers better. They had to trust themselves again. They had to believe that whatever they did in life would not automatically end in disaster. Andrew was no different, as far as Larry could see.

"You don't understand, Doc. It wasn't just because a random thing happened. I'm widely known as the screw off. The guy who always has his head at home instead of in the game here where people could die."

Andrew wasn't comfortable talking about it. He knew in his gut that if he hadn't been reading that damn letter, none of this would have happened. He knew it as surely as he knew his own name.

Larry understood Andy's guilt, but he knew that he somehow had to teach this boy to let it go. The boy needed to be here, talking, getting it out and dealing with it, so that he didn't end up like his friend Jerry. He also needed to get his head on straight before he left, because Larry wasn't the guy to push these soldiers out the door and yell, "Next!" That wasn't how he worked, and would also explain why he was sitting in this chair in this unforgiving place. He didn't feel like Andrew could function out there in the real world yet. Not until he realized that shit happens, and you just have to push through it.

"I have to tell you, son, that the longer you hold onto this idea that no one fucks off on guard duty, and that everyone belongs here but you, the longer you're going to be sitting here talking to me about this shit," said Larry, his tone stern. "To think you have to own this stuff is idiotic, to be polite. You tried to diffuse the situation. You tried to get the boy to surrender, and according to the reports I've read, you seemed to be doing just that. This was a very carefully orchestrated plan by people on the outside of that fence who used a young boy's eagerness to be accepted and to be loved to blow up a munitions shack. In all the confusion, they shot him in the chest and killed him so that he couldn't give up anything he knew. I don't think I have missed anything, really."

"I know, but—" Andy was interrupted with a hand giving him the universal sign to be quiet.

"No, you don't know," said Larry, "and that's why you're sitting in front of me. You think everything is supposed to be presented in a nice little package, a little bow on top. But the world doesn't work like that. You need to concentrate on the fact that the boy was shot not by you or by some yahoo in our army—he was shot by one of his own people to ensure that he kept quiet. You should be thanking your lucky stars that you and everyone else were as far away as possible. It could've been so much worse, son. So much worse."

Andy gestured up and down his body, "Do you call this lucky? Do you think I'm any better off feeling like I was backed over by a bus, and having this shit in my brain that's eating away at me? Do you?"

The doctor saw that he was finally making headway. He was getting Andy to actually talk about it. "I remember my dad said to me," he began. "He was a boxer, and he loved boxing metaphors. He told me that to be a man, you don't count the times you get knocked down. You count the times you get back up."

"Getting up from this is maybe more than I can do. Maybe more than anyone can do."

"Do you honestly believe that horse shit? You have your life. You have family, and you have a whole life ahead of you. Yes, you were knocked down, you were knocked down hard, but if you put your big boy pants on, I bet you could find a way to get through this and help others to do the same. You're not the only kid who has ever graced my door with a load of guilt, sorrow, or with broken bodies or broken hearts weighing them down, and guess what? They learned to live with it. No one promised you valor or war stories to tell your girl back home. What they promised you was that, in their opinion, you were doing a greater good than you could have done sucking down one of your momma's apple pies."

He paused, because if he had of kept going he probably would have had the kid crying or worse.

Andrew wasn't happy about what Larry was telling him, but he knew that his ultimate goal was to help him deal with his feelings. "It may be horse shit to you," he said, "but it ain't your body and your nightmares, are they? It ain't you who's waking up in a pool of sweat."

Larry couldn't take the pity party any longer. The boy needed to hear something. "Can I tell you a story, young man? I mean a real honest to goodness story that you might need to hear before you leave here."

Andrew was a little perplexed by the change in demeanor that Larry was exhibiting. But he nodded for the doctor to continue.

"Okay, thank you. One day, a soldier, and we will call him, uh, Barry Jackstone, came to the army because he wanted to be everything he'd read about in adventure stories and saw in the dime store movie theatres. He wanted to be something besides an apprentice in his father's hardware store. He wanted to say that he'd done something besides eat beans and fart. So Barry came over to a little place called Vietnam and found himself with a rifle, a helmet, and a bad case of diarrhea. Well, good old Barry thought that he wanted to go shoot some gooks and rid the world of communism and all the people who didn't quite look or talk like he did. He got his wish. He killed, and he killed, until one day he was faced with a soldier who was coming at him with a knife, and he fired a bullet into his brain. Up close, I could see that the soldier was just a kid, maybe twelve or thirteen at most. At the time, I thought he deserved it—I mean, Barry thought he deserved it. Barry was so sure that whatever he did was okay, because the government said it was okay. But explain to me why Barry started having dreams about that kid's face, and how many other ten-year-olds did he kill? The faces became everything he saw, and it took someone to talk to him about what happened for him to get his act together."

"So, what you're saying is that you're sitting here paying it forward, so to speak? How did you get it out of your brain?"

"Who is saying it's out? It's always there, but you have to learn to control it before it controls you, and time is your teacher for that."

"That's kind of what my dad said, too," admitted Andy.

Larry clicked his pen and started jotting some notes down on his paper. "Sounds like a very smart guy."

"What? What are you writing about me?"

"Not you, this time. Something about myself that I just realized."

"Like what?"

"That I don't have the control I thought I had with regards to this little part of my life," the doctor said with a sigh. He paused for a moment and then straightened up in his chair. "I'm not the patient today, you are, so let's get back to how you're feeling."

Andrew could not help liking the man a little more after their conversation. He'd thought in the beginning that it was just a fictional story he'd told all his nut cases, but he realized now that it was a real story and that his reactions to the story were real as well.

"Well, Doc, I guess I just need to learn how to control it."

"Control what?"

"Like you said, the worms in my brain."

"I think you have to understand that no matter what you do, or what you say, or how much penance you do, or even how many doctors you go see, you will have to live with everything you've done, perceived, and overheard. Let me tell you one thing, Andy. There is one person in this world who's our worst enemy, and it's not some guy in the army or some civilian in a far-off country. He's the guy in the mirror. He will fuck your head up so bad that you will want to just sit there and cry if you let him. The trick to a happy life is to make friends with that guy. You have to greet him with a smile and hope like hell that he's okay with who you've become. Do you understand me?"

"I guess I do," Andy said. "I try to control it, but being okay with what I think I did will take a long, long time."

He didn't think he would ever be on board with thinking that it wasn't his fault. He ran all the scenarios through his head, and still the kid had jumped the fence while he was distracted.

"A lifetime, my boy. A whole lifetime."

Andrew wasn't thrilled to hear that he was going to have this burden for the rest of his life. "I don't want to see that kid's face in my dreams every night," he said.

"You won't see him every night," Larry continued, "and the more often you help others, the less you'll see him. That's just how it works. Me, or every other head shrinker, as you like to call us, can talk to you until we're blue in the face and tell you that it's not your fault, but it will be you and only you who hands out that forgiveness. I personally think the bomb would have gone off and killed more people if everyone hadn't gathered around you and the boy. And until you aren't just hearing it, but believing it, we're just pushing air around the room."

"Thanks, Doc." Andrew did feel a little better about everything, but he knew that he wasn't going to be completely okay for a very long time. And he wasn't going to be able to get Donny to stop blaming him, even if he forgave himself. "I hear you," he continued, "but even if I can forgive myself, there are others who will never give me that merciful pardon."

"Donny?" Larry was familiar with most of it, even what Birch had confessed, but he knew that once he forgave himself, whatever Donny thought wouldn't be so important. It was up to Larry to help Birch forgive the unforgivable.

"Every time I speak with him, he seems a little more distant. He tries to act like we're still tight, but every time he comes back from therapy, he seems to be a little more withdrawn. I try to engage him in conversation about going home, but ever since his prediction came true and they took his hand, I can't get him to do anything. He just sits there and ignores me."

"I also see Donny twice a week," Larry continued, "and I can tell you that he's hurting. He's hurting because he's scared. He doesn't have a mom and a dad, and having your parents is no substitute for having his own, no matter how nice they are or what you promise him. Donny will be okay, but you have to be patient and not give up on your friend."

Larry knew that Donny did indeed blame Andy for what had happened. He couldn't talk about another patient's sessions, but he figured at some point that he would need to get them in the same room to try and see if there was a way to mend the broken friendship, and in doing so, help both of them move on, even if it meant not being as close anymore.

"I try, Doc, but he won't let me in. He won't let me anywhere close. I try to talk to him about going home and starting our company together, and he just changes the subject to something else, like what he can do with just one hand. It's so frustrating."

"I know, Andy, but at this point, you can't rush him. If you go home and he doesn't, you will have to be his friend in other ways. You may have to be okay with the fact that he might have a different path than you, and if you're meant to be together owning your own company, it will still happen. You have to believe it for it to materialize."

The doctor's alarm clock rang, signaling that it was the end of the session.

"Time's up, Doc," Andy said miserably.

"Yes, it is, but we have time to do one last thing."

"And that would be?"

"Forgive ourselves." He heard the words come out of his mouth, but he still felt funny saying them.

Andrew heard the doctor, but didn't think he was ready for such a bullshit exercise. "I think you can fly solo on this one, Doc."

"Okay, then, I will. I forgive myself," he said. "I forgive myself. I forgive myself." He meant it, and it felt good to say it and mean it.

Andy wasn't buying it. "You keep telling yourself that, Doc, and maybe, just maybe, you'll really believe it, one day."

"Thank you, Andy," said Larry.

Andy looked surprised. "For what, exactly?"

"No need to explain. A thanks is all that's needed. Hopefully, my boy, there will come a day when you understand it perfectly." He opened the door to let the nurse know that Andy was ready to go back to his bed. "See you on Wednesday."

"See you then, Doc."

HEY, MOM

Andrew lay on his bunk, his eyes fixated on the ceiling as he listened to everything happening all around him. He heard the nurses talking, the orderlies walking back and forth between rows of beds. His physical therapy had been torturous as always, and some days it felt like he was getting worse instead of better. They bent him every which way, but comfortable. They made him walk, even though his legs felt like melted rubber. Andrew felt as though every piece of exercise equipment in that room, was there was built to give him pain. They ached from strain of pushing himself up, of stretching his muscles, but these people didn't seem to care even a little bit. They just pushed him and pushed him knowing damn well that it was no use. They swore to him up and down that he was making progress, but he knew the truth. He could feel how his legs did zilch, zero, they laid there and did nothing. Andrew figured the therapists did it for fun, just to get their jollies.

He knew in his heart that he was supposed to be feeling better by now, but his spirits were in the dump. He missed everything and everyone from back home. He missed his mom. He missed his dad. And he missed his friend, who wasn't even far away physically, but felt just as far away to Andy as everyone else. He felt so alone. So many people were all around him, but not one of them even seemed to care that he existed. He thought he would've been going home by now, but between his body and his brain, he was too broken to be unleashed on the good citizens back home.

Andrew tried to read his mom's letter, but after a single paragraph, he just got even more depressed. It wasn't like the letters of old. This letter and the previous two letters also were full of chatter about how everything was great and they couldn't wait to see him, but the truth was actually that Donna had her hands full and they needed his mother to go help because Jerry was still such a G. I. Joe basket case. He could read between the lines.

He crumbled up the letter and pulled out his pen and paper. He looked around to make sure that no one was watching. He could tell that none of these guys were really his friends. He chatted with them from time to time, but Andy figured these guys would even talk to their enemy just to break up the boredom. Some of them were just waiting to go home, too, so that their mother could put them in an assisted living home, and so that professionals could address their anger situations and their other conditions. All of these suckers had no clue that they were going home to a straightjacket. But Andy knew all too well what happens when a soldier goes home and they can't fix him. They put the guy in a rubber room and let shrinks poke and prod at him until one day in the distant future he might become useful to society again.

He'd heard all the stories about how guys went home with a small problem and ended up bouncing off a padded cell trying to catch butterflies, or waking up in the middle of the night sleepwalking out of their beds and breaking their leg or ankle, or even their necks. But he knew he couldn't let them do that to him. He was going to get the hell out of there and put this shit behind him, and then forget it had ever happened.

Andy picked up his pen and started his letter.

Hey Mom,

How are you doing? How is Dad? How are Donna and Jerry? If I had to guess, I bet Jerry is in a home and not at home with Donna, right? I bet he's lying on some doctor's couch right now saying how he killed little kids and blew up villages. I bet he's telling the doctor about how it wasn't his fault, because the government made him do it for the greater good, right?

It's not your fault that Jerry came home like he did. I know it's a good heart like yours that would go out of the way to help some guy that you don't owe anything. I can't tell you how good it's going to be to get out of this place. I've been meeting with Doctor Larry, and I think we're getting a handle on this crap. We talked about it a lot the last couple sessions. He's a nice guy. He reminds me of Dad, a nice guy who you also don't want to piss off because he'll get in your face and tell you what you need to hear.

I hang out with some of the guys here, because honestly that's about all there is to do. Talking, playing cards, or writing letters to the people you love is about the only things going on here most days. I talk with Jenkins and Campbell and Ramirez a lot. They're going home soon. Jenkins and Campbell are decent guys. There are a bunch of others as well, but I don't get to talk to them much. They all got a crummy deal, but they seem to be okay, I guess. Ramirez is a lot better than all of us both physically and mentally. I wish I could take all these guys home and help them get back on their feet somehow. Doctor Larry keeps talking to me about paying it forward, and I wish I could get all these guys to come out to Virginia and help me and Donny. Some of these guys have nothing and nobody. They are just throwaways, as we call them out here. People who ended up here for no good reason other than the fact that there was nowhere else for them to go. Why do we treat people like this, Mom?

I will be home soon. My body is healing, slowly but surely. I think once Donny and I get back, we can forget about this damn place. I hate it here. I hate the crying. I hate the doctors, and I hate the fact that they're keeping me in this nut hole when they should be sending me home. I'm sure there's someone like Doctor Larry somewhere in the great state of Virginia who could treat me.

Well, I won't take up any more of your time. I just wanted to say hi and tell you not to worry about me. I'll be home helping out with dishes before you know it.

Your Loving Son, Andrew

LET'S GET IT ALL OUT, SHALL WE?

Don was trying to get some sleep. He didn't want to talk to anyone. He didn't want to do anything except be left alone, but there was one problem with that request—he knew he had to go see Larry the psychiatrist. He saw, out of the corner of his eye, Andy being wheeled back from physical therapy. He wanted to get up and punch him in his face, but there was one problem with that, too—he didn't have a fist anymore.

As Andy reached his bed and they helped him back into his bunk, Don conveniently rolled over to show his back to Andy. He really didn't care if Andy was going through issues of his own. He didn't care if Andy had guilt, and he damn sure didn't care about Andy's farm. He wished he would just leave him the hell alone and go home.

An orderly shook his shoulder gently and Don turned to see Anthony, big and black and built like a Russian tank. He was sure that Anthony could probably pick his bunk up with him lying in it. "Howdy there, Anthony," he said. "Please don't hurt me with your massive hands."

"Very funny there, patient number nine zero four," said Anthony. He was used to the wise cracks from the guys about his size. He was a big fellow, and occasionally he had to throw a guy around or pin him down. He knew why he'd been assigned to this piss hole.

"What the hell does that mean?" said Don, pretending to feel hurt.

"It means that you're just a number to me, and next time you will be six twenty-eight. You get me?"

"Wow, you have no bedside manner at all, do you?"

"You've mistaken me with Maggie," said Anthony. "Even if I were able to get into her outfit, I doubt I would look anything like that."

He pointed over at Maggie and took a mental picture of that cute booty, as he called it, as he was no different from every other horny guy in this place. Maggie was the picture in many guys' minds as they took their showers. He was no different.

Don looked around the big man's hand and took his own mental picture. Even though she was older than the women he would normally date, her kindness and that bright smile made her attractive to everyone there. Then he lay back and just gave Anthony a big smile. "I hear you loud and clear."

Anthony grabbed Don by his good arm to help him get upright. "You ready to go see Doctor Larry?"

"I guess I need my head shrunk a little bit today," Don admitted.

"I think that's between you two. I know he's a good guy with good advice, if you give him the chance to share it with you."

"Oh, so you've laid on his couch once or twice then?"

"Let's just say he gives good advice and leave it at that, shall we?"

Don was curious about Anthony's comments. He didn't seem to have any mental issues. He didn't seem to be filled with rage, or guilt, or depression. Maybe he'd hit a captain and knocked his teeth out, or broke a jeep in half. "Okay, we can talk about that later," said Donny, "when I get back."

"Doubtful."

Anthony tried his best to not get close to any of these guys. They were walking head cases—the ones who could walk, that is—and the ones who couldn't were even worse off, and Anthony wanted nothing to do with any of them. He didn't want to be like Maggie who snuck off into a closet to cry because some nutcase was fucked in the head and everyone could read his outcome like it was advertised on a billboard. If you got too close, you started caring, and in this place, all that did was suck every bit of energy out of your body. Anthony didn't want to be that guy.

"Why don't we go see Larry, shall we?" said Anthony.

As he was helped off his bed and into the chair. It was customary to be wheeled down to the doctor's office, even if you could walk. Don could see

Andy watching him as if something was on the tip of his tongue. But Don acted like no one was there. "Let's get out of here and get this over with, shall we?" he said to Anthony.

Anthony didn't say anything. He just pushed the wheelchair. He could see the tension between the two soldiers, but he wanted nothing to do with their little feud. As he reached the doctor's office, he turned to pull Don into the office as opposed to pushing the chair ahead of him. He pushed him up towards the nurse's station, waited until the nurse acknowledged his presence, and then turned and walked away without a word. He had a hundred other things that needed to get done before he could go off duty.

Don was left there like a sack of potatoes on a loading dock. He sat and looked at the nurses, the paintings on the wall, the dirt on the floor; he looked at everything but the stump where his hand used to be.

Larry came out of his office and saw Don sitting patiently in his chair, waiting for him to come out and fix him up. This guy was a tough nut to crack, but Larry was willing to do his best to not only crack it, but to help him learn to deal with his injuries. Larry's profession was not an easy one, especially in a place like this one. "Ready?" he said.

"I guess so, Doc."

Don's sessions with Larry seemed to be going nowhere. There was nothing Larry could do or that any other doctor could do. If they couldn't put his hand back, what good were any of them? This was unfortunately Don's outlook on any doctor he met.

"Where do you want to start?" said Don.

The doctor was not used to this much compliance from Don, which meant that he was drawing even more inward. But he had to get the helplessness out of his head if he were to help him in any way.

Larry pushed him over to the couch, where it was his choice to stand and move to the couch or sit where he was in his chair. "Let's get rolling, shall we?" said the doctor. Larry moved over to his own chair and picked up his writing utensils. He sat back, got comfortable, and said quietly, "I'm ready when you are."

"Ready to tell you how life has treated me so unfairly? How no one likes me and I have to learn to wipe my ass with my left hand now?"

Larry cleared his throat. "Okay, let's see now. We already know that up until now, your life has been difficult, right? We know that you were an orphan. We know that your parents died. We know that no one wanted you, but let's talk more about what has happened during the past six or so weeks. Let's talk about your hand. Let's talk about your friend who is killing himself trying to get you to forgive him. Hell, why don't we talk about the tens of thousands of guys who have gone home without arms, hands, legs, eyes, noses, and even jaws, and have learned to not be such a dick to the people around them? Let's start there, shall we?"

Don just stared off blankly as he usually did during these sessions. Then he turned slightly toward Larry and sat up straight in his chair. "Really, Larry? That is what you are going with today, tough love?"

"Is it working?"

"Not really."

"Okay then, do me a favor and explain to me why you won't forgive your friend? Answer me that question, and I'll leave you alone."

Don just held up his arm from his lap to show Larry the stump where his hand had once been. "I'm not Donald Birch anymore, Doc. I'm now Donny Crabclaw."

"You're going to act like a kid on the playground who just got teased by a bunch of stupid children?" said Larry. "That's going to be your defense for being a jerk to Andy and everyone else? I think you'd better come up with something better than that if you want me to leave you alone today."

"Wow, Doc," said Donny, the irritation and resentment audible in his voice. "I'm cured. I think I'm ready to go home now. I think I can do anything now."

"Is this how you plan on dealing with everyone who sees you in your prosthesis? Is this how you're going to react to some kid looks at you who's just curious and doesn't understand? Why are you not forgiving Andy for what happened?"

"It doesn't matter, Doc."

"I'm afraid it does, my boy. Until you give me a straight answer, we're going to eat, piss, and shit in here together. Do you understand me, corporal?" Then Larry took on a more rigid and military posture. "Why won't you forgive the man who has been crawling on his knees for you to forgive him?"

Don blurted out in anger, almost screaming at the top of his lungs, "Because, dammit!" His voice calmed after a few seconds of silence. "Because he was the one who acted like such a kid out there, and I couldn't protect him from everything. If he'd have just done what I told him to do, this shit would have never happened."

"I see," said Larry. "So the fact that he almost got killed was your fault, somehow?"

"That's not what I said, Doc. I said that if he hadn't been such a jerkoff kid, we would be sitting at his house right now fishing or hunting or screwing some farmer's daughter."

The pain he was feeling was evident in his eyes. The small pools of tears were too heavy to hold back any longer. He wiped them vigorously with his good hand.

"Do you want to know what I think?" said Larry, more gently than before. He did not wait for a response before he said, "What I think is that you hate him for making you fail at your duty of protecting him. What I think is that you hate him for getting hurt, not getting *you* hurt. I also think that if you don't forgive him, you will hate yourself so much more than you do right now. I think that Andy's injuries, both mental and physical, will be a test that he may not be able to pass without you. If you don't get your head out of your ass and be there for him now, you're going to think this is a carnival compared to how you'll feel later." He took a deep breath once, then again. "Now I'm done being on my soapbox."

Don didn't know what to say. He just sat there and stared at the doctor, trying to formulate a response. He finally pulled himself together and began, "Are you finished? Just because you're a doctor, you figure you have everything figured out about me?"

"No," said Larry. "I don't have everything figured out about you, or anyone else, because if I did, you'd be all better and on your way back home with a big smile on your face."

"A big smile?"

"A *huge* smile?"

"And just why would I have this huge smile on my face?" said Don. "Please tell me, I really am curious."

"You would be smiling because you'd be okay with what has happened, and you would be okay with living with yourself. People who are okay with who they are smile a lot more than folks like us. Folks like us make ourselves and everyone around us feel like shit. Just ask both of my ex-wives. Misery loves company."

Larry had given Don a good bit to think about. This was the first session that actually made Don feel something besides more anger and condescension towards Larry. Through all the crap, through all the fake toughness, it seemed that helping his patients actually was a top priority to Larry. It must have been his own kind of therapy, he figured.

"I hear you, Doc."

"I hope so, because I can tell you first hand that if you stay on the path you're on at the moment, you'll look back on today and see these as the good days. Do yourself a favor and forgive yourself."

Don gave the doctor a quizzical stare for a few seconds, and then said sheepishly, "I said, I hear you, Doc." He looked at his stump where his hand used to be, but he still couldn't find anything hopeful to say about it.

"Look at it hard, my boy," said Larry. "Life sold you a raw deal, and as much as it pisses you off, you have to come to terms with this being who you are now. You have to decide if a plastic hand is better than nothing at all. As long as you see yourself as Donny Crabclaw instead of as a soldier who has done his duty, you'll always feel hatred towards every single person who has both of their hands. This is the turning point where you need to come to terms with the new Donald Birch, and that's when I'll be happy to put you on the next transport. But until I can see that transformation, your ass is going to sit right here and feel sorry for yourself."

The truth, though, was that he couldn't hold Don much longer. He wasn't the kind of case that the army allowed to stay there indefinitely. Guys like Don got shipped home where a counselor would take over. Larry would try to do what he could while Don was still here, but if he didn't change his outlook soon, he would live a life of self-pity. And with no family, he would probably end up in jail or a psych ward before he even turned twenty-five.

Don heard what the doctor was saying, but he was so angry, and he just wasn't sure yet how to release it as easily as Larry was making it sound. "If it's that easy, how do I deal with kids staring at me in restaurants, girls making excuses when I ask them out, people gawking at me like I'm some freak when I walk down the street?"

Larry was tired of the pity party. Sometimes he just wanted to get out of his chair, go up to the patient, and beat them in the head with the biggest bat they make. Of course, he couldn't do that, but there were times he wished he could.

"What about the guys who have never seen the war who are wheel-chairing their way down the street without any help?" said Larry. "What do you think is running through their minds? You, on the other hand, are going to get people walking up to you all the time shaking your hand and saying 'thank you for your service.' You're going to have a family of brothers who know exactly how you feel. Bottom line is that if you stay half-empty, I wouldn't blame anyone for treating you like shit. People are going to treat you like you treat yourself."

He clicked his pen and starting writing in his pad. Meanwhile, Don was starting to tear up. He took his nub and wiped the tears streaming down his cheek. He hated Larry for making him cry. He finally yelled, "I don't know how!"

"But that's the easy part," said Larry. "You help others. You go out there and find anyone who might need a friend or a helping hand, and you help them deal with the crap that we call life. Maybe just lend an ear so they can get all those tears and negative emotions out."

Don took a second swipe of the waterworks pouring down his face. "Is that what you're doing?"

Larry didn't talk much about himself to anyone, but in this case, he thought it might be therapeutic. "Affirmative, young man. I've been doing this for over twenty years, and it's probably the only thing in my life that keeps me sane. Failed marriages, kids not wanting to talk to me, and the deepest of depressions are things that people deal with every day. And I have both of my hands, but I would switch places with you in a heartbeat."

Don now felt a bit closer to the doctor. He looked at Larry and wondered what had fucked him up so badly. He could speculate all day, but probably wouldn't even come close to the truth. "I hear you, Doc. I'll try to get this stain out of my soul."

"Did you just say *stain on your soul*? I think you need to explain how your soul got stained."

"That's how I feel," said Don. "It's so deep that I can't get ahold of it, so I say it's attached to my soul, and I don't know how to get it off."

"Okay, good enough." That was a new one, and he definitely had to write that one down. If he heard it again, maybe there might be a paper to be written on stained souls. Larry got a small wrinkle of a smile from imagining a commercial with some lawyer saying, "Did your soul get stained in the army? If so, please call my law firm. You may be entitled to compensation."

"So, what do I do now?" said Don.

Larry pushed away the vision of the lawyer. "Well, son, that's kind of up to you at this point. I can help you, but when you go home, you're going to have to learn to live with whatever comes your way. You're always going to be reminded of what happened when you try to use the hand you lost. You're going to be reminded every day, and you have to learn that you have it worse than some people, but a lot better than others. Do you understand me?"

"I do, Doc, I do," said Don. "I don't think I can do it today, but I do understand you." He looked at his hand and then at his nub. He started to laugh when he thought about how one of the things he'd have to learn to do with his remaining hand is pull his peter.

The laugh turned more and more boisterous. *This feels good*, he thought. *Maybe this is where healing starts.*

Larry was pleased to see the spark of recovery in the boy's eyes, and he laughed along with him. He was very pleased with the fact that he'd actually helped the boy today. He had been getting used to the silent treatment, but he knew from experience that people talked when they had something they wanted to say, and today, Don had had something he'd wanted to get off his chest.

"See you on Wednesday," said Larry.

WHO IS THIS?

Marie sat at the kitchen table with a stunned expression on her face. She stared across at Mike with a look of stone. She didn't know who had written this last letter, but this was not her son. These words had to be from someone else altogether.

"Mike, what the hell is going on here? This is the second letter in as many days that expressed nothing but anger. What is going on with him, Mike?"

Mike too was completely flabbergasted, and he didn't know what to say. It broke his heart to not have his son here and be able to help him through this tough time in his life. His last few letters had had more profanity in them than Mike believed Andy had ever spoken in his entire life. He was speaking to his parents as if they understood the hate and anger that was boiling inside of him. "Whatever it is, Marie," Mike said, "I hope the doctors can help him with it."

"He was better before he started seeing Doctor Larry," said Marie bitterly. She was beginning to think that this doctor wasn't much help for her son. "What happened to the kid who was so excited about getting home and doing dishes and helping mow grass? What happened to Andy?" Marie started to tear up, so she put her hand on her breastplate and took a deep breath. "Why, Mike? Why does my boy hate us and everyone else?"

Mike said sharply, "He doesn't hate us at all. He hates his circumstances. He hates the war. He hates the hospital that he feels trapped in. Right now, he hates a lot of things, but you and I are not among the things he hates. It's hard to believe after his last letter of rantings, but he doesn't hate you. He doesn't hate me. At the moment, he hates himself a lot more than anyone else."

"I want Andy back, Mike. I want our son back."

In the back of Marie's mind, she was terrified that Andy was going to come home and be like Jerry. He was going to fester into this big pile of hate until the point where no one could help him anymore. Jerry had become just that. He'd become someone who couldn't get past the fact that life had dealt him a crappy hand, and he just couldn't play it.

"I know, Marie," said Mike. "I want little Andy back too, but I don't think we will ever see little Andy again. Who we need to worry about now is the man who will be coming home to us, and how to help whoever our son has become. He doesn't know how to deal with the grief that he's processing. But the doctors will help him with that, and when he gets home, we will help him with the rest."

Mike kept talking, hoping to be able to believe the crap that was coming out of his mouth. He'd seen this so many times with his buddies from the war. Guys who just couldn't get it together. They had flashbacks; they had bouts of utter mind-numbing depression. They had families that just gave up on them because they couldn't take the anger and what they considered to be pity parties.

Marie wasn't convinced of her husband's sincerity, but she wished with all her might that what he was saying was true. She wanted to believe more than anything that Andrew was going to be himself again someday, and she had to accomplish that seemingly unobtainable goal by simply being patient. But she had to admit that patience was not one of her strong suits. She was more likely to shake him until she saw her boy reappear in his place.

"What if he turns out to be like Jerry?" she asked. "Or worse? What if we can't reach him?"

Mike hoped upon hope that having Andy home would help his recovery. The fact that Andy would have someone there to help him who had gone through the anger and the guilt and the depression was Mike's only source of comfort. "If he does, then we will have to live with it," he said. "We all knew that this day and this possibility could occur, and for us to sit here and act like we are totally blindsided is not fair, nor accurate. What we have to focus on is our boy, and according to his letters, he's hurting. He's hurting badly, and judging him before he even gets home is not the answer. What we will do is give him space and time to heal. Knowing that he has us to turn to is all we can offer until he's ready to get his life together and move on."

"I don't like your plan," said Marie with a pained look on her face.

"Don't have to like it, just have to follow it."

"Who made you the doctor?" she said, but then she sighed and leaned toward him.

"Okay," said Mike, "now that we have that settled, we can move forward. I think we should write him a letter and remind him of everything he loved about this place, from the animals to the way he and I would mend fences and take in the harvest."

"Are you sure he loved that?" said Marie. "Because that sounds like a lot of work to me. How about my food, and my hugs, and especially my pies?"

"Yeah, put all that in there," said Mike. "It's important we stop talking about Donny, or Jerry, or getting better, or who said what or when or where. We're going to get that boy on our doorstep sooner than you think, and if we're not prepared, we're going to lose him before he even sets foot in the door. Trust me, I know."

Mike was agitated, but calm. He was frightened, but strong. He was scared to death, but he was also ready to push fear aside if it meant helping his son.

Marie agreed with him, and she too was willing to do anything and everything to help her son, but she knew it wasn't going to be easy. "What do you want me to do?"

"Go get your pad and paper, and write the most loving letter you can think of, but replace 'I love my little boy' with something like 'the animals sure do miss you feeding them in the morning,' or 'the peppers don't look nothing like they did when you were tending to them, but don't tell your father.' That kind of thing is what your letter needs to say from now on. Write him a letter every day, but don't mention things like the doctors. No more questions about Donny and his ailments. Make sure you put in something about how it's going to take time for Andy to teach Don everything he needs to know, but we know Andy can do it. Those are the kinds of letters that we have to start writing from now on, okay?"

"I think I can handle that, Colonel Mike," said Marie teasingly. "I think I can put something together that you will be happy with."

"How is Jerry doing since they put him in that assisted living place?"

"We are not doing that to Andy!"

"No one said we were," said Mike, raising his hands in defense. "What I asked was a simple question about our neighbors kid, who you've spent a great deal of time with as of late."

"Good, because Andy isn't going anywhere," said Marie. "I don't care how many pots and pans he throws through the window."

Marie suddenly started crying. Her pain, her fear, and her grief came pouring out in a gush of sorrow and anguish. This wasn't something she thought she could fix. The letters that she was getting from Andy were from someone who was hurting, and hurting very badly. Someone who couldn't fix what was wrong with himself.

"Message received there, little lady," said Mike. He reached for his wife. "I happen to agree with you completely."

Eventually, after consoling Marie, Mike walked off and left her to her letter writing. He gave her the tools to help; now it was up to her to write whatever she thought best. He just hoped that she took his advice and left the overprotecting out of the letters, at least for now. It was the last thing Andy needed.

Mike had gotten the picture from a few of his boy's letters, and it was no small task getting the image of a young boy being blown to bits in front of you out of your mind. He wept for his son, having to deal with blocking out that image on a daily basis. He wished with all his might that he could take that pain away from his son, but the truth was that Andy was going to have to rise and demand everything that his intellect could give him in order to get through this. He would have to come to terms with seeing that boy for a very, very long time, no matter what doctor he saw or what pill he took.

Mike knew that doctors and pills didn't fix anything. It was the will and the fortitude and their trust in God that got guys through this kind of ordeal. It was all about concentrating more on hope than hurt, and it would take Andy through a hellacious ride that few people came out of unscathed. Most guys, if they were really lucky, learned how to mask the panic attacks and the depression and the nightmares from their loved ones. Mike knew all too well that it wasn't going to be an easy ride for his son, and that made him very sad for his boy.

HEY, DOC!

octor Larry pushed Andrew into his office and wheeled him so that he would be facing the chair that Larry would be sitting in. "So, Andy, what's been going on?" he said.

"Well, Doc, what can I say that I haven't already said to you?" said Andy. "The food sucks, the beds suck, and the view most certainly sucks. Can I go home now?"

"Oh, how I wish it was that easy, Andy. I really do."

Larry got out his pad and paper and sat back in his comfy chair. Larry was ready to repair some minds. "So, what's been going on, really? The nurses say that you've been exhibiting some anger towards them and your fellow patients. What's going on there?"

"Nothing," Andy insisted. "I just want to go home. I'm sick and tired of being in this place, and I don't understand why I can't do this back home."

"Well, as we have discussed before, I have to feel like you're ready to go home before I can feel good about sending you there. You have family members who will be affected by my decision, so I have to take it very seriously."

But Larry's true motivation was that he knew those quacks back home were just going to push Andy through the system so that they could get a paycheck. He'd seen the results of their work with these kids, and he and everyone else knew that a duck with a pad and paper could have done just as much.

Andrew wasn't happy with the coy way that Larry was saying that he would stay there forever if Larry deemed it necessary. What he saw was a man standing in his way of going home and forgetting this place ever existed. "I hear you, Doc," said Andy, desperation creeping into his voice. "But what do I have to do, really, to get you to believe that I'm ready?"

"Well, first we can start with not getting reports that you're being angry with the patients and the nurses. Why are you getting so upset? I thought we were working through all the guilt. I think there's something you're not telling me, so do you want to make this easy on me and just go ahead and tell me what it is?"

Larry knew what was bothering Andy, but he needed him to say it out loud. It was the only way the door could be opened up to fixing the issue.

But Andy didn't want to play this game anymore. He wanted to go home. "I'm not upset with anyone," he said. "I'm sick and tired of you people making me go to therapy when I don't want to. I'm sick of you making me explore my feelings," he finished, accentuating the last word with air quotes.

Andy sighed deeply. "I don't get it, Larry. I thought we were on our way to the airport, and now it seems like you're driving me to the nearest nuthouse."

Larry wasn't seeing anything he hadn't seen a million times, but this was one of the rare times where the war wasn't the thing screwing this kid's head up, but rather his boot camp buddy not wanting anything to do with him, and especially his therapy not going as well as he'd hoped, which was the root of this boy's issues. It wasn't that odd, and definitely not unheard of. He couldn't Blame Don for how he felt, and Andrew needed to give him the space to figure things out for himself, so that he could conclude that they were actually still friends. Each time Andy blew up at Don, a doctor, or a nurse, it made Birch that much more uncomfortable around him, and unfortunately, Andy was just not getting it.

"I think we need to talk about why you keep getting into arguments with your friend Don," said Larry. "What's going on there?"

"Good question, Doc. If he talked to me, I could tell you."

"Can you at least tell me what you think is the problem? I mean, do you think he's having a problem with his hand amputation? Do you think that's why he won't talk to you?"

Larry knew all too well the reason why Don was avoiding Andy, because he talked with Birch about it, and Don was quite plain about why he was upset. He didn't want to be, nor did he quite understand why, but he did feel like he had to blame someone for what happened to him, and Andy was the only physical being that he could blame. Larry knew that Don was a work in progress. He thought that a few more sessions with him would help Don understand that he wasn't mad at Andy for the hand, but more than likely mad at Andy for not allowing Don to keep him safe. He had to keep this in mind while dealing with Andy, too.

"C'mon, Doc, don't be coy with me. We've only talked about this a million times. Why don't you play a different record already?"

"Why don't you tell me one more time about what happened, then?" said Larry. "I mean, we may have missed something the last time we went over this. I think you told me that it was your fault, or that you think Don thinks it was your fault, that he lost his hand."

The idea of this exercise was for Andy to come to the conclusion logically that even if Don did blame him, it didn't make sense, and he would see that it was baggage that Don was carrying and that Andy should stop trying to carry a bag meant for another.

"Fine, Doc, fine," said Andy. "I'm a goof off and it got me and a bunch of other guys blown up, and my best friends hand blown off. My stupidity got a guy who like a brother to me to look at me like he wants to spit in my face. Did I leave anything out?"

"You left a few things out. Do you think it was your fault? Do you think Don is justified in thinking the way you think he does?"

"If I'd been paying attention, and if Don had been paying attention instead of warning me to put my mother's letter away before Brey saw me, then maybe one of us would have heard or seen something that would have let us avoid this whole thing. I'd be sitting home right now and Mom and Dad would be grinning from ear to ear to have me back. So yeah, Doc, I don't just *think* it's my fault. All the evidence points to it being my fault."

"So, you reason that because you caused all of this, you can't be happy at all? Do you think that your friend hates your guts because he blames you?"

"Are you paying attention to your notes, Doc?" said Andy. "It seems obvious. He won't talk to me, he barely even looks at me, and he just sits there staring out the window like a man who's waiting for a bus to come by to pick him up, or something."

Larry hated these stubborn cases when the men just refused to give themselves a break. Andy was now in that category of guys who would never let themselves be happy as long as they felt that someone was unhappy because of them. It was a shame, but it was like pouring water into a bucket with holes in the bottom. Nothing ever was accomplished besides making a mess.

It was a shame that Larry couldn't get Andy and Don in a room together and make them hash it out instead of acting like five year old's, but that wasn't an option here. His job was to give them the idea to do so on their own, and unfortunately, he knew that the odds weren't in his favor this time. He needed to help Andy see that not everything worked out the way you wanted it to, but that doesn't mean you just give up and crawl into a hole because you didn't get your way. That was guilt with a twist of immaturity mixed in, which never works. And Larry knew its outcome firsthand.

"I can't make him talk to me," said Andy, "but if saying I'm sorry doesn't fix anything, then it will never get better."

"Did you try just giving him some space to cope with the anger and the guilt and the self-pity that he just needs to get out of his system?" said Larry.

"I understand the anger part. I even understand the self-pity part. But what does he have to feel guilty about? I mean, he was telling me to get up and run from the very first second when he saw me kneeling down with that kid. I don't get your meaning, Doc."

Larry knew he had to tread lightly. He couldn't talk about his and Don's sessions, but he was sure that Andy would never think about any other scenario other than everything being his fault. "I'm sure he has a lot of guilt to deal with, actually," Larry began. " And I also think he'll come around and be your friend again, but only if you give him the space to figure things out on his own. Every time you try and drag him onto your side, he's always going to push back. It's just human nature."

Andrew was not sure what to make of what Larry was saying. It didn't make any sense to him for Don to feel guilty. "But why would he feel guilty?" he insisted.

"According to both of your charts that I've read, it seems that he has saved you from yourself quite a lot. He has saved you from your fellow bunkmates, he has saved you from getting kicked out. The one thing he has seemed to do from the beginning is make sure you got through this and back home in one piece. He failed at that, Andy, and so that's where the guilt stems from."

Andy had to think about that for a moment. He wasn't sure if that was just doctor mumbo jumbo to get him to stop blaming himself and being such an asshole to everyone that came near him, but he did think about what the man said. "He can't blame himself, because he wasn't close enough to throw himself on me so that I wouldn't get hurt. That's ridiculous."

"You are actually one hundred percent correct about that, but nonetheless, I think that's what's going on here," said Larry. "He sees you not as the culprit, but as the reminder of his own failure. He's going to have to give up on the big brother complex that he's had with you and just be your friend, but until he can do that, he will need space."

Larry hoped that the way he stated his thoughts wasn't a violation of patient/doctor confidentiality. But he really didn't care if it was, really—not if it helped these kids get their act together. "You have some very serious injuries, my boy, and your physical therapy will help, but it's not going to be enough. Not even close."

"What do you mean? I mean, I'm working my ass off to get back home. If you want, I'll crawl to the airport, but just let me go home, please!"

"You're making great improvements, you really are," said Larry. "I just want to make sure that you're willing to let all the crap go and be okay with the new you, the one that will need help all the time in the beginning and then a little less and a little less until you can take care of yourself. That's how this works. You'll have to cry from time to time, because you're not a little kid any longer. You're now a wounded veteran who gave himself to his country, and you have to be proud of that, not ashamed, because someone might look at you and point."

"But I just want to go home."

"I know, I know, we've established the fact that you want to go home. What you should want is to get better, with or without Mister Birch. Now, let's talk about your physical therapy. How is that going?"

"It's like it always is—it's boring, it hurts, and I'm pretty sure those people get their rocks off on hurting people."

"Do you really think that?"

"No," Andy admitted, "but they don't cry with me, so I take it that they're enjoying every bit of my agony. Sadistic bastards."

"Well, I haven't heard that before about Maggie and Karen," said Larry. "Usually, I get the 'nice rack to stare at' or the 'she smells so pretty' or 'is she seeing anyone?' Karen hasn't ever been categorized as sadistic before." Larry was a bit shocked at Andy's description, even if he was only blowing off a bit of steam. "So, do you think therapy is helping at all? I mean, you have a long time of dealing with this. I always see you sitting in that damn chair. Are you walking better, or at all?"

"I think they're trying to help me, but I hate it here so much that I think my recovery would happen quicker someplace else."

"Let me guess," said Larry. "Someplace in Hicksville, Virginia, perhaps? Without staring at Mister Birch, perhaps?"

"Perhaps."

"Okay," said Larry. "Why don't we talk about what you're going to do when you do get home."

Larry couldn't keep Andy there forever. Sooner or later, well or sick, they would ship him home to Mommy, and Mommy would treat him like a kid who just got his first scraped knee and then baby him right into a bottomless depression. He could map out his whole future from the day he gets home, and the unfortunate party was that Andy wasn't doing a damn thing to help himself. He was welcoming the future that Larry feared for him.

"I don't know," said Andy. "I know for sure I'm going to have to get my shit together and get these doctors to help me with my leg, and then figure out a way to help my dad on the farm. I'm going to have a lot to figure out, really. I think I have to come to the realization that Don is going to be heading in a different direction than I am, and I have to be fine with it. No matter how I try to fix things, I'll always be a constant reminder of this place and why people are staring at him. I wish with all my heart that I could fix it, but I can't."

"Now, that's the first intelligent thing you've said today, my boy. I see you going home rather soon, and having that potpie and brown gravy. Damn, now I've made myself hungry."

"I think that truthfully, I could say that I'm sorry to Don a million times and he wouldn't give it a second thought. I think too that if Don doesn't want to come back with me and start a business together, then that's something he'll miss out on."

"Is that what the two of you planned on doing when you got home?" said Larry. "You were going to start a business together? Why don't you think it will happen anymore?"

"I can't wait for Don to decide whether he wants to be my friend or not. I think I have to move on and find someone that actually wants to talk to me."

It broke Andy's heart to say it, but he was smart enough to know that Larry wanted to hear how he was ready to move on, so he was going to give Larry just what he wanted to hear.

As far as doctors went, Larry was a good one, and he knew the difference between a heartfelt statement and a bullshit one when he heard it.

"Well, if that's true, I'm glad to hear it," he said. "I think if Don wants to be your friend, he'll find your address and look you up. I think it's the only way the two of you can put all this crap behind you. You'll have to start over, and you can make friends with the new Don. And he can make friends with this new Andy."

"Yeah, I think so too, Doc. I think if he wants to start a business with me, then he can come down to 816 Windy Road and knock on my door."

He wasn't sure totally that Larry was buying it, but at this point he would do anything if he thought it might get him out of there.

"Let's call it a day, and I'll see you tomorrow," said Larry. "I have a few calls to make, and I'll see when we can get you home."

Truthfully, as soon as the physical therapist released Andy, he was going to be shipped out anyway. Larry figured he might as well make Andy feel like it was himself that got him home, because to Larry, it was the mind that was a hundred times harder to heal than the body in these situations.

"Sure thing, Doc," said Andy. The prospect of going home made him feel like jumping up and down. In his current condition, though, he figured the happy dance would have to be done in his head, and in his wheelchair.

ANGRY, FURIOUS, CALM

Marie and Mike were sitting on the porch when Marie heard the rumbling of the mail lady's truck coming up the hill, which had become a double-edged sword lately. Andy's letters were not about missing home and home-made cooking. It was anger, and depression, that she saw in his words. He sounded like a boy who could not accept the fact that the other kids were picking on him. There was nothing he could do but act out. Marie wasn't sure if there was anything at all that could be done. Mike was silent and solemn, and there was no talking about bringing back the good old days. She was quite sure that he didn't believe they would ever fully come back.

Mike watched as the smoke from the truck's exhaust billowed into the air. He didn't get up to go get the mail as fast as he'd done in the past. He sat and watched the birds in the trees, the cows moving along as if they had no care in the world. He wasn't quite sure he wanted to hear another rant from his son about how life was so unfair. The heartache he felt for his son was rivaled by the need to shake him and tell him to stop being a kid, and just deal with it. It was he who'd wanted to go out and see the world. It was he who'd thought that he would come back a man that all of his peers would be jealous of, and it was he who'd thought he needed to do this to make Mike proud of him. Seeing the world under his conditions was never an option, and Andy needed to come to that conclusion before he got back home, or there was going to be another war fought right there on the farm.

Neither Mike nor Marie got up from their chairs when the mail lady drove off after depositing a few envelopes into the mailbox. Wife looked at husband, and husband to wife, with no verbal communication at all. And after a moment, when the mail truck was completely gone, Mike finally got to his feet. He still had the tiniest bit of optimism that this letter might be different. It might have a spark of the old Andy between the lines. He felt ashamed to feel like not wanting a letter from his son, but what was there to say? In the past two months, Andy had gone from being a good kid with hope to a bitter and angry young man who saw nothing but the raw deal that the world had dealt him.

Mike knew what he wanted to say. He knew what he *needed* to say. But that could wait until Andy got home.

Mike perused the mail on his way back to his normal seat in the kitchen, his wife's eyes full of hope. Maybe this one would be different. Maybe this letter, if there even were one, would be the one in which Andy came to his senses and realized that he would be fine, but he had to believe it and not live inside this one moment of his life every day forever. "Two letters and an advertisement for Lauer's," said Mike. "It looks like the grocery store is giving decent prices on eggs this week. Andy sent us two letters, too." He left that announcement for last, because he wasn't sure he even wanted to read these new letters.

The last two or three letters that they'd received from Andy were about how he'd gotten a shitty deal and he just wanted to get out of there. It was obvious that the doctors were not going to be able to help him, and blah blah blah. Mike knew one thing for sure, though. If Andy didn't have faith that his physical injuries would heal, and more importantly, that the nightmares, the face of that little kid, and the guilt would all fade into distant memories someday, then he was never going to have a future. He would never live at all; he would only exist. It didn't matter how many letters Mike or Marie wrote; Andy needed to come to the conclusion himself that someday everything would be okay.

It had to be tearing his son's guts out to be so close to having been a hero, and then have it all be taken away by one bullet. Mike had spent many a minute thinking about it, and each time his conclusion was that Andy had been given one of the rawest of deals, and even though he didn't understand why, he figured it had to have some purpose. What was the alternative? This was one of those things that could test a man's faith in God.

Marie sat there with that doe-like look on her face. She wanted to yell, "Well, read it already, you silly bastard!" But she didn't say anything. She figured Mike would open it up and read it at his own pace, or just hand it to her to read. Andy's last letter was so irate and full of hatred for everything and everyone, and more than anything, just full of self-pity. She wanted to hug him and make all the bad things disappear, but the truth was that she totally agreed with Mike. He had known that this was a real possibility, and he couldn't complain now just because it came to fruition. She too thought many a night about what her baby must be going through and what must be rattling around in his head, but the reality was that this was where all of them were, and they all needed to deal with it instead of throwing blame around. It happened, and what she tried to convey in her response letters was that she knew one thing for certain, and that was that she loved Andy and that they would get through this.

Mike started reading the great deals at Lauer's until he heard his wife clear her throat, giving him a clear signal to read the letter from their son. He put down the advertisement and picked up the letter. "Okay, babe," he said. "Happy place, happy place."

"Just read the letter, and don't make me tan your hide," said Marie, surprising herself. Obviously she had the jitters about how bad this letter might be. She didn't think it could get much worse than the last rant-fest that he'd sent. She didn't think she could take another one like that. It broke her heart.

"Here goes." Mike cleared his throat and continued, "Dear Mom and Dad," then turned to Marie and said, "It sounds promising so far."

She frowned, and Mike continued to read.

Dear Mom and Dad,

First of all, I want to apologize for all of the hatred I've been spewing lately. I was so mad at everybody. I thought everyone here just wanted to keep me from going home, but I had a really good session with Doc Larry, and he did help me realize something about why I was so pissed at everything. I was upset that my best friend hated me, but not for the reason I thought. I think now it's time for me to realize that as much as I wanted Donny to come home with me and to have a best friend, a brother, and a business partner, it's not what he needs right now.

I talked with Larry about it and as much as it tears my guts out, I can't change that, either. I don't have the power to figure out why the people here hate us to the degree they do, but I'm starting to figure it out. They don't want us here no more than I want to be here, and when people realize you don't really want to be here, they ask... so, why are you here, then? The answer I think lies in what can we take from them while I'm here. It makes me so sad, because I really wanted to be the guy that came over here and created a bond between us and them, but I know I can help people, it just doesn't have to be here in Afghanistan. I can help people back home who are like me. I can help them get themselves back together. Larry says it's going to be a long, hard road to recovery, but each time I help someone, I will get a little closer to acceptance.

I don't want to be mad anymore. I don't want to be angry at my commanders. I don't want to be angry at their commanders. I don't want to be angry with the stupidity and the greed and the hate and the total lack of love for your fellow man that I've seen here. I just want to be able to figure a way to live with what happened, and try to use my disability to make others aware of what can happen.

I don't want to be anyone's poster child for disliking the army or anything, but I just want people to be educated about what you really have to do to get those cool war stories, all the things you have to give up for those stories. I love you both very much, and if I made you cry, Mom, I'm so sorry. Dad, if I made you mad or disappointed in any way, I'm so sorry. I don't want to come home and have you two dislike who I am now. I love you both.

As far as Donny goes, I think he needs to work out his own demons. I try to get him to understand that we can do it together, but he won't even talk to me, and that made me so mad at first, but now it makes me sad. Larry was right, I can see that now. It should make me hopeful, but I personally think that's crap. I know he can't come to terms about losing his hand, but hopefully one day he will be able to find peace. I'm not saying I have. Sometimes I'm so mad and I can't really put my finger on why.

Mom, Dad, I just wanted to apologize again. I know I have a long way to go, and I know I will do everything to make you proud of me; more gratitude and less attitude. That is a catch phrase of Doc Larry's. He is such a jerk. No, I'm kidding, he's pretty cool as far as doctors go. He acts like he doesn't care, but he gets so upset with me when I act like I don't care about anything. He says he's going to keep me here until I get some sense in my head, which means I may be here for quite a while. I'm hoping to be home soon, though, but I'm going to try to take advantage of the fact that I need to be here right now. I want to be home as much as anything, but I need to get better and learn to live with myself and everything that goes along with what has happened to me in the past few months. What Donny does with his hand, or how he learns to deal, cannot be my problem anymore, as much as it eats my *gut out to admit it. I can't help him until he wants to help himself.*

Well, I just wanted to say I'm sorry, and let you know that I might be home by the time winter comes. I think Larry is happy with my progress, and when I get home, I will try to get as well as I can get as fast as I can so that I can help out around the house. Thanks for being my mom and dad.

Your Loving Son, Andrew

Mike folded the letter and placed it in its paper sheath, only to find that teardrops had fallen on it. Then he started crying uncontrollably. There was so much pain in his heaving that he immediately received a warm embrace from Marie, who was also sobbing with relief. Mike stood to his feet and pulled his wife's head to his chest. In almost a whisper, Mike sniffled and said, "Thank you so much, Lord. Thank you for hearing our prayers."

Marie pulled herself away from her husband's chest, looked up, and silently thanked the Lord as well. "Mike, is this a dream?" she said. "Can he really be back?"

Mike wanted to believe it with all his heart, but he also knew that thinking that his son had made some miraculous recovery was naïve at best. It was a good sign, but the truth was that something may piss him off in the interim and have him ranting worse than ever in the next letter. "I wouldn't get too excite," he said. "I mean, I want him back as much as you, but we have to be real about the damage that has been done. He's broken up and that is something we just have to deal with when he gets here, and don't ever forget it. One day he is going to be all smiles, and the next he could very well hate the world again. I'm glad that he's making progress, but he will never again be that kid we let get on that bus."

"I just want him home," said Marie. "I just want him home now, right now."

Marie started tearing up again. She was so excited at the prospect, but she also knew that her son could turn into a Jerry with the flip of a switch.

"I do too," said Mike. "I want him home more than anyone knows. Not having him around tears my guts up sometimes, and the thought that our Andy may be locked up in some guy's head and can't get out makes me so furious." Then he sighed and tried to spin the conversation in a positive direction. "Why don't we read the next one? Maybe it's even better."

He started to open the next letter, but before he could start reading, Marie said quickly, "If it starts off with anything hateful, just put it back in the envelope and throw it away."

Mike examined the letter for a few seconds and then said, "Well, I don't see the word 'kill' in here anywhere, so I guess that's good?"

Mike cleared his throat and leaned back against the counter. He took a second to get his thoughts together, praying that it was as good or even better than the first had been.

Hi Mom and Dad,

It's Andy again. I just wanted to write you so that I could let you know how things are going here. I wrote you a letter yesterday, so hopefully you will get them both on the same day. I'm so bored here that it makes my teeth hurt. I know that makes no sense to you, but neither does a lot of sayings I hear at home from Dad's friends, like "Those brothers are closer than two front teeth." Really, Dad? Or how about "dumber than a bagful of hammers?" That one is not the dumbest, but it's up there.

So, anyway, as I was saying. I'm bored out of my skull. Most of the guys who were here when I first got here are back on duty, or else they went home. Don left today. He went stateside. No goodbyes or anything, but I wish him well with everything. I hope he has a long and happy life. God, I'm so bored here. Please let me come home, for

God's sake. I'm waking up tasting Mom's mashed potatoes at three in the morning. I'm assuming it's the pills, but sometimes I swear I can still taste them when I wake up.

Oh, I saw Doc Larry today. I think he's finally beginning to believe that I can make it on my own. He seems to be wrapping things up with me. He's not asking me a lot of questions. He is just letting me talk and figure stuff out on my own. I swear it's just like Dad does. Walks me over to the answer, but makes me pick it up. Just like you, Dad.

The nurse is here taking my temperature and telling me it's time for therapy again. I will talk to you later, Mom and Dad.

Your Loving Son, Andrew

Marie lit up like a slot machine at the casino a few towns over from where they lived. Then she blurted, "Let's write him a letter letting him know how proud we are of him, and how if Don doesn't want to come back and be his friend, then it's his loss, not Andy's."

"Let's do it." Mike chuckled a bit. "There was a time when that meant something else. It meant, 'let's go upstairs.' What happened to that?"

"We got old, dear," said Marie. "We just got old."

Mike put his thick arm around Marie's waist and walked her back to the table. He felt good. He hadn't felt good in such a long time, and it felt very nice to have a smile on his face and to see one his wife's face as well. He pulled out her chair in the kitchen and let her proceed to plop down.

"I'll get the pad and paper," said Marie. "Do you know what you want to say?" Marie was almost so giddy she couldn't contain herself. No matter how *realistic* Mike wanted her to be, she was going to stay hopeful.

"Yeah, I think I know a thing or two I'd like to say to the boy," said Mike. He sat down at the kitchen table and watched as Marie followed her ritual of how to write Andrew a letter. She got her favorite pen out, her spiral notebook, and sat at the table with that grin that said she could not be any happier than right at this moment. "Ready?"

Marie got herself situated and flipped to a blank page in her book. She was ready to write the most heartfelt letter ever written to a son sitting in a war zone hospital who wanted to come home more than anything. "I'm so glad to hear him joking. That means he's better, right?"

"It means that he's *getting* better. It means that he's started his journey of dealing with his pain."

Mike sat and just watched silently. He'd seen this ceremonious ritual so often that he could pretty much close his eyes and still see Marie's movements. She began to write the letter.

Dear Andrew,

We got both your letters today, and first of all, I just want you to know we love you and miss you too. We're so happy that Doc Larry is helping you deal with some things. Let him help you, son, and take advantage of what he knows. We can't wait til you get home. There are so many places I want to go. Your Aunt Joan always asks how you're doing, and I think we should drive down and see her one day after you get settled. But one thing at a time.

Your father is right here next to me, and he's telling me to tell you that he loves you and that he is proud of you. We've been talking a lot about what we're going to do, and we just want you to know that this is your home and we're here if you need anything. If you want to talk or want to just be left alone, please let us know. Don't keep things bottled up inside. It's not healthy for anyone.

It sounds like this doctor could have his own show and be on Oprah, telling people how to handle being a strong person inside and out. He sounds like a good friend who is always welcome at my house for dinner. Please let him know.

Your dad just brought up something that we would both like to tell you about your friend Donny. Your doctor is right, Andy, when he says that not everyone heals at the same speed, and he can't heal at your pace. He may need to be somewhere where the doctors can help him more than you or us can. He has to be okay with his hand being gone, but he also has to be okay with the fact that life goes on.

We're getting up there in age, Andy, and if Donny wants to come here and live with us, that's great and he is more than welcome, but we nor anyone else can do what he needs done for him. He has to want to overcome this and become someone who doesn't need his hand in order to be happy. Until he gets to that stage, I don't think anyone can help him. I think you should continue to be his friend even if he's not in front of you, and let him know that when he's ready, you will be home and look forward to the day that he knocks on your door. Until that day comes, Andy, you will just have to give him the time and space that he needs to get well.

Andy, your dad says that Don is always welcome, but make sure that he wants to be here for the right reasons, and not just be here so he doesn't have to face the real world.

Well, anyway, Andy, it was so great hearing from you, and we're hopeful about what life has in store for you. I'm also so glad your sense of humor is back. Keep us up to speed about what's going on and write us anytime.

Your Loving Parents,

Mom and Dad

Marie was choked up. There was so much more she wanted to say. She wanted to write a letter the length of a novel, saying that she loved him and missed him and couldn't wait for him to get home and for them to be a real family again, over and over again on each page.

She ripped the page away from the notebook, reached behind her, and pulled the drawer next to the sink open. She removed a pair of scissors and an envelope. Marie cut the fringes off the paper and folded it up to the size that would fit perfectly in the envelope. She stuffed the paper into the envelope and licked it shut. "Ready to go?" she said to Mike.

"Where?" he said, confused.

"To the post office, of course," said Marie.

There was a chill in the air, so she grabbed her shawl.

Mike wasn't going to argue, mostly because he was anxious to get the letter to Andy as well. It could've been given to the mail lady, but that would not be as fast as dropping it in the box outside the postal building. With keys in hand, Mike and Marie walked outside to the old truck to deliver one of their most important letters.

FINAL SESSION

Larry Jackson's next-to-last patient for the day had left. He was glad that the day was almost over. He only had to see one more patient, and then he could go get a drink somewhere, anywhere besides the hospital. He'd heard too many lies and saw too many crocodile tears today to not drown them out with anything other than a stiff bourbon.

He grabbed his notebook and started going over his last patient's notes. He flipped from one page to another to see how much progress that Andrew Knox had shown in the past two months. Three times a week was a pretty aggressive schedule, but he was pretty sure that Andy needed it. He was definitely better, a whole lot better, but it was also pretty evident that this young man was acting healed so that he could go home. Larry was running out of time, because he knew that physical therapy was getting ready to sign off on him this week, more than likely, due to the government's not caring how its former soldiers are feeling or functioning in society. This particular government only cared about unborn babes still in the womb who didn't have names yet. After that, you were one hundred percent on your own. This was their policy, and unfortunately, Larry knew that a week or ten days was all this kid had left to be there. He had to figure a way to help this kid deal with the crap in his brain before he became just another old case file in a sea of case files, and eventually forgotten altogether.

He read over his notes from Andy's last session, and it was definitely encouraging, but there were key things that he never wanted to talk about, and that was a definite sign that he was still struggling with something, even if everything he did say was all butterflies and rainbows. In this case,

Larry couldn't come right out and call Knox a liar, even though he wanted to. He needed to tell this kid to wake up and stop trying to pull some horse shit just to go home. He needed to take this stuff seriously. No one but him was the cause of his physical and mental detriment. He needed to be okay with the fact that sometimes things just happen, but as long as he was going to pull his chain, Larry was going to keep him there every minute that they would let him.

His notes clearly stated that Andrew was not getting the whole picture. If he didn't try to make friends with someone, anyone at all, he more than likely would have long-lasting issues with relationships. Guilt was a debilitating disease that was almost impossible to overcome, and to some degree, it was Andy's own fault. If he'd have ran and let the sharpshooter do his thing, who knows what would have happened. But on the other hand, it may have been a lot worse. The unknown was a bitch, and those *what ifs* could drive a man crazy.

Larry was glad to hear that the outbursts had all but gone away, but in his heart, he felt that it was a controlled anger under wraps, as opposed to an anger extinguished. He knew that this kid had to come to terms somehow in order to move on with his life. He had to forgive himself, forgive the government, and forgive the guy who shot the kid, or he was going to be one of those sad vets living thirty years in the past when he got to be Larry's age.

Larry tried his best not to get overwhelmed with his caseloads. He also tried not to just blow them off because he was tired. He knew all too well the ramifications of not getting help early for these guys. The guilt, the self-pity, and the nightmares had a habit of turning these guys into wrecking balls when they went home. Some ended up in jail, some ended up in homes, but they were all human beings who deserved better. It was a damn shame what happened to these guys, and truth be told, even to himself. He'd deserved better when it was his turn, and he knew from his own experiences that dealing with the gawking ignorant kids and the adults who couldn't help but stare was worse than this place could ever be.

Kids like Andy just didn't know it yet.

Larry heard the nurse talking like she was about to bring Andrew in, so he took the next thirty seconds and perused the notes to see if anything jumped out at him. He seemed to talk a lot about Don, so Larry thought he would start there.

He heard a small knock on his office door. "Come in," he said.

The door swung open and the nurse stood there next to Andrew Knox in his wheelchair, and he did at least have a smile on his face. He wasn't happy to be there, but he was trying to make the best of things, or so he wanted Larry to think. His whole goal in the past weeks was to get home, but recently, Larry's goal was also to get him home, but without the nightmares. And it seemed that Larry was his best shot at accomplishing that.

"Hey, Andy," said Larry.

"Hey, Doc."

"Well, let's get started, shall we? Are we ready to start?" He was tired, so he was really hoping that Andy would do all the talking during this session.

"Yeah, I think so," said Andy. "Do you think I am making enough progress to go home pretty soon, Doc?"

This kid was an obvious broken record that only knew one tune. Larry was under the gun. He could say *yes* and not mean it, or say *no* and take away Andy's sense of hope. He used the oldest psychiatrist trick instead. "What do you honestly think?" he asked. "Take a second before answering."

"Well, Doc, I honestly feel like I'm a basket case, but I don't know what to do about it. I try to get myself to a place where I'm okay with everything, where I'm okay with how everything happened, but I feel like such a sucker. I feel like everyone lies now. Everyone from Uncle Sam to my commanding officers, to my friends, to everyone."

"Why do you think people are lying to you?"

Larry had seen this a hundred million times in his career. A patient couldn't make sense of the tragedy, so they tried to find someone to blame just to put a physical face on their foe, trying to rationalize what happened so they could move forward.

"People told me to come over and help these folks, so I did," said Andy. "I didn't help anyone, though. I just hurt them. No one here is getting a damn thing out of us being here. We are here for one purpose and one alone. To pillage what we can before we go. It's obvious to them, and now very obvious to me."

Larry didn't like this anxious Andy. He wanted smiling Andy back. "So, now that you know this, what can you do about it?" he asked slowly.

"What I can do is not be so damn stupid from here on. What I can do is not believe everyone who tells me they're my friend. What I can do is not be such a pushover."

"Okay, so there is a lot you can do, I get it, but what I'm getting at is why do you think you have to blame anyone? Do you understand that sometimes things just happen, and neither you nor anyone else can stop it? This, I think, is one of those rare times when you have to accept that the universe threw you a curve ball, and you have to be okay with not having anyone to blame."

"Crap, Doc, real crap."

"Really?"

"Yeah, really," said Andy. "I think that there are a lot of people on our side who helped that boy get over that wall and have the awareness and understanding to do what he did. From the senator who is very willing to step on every soldier's neck to make a buck, to every soldier who looked at them like they were pieces of shit, to the guy who was salivating to blow his head off and then shot him. Like a guard dog being let off his leash. It's sickening, Doc. There are hundreds if not thousands of people I could blame. You want this to be some metaphysical divine occurrence, and it's not. It happened because of greed, fear, and ignorance, and everyone exhibiting these traits should be to blame."

Larry had to admit that Andy was absolutely right, which made it that much harder to rebut his statement. "Even if I agreed with that, and I do," Larry began, "what good is there to hold that inside? Let me tell you something that a wise man told me once: 'Don't look back and see the muck you were in, reach back and help someone out of the muck you were just in.' That's the best medicine for someone going through what you are."

"I hear you, Doc," Andy said with a sigh. "Sounds like something my dad would say."

"It was something *my* dad did say," confirmed Larry.

"How can I help anyone in my situation? I'm broke from the head down. I couldn't help anyone even if I wanted to."

"That's where you're dead wrong, my boy. You can talk to someone standing upright or sitting in a chair. You can be using a walker or a set of crutches and still help someone out of that muck. It's all up here." Larry pointed his finger to his left temple. "All up here, my boy."

"Okay, Doc. I get you. I'd like to help others, but I don't know what I could do or say."

"Tell them what you just ranted about at me. It would probably be more therapeutic for you, and probably whomever you're speaking with as well."

"Well, I'll try anything to get out of here. What do I have to do?"

"You won't have to wait much longer," said Larry. "I spoke with your physical therapist, Doctor Park, and he says that he's done all he can for you. The rest is up to you, and time, to heal. Your spinal injuries could take a long time—I mean a *long* time to heal—if they heal at all. If they don't, you have to learn to live with that fact somehow. I think you're getting better, I hear from the nurses you're fighting to get better, but don't ever think you're totally cured, because that's the one mistake so many of us make. We are never cured; we just learn to live with ourselves better and better each day."

"Are you serious, Larry? I'm going home? I'm really getting out of this place?"

"Unless you want to stay and talk with me three times a week. I mean, I can arrange it for four to six more months, if you think we need to talk more?"

"Hell no," said Andy. "I think I should be on a plane in the morning."

"Well, how about ten days or so? All the paperwork to get you home takes a lot of signatures, and when that's done, there are schedules that need to be set up. You will not be flying Delta." Larry was glad to see Andy excited, but he was worried about him at the same time. "There are a few other things I want to talk about. We do still have a half hour."

Andrew was so excited he thought he might pee himself. The words he thought he'd never hear were just said to him, and he still couldn't believe it. "I swear, if I could get out of this wheelchair, I'd kiss you," he said with a grin.

Larry gave him a big old smile. Then he said, "I think we should touch on your friend Don and how you feel about him and his being gone home, and whether has anything changed."

"Everything has changed, Doc. I'm going home."

"You going home doesn't resolve the issue."

"You're absolutely right. I can sit here and be as miserable as I want to be, but the decision is Don's. He can be my friend. He can be my enemy. But either way, it's his call. I mean, I've extended my hand so many times, only to get it slapped. I'm not doing that again. I know what you're going to say and you can save it. I never said he couldn't be my friend, but I'm damn sure not going to beg him any longer. He can stay miserable for the rest of his life, wishing his hand back. I lost a lot, too, and I'm willing to try, and if he can't, then screw him."

Larry let the kid vent, which was probably the best thing he could do for him. "I think you're right," he said finally. "Giving him the time to figure out his own life is probably the one thing he needs."

Larry had spoken to Don on several occasions, and at their last encounter, he'd thought for sure that Don was beginning to crack on the guilt trip thing. He was sad to hear that that was not actually the case. He thought for sure he would've said something to Knox before he left.

"I hope with all my heart that he finds whatever he needs to live again," said Andy. "But it's not my turn to watch him, burp him, or change his diaper." Andy was sad, but also angry. He'd lost stuff, too, and at least Don could walk. At least Don could dance with a girl, and drive a car, and a million other things that Andy couldn't do. *So he can go fuck himself,* Andy thought in a split second of self-pity.

Larry could see that there was a lot of pent-up anger that Andrew was trying to deal with, but definitely not in a constructive way. "Knox, you have to be okay with giving him the time he needs, and just let him know that you're still his brother if he ever needs one."

"I told him that a couple days ago, before he left, and got nothing for my trouble."

"If that's so, then you just walk away, and give him his space."

"He has all the space that he could ever want, as far as I'm concerned," grumbled Andy.

Larry stood up and walked over to Andrew. He stretched out his hand, and the two men shook solemnly. "Congratulations, my boy," said Larry. "Just remember all that we've talked about, and make sure you make friends that can relate, and help them through the bad times. It's the best way you'll find your own path."

He was grateful, but all he could think about at that moment was getting the hell out of that room, out of that hospital, and out of that country. He couldn't wait to send his mom a letter letting her know. "Thanks, Doc," he said. Then he turned his wheelchair around and sped out as the door was opened by the doctor.

Captain Jackson watched as the boy raced out the door and down the hall before he could blink an eye. He was cautious about his patient, to say the least. He knew that the boy was hurting, and was trying his best to mask it with smiles and happy thoughts, but he'd been around the block too many times to fall for it. Larry shut the door slowly, walked back to his desk, and unfolded his notebook. He flipped to a new page and began writing:

> *Andrew Knox, final session... Andrew Knox will need more than I'm able to give him here. I can talk to him until I'm blue in the face, but unfortunately he doesn't see me as an ally. Not yet, anyway. His only safe space is going to be back on his farm petting cows. He has made good progress, even if he doesn't know how to process some of it yet. I'll release him as of tomorrow with his commanding officer, and wish him, just like all the others, the best of a physically-and more importantly, mentally-healthy life.*

Larry placed his pen down on his desk and he closed his book. He yawned deeply and stood to his feet. Tonight, he was no help to anyone. The only thing he wanted to talk to tonight was his bunk, and maybe his flat lifeless pillow.

He whispered softly, "Good luck, Andy. May you have a long and wonderful life."

Larry closed the door behind him. He was done for the night, and it would just be another new face greeting him tomorrow.

DEAR SIGMUND

Doctor Larry Jackson was done for the day, and he was so glad. Many of the kids he'd been seeing for the past few months were shipped out a few days ago, and that only left him with two or three patients who really even needed his help. He was sure that he would get bombarded soon, as always, but for now, he was going to appreciate the lull in his schedule.

He liked to delude himself into thinking he was making a difference in these young people's lives, but the reality was that most of these kids he'd seen over the past two years were headed for one future only. Not the kids who just got a scraped knee or were glad to be killing those bastards, as they would say, but the ones who were really fucked up in the head. The ones who couldn't wrap their heads around what had happened to them, or what they themselves had done. Those were the ones he tried to reach, but unfortunately, the majority of them blew their brains out ten minutes after reaching American soil. He was so sick of writing *PTSD* on every scrap of paper in this office. It made him so depressed at times, a gut-wrenching sadness that booze and top shelf pain killers couldn't always make go away.

He had no couch to lay on and tell someone his woes. No one cared even a little. Some days he just needed a cathartic scream, but unfortunately, most days it was in his pillow that bore the brunt before he passed out from a mixture of booze, pills, and emotional exhaustion.

Because he was a decent therapist, and knew this, he had devised a way to help himself through these particular days. He couldn't ask his assistant to do anything because he might as well blow his brains out, too, or hand a pad and paper to a tabby cat. His female assistant, before she got transferred, hid behind her pad to keep the boys from staring at her chest. She was pretty much worthless in a setting such as this one. He started his own form of therapy and came up with the brilliant idea that he would write a letter to one of his famous friends. Alfred Adler, and Carl Jung, and mostly, his best friend Sigmund Freud, were now his sounding boards.

But he didn't stop there.

He had also written Plato and Socrates over the years, and many others who he considered to be real thinkers, and it helped when he was floating in a sea of the exact opposite kind of people. Today, though, he wanted to write Sigmund a letter and catch him up about these stupid, selfish, and mostly dull people there, and how he had navigated the mine field of becoming just like them.

Larry reached out and grabbed his pad of good paper. This wasn't paper for doodling on or taking notes describing some kid's bed-wetting in detail. This was thick, refined paper that should only be used for writing letters to your best friend, as far as Doctor Larry Jackson was concerned. He and his pad made their way to the nice comfy chair where he'd spent so many hours trying to help his patients. In some patients, he saw that glimmer of hope, and some he knew instinctively were heading down a dark hole that only their bullet or a cop's bullet was going to put an end to.

Larry looked up at the celling for a moment, as if pondering what his first words would be. He couldn't help but notice how dim and dismal the lighting was in his office at that hour. When the sun was shining through during the day, he never noticed what poor lighting there was in his tiny office.

Larry relaxed and crossed his legs. He tried to exhale out all the bad crap and inhale some positive thoughts. He knew just what he wanted to tell his friend. He wanted to tell him all about how prejudiced, unfair, unempathetic, and greedy the people seemed to be who were ruling the planet, but instead he just picked up his pen and pad and started writing.

Dear Sigmund,

*It's been a while, old friend. I would say I hope heaven is
everything they say it is, but we both know I don't believe
in that stuff, and we have never lied to each other yet,
so let's not start now. It's been rough here, Sigmund. If
I'm not wanting to punch some dipshit officer out, I'm
wanting to cry mid-session. I'm so tired. I think I'm ready
to go back home, but I'm so fearful of leaving these kids
to John, who thinks therapy is just a paycheck. John is
about as good as a fart in the wind, and just watching
him with these kids makes me want to throat chop him
sometimes. If I seized his pad from him, I think I would see
sketches of tanks and airplanes. Where the hell do they
find these inexperienced, unknowing test dummies?*

*Most of my kids have left, Sigmund, and they're on their
way back to their families, and some are just back to be
thrown on the street to be picked up with the rest of the
trash after they step out in front of a bus. I know the
ones that will, too. They all have different reasons for
doing it, and I can't seem to help any of them. What am I
doing here? I feel so useless here sometimes. I wonder how
you coped with it? I wonder how you dealt with the guilt
and the shame of not being able to do your job? How
did you talk to a kid who didn't love himself or the world
or anything at all? How did you get through to the ones
who were so fucked up that, you knew their future better
than they did?*

*I have this one guy, Andrew , who left a few days ago,
and who asked me constantly, "Why am I here? Am I
doing the right thing? Did I make the right choice? Why
am I not a good guy?" Sometimes I just want to scream.*

The rare few who can reflect on their decisions find out that it's the person in the mirror who hands out respect, and only that person can make them feel unbroken and whole. Actually, in my opinion, it's the ones that earn respect and pride of that person for their life choices and not on some battlefield who stop existing and start living, but it's so hard to get these kids to wake up and realize it. It's not always about whether or not someone made the right choice. Their whole life is about making one choice after another. Old or young, good or bad, everyone makes them. Sometimes the honorable, customary, or even noble choice is not the right option. You can do anything for all the right reasons, to be one of the good guys, to make a difference, but walk away feeling not good and definitely not honorable. It's called life, and some of these kids don't want to live it.

I try and tell these out-of-touch-with-reality, wanna-be-GI Joe's that you can't chase someone else's glory, and I know what you're going to say and what Carl would say, and even what that pussy Plato would say, but it's true. At some point, the lucky few realize that it's not about making Mommy and Daddy proud, or making your uncle Joe or even the next-door neighbor proud. It becomes more about making the person in the mirror proud. I feel so useless. I don't think I have what it takes any more, my friend. I really don't. I couldn't get through to an overripe peach pit.

With a heavy sigh, he reached out for the right words for what he wanted to convey.

I have this one kid who wants to just die, because his friend died, because he should have saved him. How do I

*convince him that he's wrong? Is it better to live with the
guilt that is going to make him feel like shit until he finally
comes to terms and splatters his brain everywhere? How
is he going to come to terms that he's not the good guy
anymore? Are there any more good guys in this world?
He doesn't get to brag about making a difference. How
does he look at his superiors and feel like he's one of the
good guys, knowing what he knows? Knowing that nothing
here makes any sense except for greed and corruption
and the insatiable appetite to fuck people over to get
what you want? How do I keep doing this? How?*

Wow! he thought to himself. At first he hadn't even realized that he'd used the first person and somewhat gone off the rails. How could he tell these kids to keep the lie going to the next generation to make them feel better about themselves? We were there to dig for oil, and dig for gold, but the media had the world believing in fake water wells being drilled to help the poor and thirsty. Anyone who spent ten minutes over there would know that that's a crock. How could he keep telling these kids to lie to the world so that they can get a good night's sleep?

He felt cleansed, in a way. He knew that Sigmund would say something like, "Well, Larry, why are you there then? Don't tell me you're here to save these guys lives. Don't tell me you're here to make a difference. Why do you not help people back home, Larry? Why do you feel as though you're the only one that can sit in that chair? You know there are boys needing help back in South Bend, Indiana, and Baltimore, and New York City. Why are you here, then?'

Larry chuckled a bit at the revelation. "Yeah, why am I here?" He tapped his pen on his pad. "Why are you here, Larry? Answer the fucking question."

He sat back with a cathartic grin and started writing again.

*You know what, Sigmund, you're absolutely right, as
always. I don't have to help kids in this shithole. I don't*

have to help kids while begging for basic supplies from some dipshit, brown-nosing officer with his head up his superior's ass. I don't have to sit here popping pills and taking swigs from a bourbon bottle to feel something besides depression, despondency, and grief. I don't have to label kids as already dead while they're sitting five feet away from me. I can actually help kids back home. I can help them deal with the lie they'd been told a hundred times at the barber shop. It doesn't have to be here.

Larry got up to stretch his legs and to also visit his desk. "Speaking of bourbon," he said under his breath, "where are you, my pretty?" He set his pen and paper on the arm of the chair and made his way to the corner of his tiny desk. He got a clean glass from his desk drawer and poured himself a healthy serving of Old Grand Dad bourbon. It was his favorite, as it had been for his father as well.

After taking a big gulp and gritting his teeth while feeling the burn as it went down, he said, "Here's to my retirement from this shithole place."

He took his drink, sat it on the table next to his chair, picked up his pad and paper off the chair, and then spun and plopped down once again. He couldn't remember having an actually happy thought in his head for such a long time. "Here's to you, Sigmund." He took another big swallow and after placing it back on his side table, then resumed writing.

Sigmund, I don't know how to thank you. I think that my penance is finally over. I don't need to be here anymore. My friend died, and that is that. I can miss Tommy every day if I want, but I can't blame myself. It doesn't honor him; in fact, it dishonors him. If I wanted to honor him, I would get my head out of my self-pitying ass, sober up, and get my shit together, right Sigmund? I don't need to be here anymore. I know you would say that I knew this the whole time, and maybe you're right, but it always helps to talk things out with a good friend. I will write soon. I can learn so much more from you, I think.

Larry raised his glass once more, "Here's to Tommy. I still miss you, man. Here's to all the kids I helped. And here's to all the kids that I couldn't help. Here's to you, Sigmund. You never let me down."

Larry held his glass up in the air for a few seconds, paying homage to all who had passed through his tiny little office, and quickly took another big swig. He tore off the letter from his high-dollar pad and folded it in half neatly, then placed it in the drawer on top of the other few dozen letters that he'd written over the last two years. As he pushed the drawer shut, he remarked, "Maybe someday I'll write a book of letters written to history's philosophers and thinkers."

He thought about what a great day tomorrow would be when he put in his two weeks' notice, so to speak. He couldn't wait to see his superior's face when he said, "I'm outta here."

There were so many things to do there at the office and also back at home to get himself ready. He had to call his brother. He had to call his sister. He had to get a place, and then find a hospital that needed someone like him and his talents. Who would need him the most? It was so exciting just thinking about it. It would take him a few months to get home, but he knew that this was the right thing to do.

He took the last swig from his glass that only offered him a couple drops of bourbon, and with a big smile from ear to ear, he walked out the door feeling a hundred pounds lighter, and flipped the light out just as he closed the door behind him.

I'M SO HAPPY

Mike and Marie sat at the kitchen table talking about this and that when, in the distance, they heard the unmistakable rumbling of the mail truck. They looked at each other and Marie produced a big smile on her face. But before she could say a word, Mike interjected, "Now, you know the last three days you've been nothing but disappointed every time you go out there."

"I know, I know," said Marie. "I can hope, can't I?"

"Hoping is fine if you're not going to get crushed when all you see is the latest electric bill. She's not even on our street yet."

"Yeah, but I bet if we walked slow, we would be there at the same time," Marie said hopefully.

Mike didn't want to disappoint her, but she got so dejected when a letter from Andy wasn't there. Ever since they'd received the letter saying that he would be coming home soon, she couldn't keep still at all. She was walking on hot coals, as Mike had told her over and over. Every time the phone rang, she lit up like it was going to be Andy telling her that he was at the bus stop. He couldn't control her, though, so he just went along with it. Hopefully, after Andy got home, she would calm the hell down and start acting normal again.

"Sure, I'm pretty sure I can walk that slow," said Mike.

Marie got up from her chair and interlaced her hand with her husband's. She was gripping it firmly, but she didn't want him to let go. "Come on," she said. "Maybe today is a good day for letters."

Mike didn't like her getting her hopes up every day, but he'd learned that trying to warn her, or talk reason or logic to her, was useless, so he just kept quiet. "Well, what are you waiting for?" he said.

They left the coziness of their warm kitchen and walked hand in hand towards the mailbox. The driveway was a good fifty yards long, so it would take a minute or two to get there, especially walking around the potholes. Marie's pace quickened when she heard the mail truck turn onto their street. She was still a hundred yards away or so, but it wouldn't take her long to reach their mailbox, since there were no others on their road.

"Hold on, these old bones don't run like they used to," said Mike. He wasn't an invalid by any means, but he wasn't a track star, either.

Mike saw the wad of paper being placed in the box, and before they could reach it, the truck had sped off, backfiring when she hit second gear.

Marie was almost as nervous as a schoolgirl. There was so much to look through. The advertisements were handed to Mike to hold onto, so that she could look through the few envelopes. She stopped short when she came to Andy's letter.

The look on her face was that of delight.

"Well?" said Mike.

"Let's go inside and see what he has to say."

Marie hurried her old bones back to the house as quickly as possible, walking on the edge where there were the fewest pot holes to dodge. Mike was right behind her. He too wanted to know what was in the letter. *Good news*, he thought. *It just had to be.*

Once they got inside, Marie sat down at the table and ripped open the letter. She read the first few lines silently, and then started crying.

"What is it?" Mike's mind raced to the worst. "What happened to Andy?"

She smiled through the tears. "He's coming home. Our boy is coming home, Mike."

She started crying again, her tears falling like rain on a spring day. She wiped her face and started reading.

Hey Mom and Dad,

Doc Larry says I should be home in a couple weeks. If I leave here on the tenth, I should be home around the fourteenth. I still have to be discharged, but that should only take a few days. I want to come home so badly. I want to be home and watch the sun rise over an oak tree instead of a sand dune. I want to smell something besides my own tears and sorrow. I'm so sorry I put you all through this. I'm so sorry, Mom, that I was such a jerk to you and Dad. I have a lot of making up to do. I want to get better. And I want to help others get better, too.

I'll let you know when I'm back in the States. It should be in that ballpark. So, you might not hear from me until then. Take care of everything until I get home, and tell Dad that the best way for me to get better is to fix that place up with him.

Your Loving Son, Andrew

Marie released a big sigh of relief. Then she spun around and looked at the calendar. "Mike, today is the ninth. Our boy is going to be home in a couple days. Mike, are you hearing me?" Her giddiness was almost uncontrollable.

"I hear you," said Mike. "We have a lot to do to get the place ready."

He didn't really think so, but he knew she thought so.

"We have to go shopping," he said, "and we have to wrangle the dust bunnies up in his room." A small smirk formed on his lips.

"Are you making fun of me?" said Marie. "Are you making fun of my pain?" But then she too presented a smirk of her own.

"Never, babe, never. It's not in my nature."

"That's what I thought." Marie grabbed Mike and squeezed as hard as she could. "He's coming home, Mike. He's coming home."

6 MONTHS LATER

Marie looked out the window to see Mike walking around the yard as usual, feeding the critters, but she knew that his own well-being was nowhere near the top of his priority list as of late. She wanted to give him space, but his disorientation and confusion broke her heart. There was nothing anyone could do for him. He had to fix it himself. *He's like an old tractor that needed a part that they don't sell anymore,* she thought to herself.

As she watched her husband tinker aimlessly, she caught the outline of a car coming down their road. Definitely not the mail truck. She figured it must be a visitor of Donna's, who lived down the road. The car was in no hurry. And the one thing that amazed her more than anything was that it turned into their driveway. Even Mike's head was turned by the sudden noise coming up the driveway. The last unknown car that was in that driveway had appeared six months ago.

Marie pulled the curtain back in place and walked out the kitchen door. She saw Mike throwing what seed he had in his hand down onto the ground and walking towards his wife.

Mike was a bit surprised, to say the least. He had never seen this car before. Most of his friends drove pick-up trucks. This car was an old, beat-up Ford Taurus with faded blue on the hood and roof. Mike stood next to his wife as the car came to a stop a few feet in front of them. Mike had no clue who the man inside the car was.

Marie watched in total bewilderment as the man emerged. His clothes were a bit disheveled, his beard was a bit unkept, and his eyes looked lost. Like they were searching for something. *Who is this guy?* she thought.

Mike spoke in his usual soldier-like tone to the young man. "May we help you, son?"

The man closed his door firmly and turned to the man and woman standing just a few feet from the front of his car. "Hi," he began. "My name is Donald Birch, sir." He walked forward and shook Mike's hand.

Mike and Maria both looked at each other and then back at Don, who said again, "I'm so sorry to bother you, but I had to come up to talk with you. Do you know who I am?"

"Yes, we do, son," came an almost inaudible sound from Marie's lips. "Please come in."

They walked to the house and then Marie opened the door, and she and Mike entered after Don. "Please sit down, and what drink can I get you? Coffee?" She didn't know what to say to this kid. What was there to say? She knew him, but she'd never met him.

"No, thank you, ma'am," said Don. "I just wanted to say this before I lost my nerve."

"Say what?" Mike's voice became very serious.

Don looked around and was a bit sad that Andy was nowhere to be seen. It was obvious to Don that he'd done the unthinkable, but he wasn't even a little bit surprised. He'd known that Andy was going to take the easy way out.

He blurted out, as if the words were pushing their way out by force, "I wanted to be there for Andy, but I failed him. I wanted to be there, but I couldn't get my head out of my own butt to help anyone, and I just wanted to say that I'm so sorry. I should have been there for Andy."

Just then, from behind Mrs. Knox, a voice called out, "Who keeps calling my name?"

Andy wheeled out and saw Don sitting at his kitchen table. "Don?" he said incredulously.

Don's mouth fell open. "You jerk," he said. "I thought you were dead."

"Why the hell would you think that?" said Andy.

"You know why."

Mike stood up and motioned to his wife. "Marie, will you help me outside for a minute?" He was sure these two boys needed some space to grind out whatever they needed to work out.

"Sure." Marie got up and joined her husband walking out the back door.

Don was flabbergasted, to say the least. "What the fuck?" he said, mostly to himself.

"Are you sad that I'm not dead?" said Andy.

"No!"

"Then why are you here? I thought you hated me?" Andy pushed the chair aside and wheeled himself a bit closer.

"I don't hate you. I never did."

Andy's feelings of hurt and betrayal came rushing back in full force. "Why are you here, Don? What on earth could you want from a cripple like me?"

"I wanted to make sure you got home, is all."

"That's all?"

"I wanted to see if you were okay, okay?" Don said, his voice rising.

"Well, I'm still in a chair. I'm still fucked up in the head, I still have bad dreams, and I'm definitely still hating myself for doing the most stupid thing one person can ever do. I hate so many things and so many people, but I can't cry about it anymore. My mom needs me, my dad needs me. Doc Larry helped out a lot in showing me that a bullet in my head wasn't going to help my dad in any way. I can't run off and be a little bitch."

"Like I did?" Don pointed to his chest.

"Yep," Andy said coldly. "Just like you did." He wanted to punch Don square in the face. So why didn't he? He figured he just didn't want to feel any worse than he already did. It was time to put all that crap behind him. Or at least try.

" I'm sorry," said Don.

"Save it, dude."

"I came here to say I'm sorry."

"And you said it."

But Don wasn't going to give up that easily. He had a lot of demons himself that needed slaying. He could get up and tell Andy to fuck himself and the horse and all that crap, but he decided to just change the subject. "How are your legs coming?" he said.

Andy was quiet for a moment. Then he said, "Well, to be honest, I won't be running any quarter miles any time soon."

"But someday, though, right?"

"Yep, someday," Andy confirmed. "The doc says I have a long, long road ahead of me, but with a lot of hard work, a lot of physical therapy, and a lot of time, he thinks I could be up and walking again someday. I'm making some progress, which I'm trying really hard to remember when I want to punch a wall, or someone's face."

"That's great news," said Don, visibly relieved. "Keep positive. You have to."

"No, you try, that's it," said Andy. "But realistically, the diagnosis is better than if someone tells you that you absolutely won't walk again. I repeat it to myself every night, almost like the Lord's prayer."

"Yeah, I guess that will work."

Don wished that there was something he could do. He felt so badly, but he couldn't do a damn thing about it. He had his own shit to deal with.

Andrew sized up his friend. He could tell that his life was no picnic, either. "How about you and your hand?" he asked.

"You mean my ol' crab claw?"

"I wanted to say it so bad, but I thought you'd hit me."

Andy took a big sigh and let it out slowly. "Look, dickweed, I know I should apologize. I forgive you, I forgive you. I'm not mad at you. Not anymore, anyway. I did hate you for a long time for not being there when I needed you the most. I hated you more than I thought it was possible to hate another person. But I can't do it anymore. I can't afford to. I'm trying my best to put all that crap behind me and leave it there. I'm not doing it for you, or for me, just so you know. I'm doing it for my mom and my dad, and all the guys like Jerry, and all the other guys who didn't come back at all. They deserve more than me acting like a whiny little bitch. So, if you want the truth, I forgive you. I really do." He took a deep breath like he'd just dropped a huge rock that he had been carrying around for a very long time.

Andy took another deep breath and continued. "I've learned recently that the fight is not to get my legs back as much as it's fighting to look myself in the mirror and forgive myself. That's the real fight, but to do that, you have to be honest with yourself. There isn't one person on this planet who owes you a damn thing. They don't owe you love, or respect, or loyalty, or friendship. No one owes you a thing. When you get that through your skull, you might find yourself a better person, and a whole fucking lot easier to live with."

"Is that what your doctor has been helping you with?" Don asked.

"Shit, that quack couldn't help me if his life depended on it."

"Your dad?"

"Yep," said Andy. "My dad is really helping me. He's helping me so much more than that hundred-dollar-an-hour quack asking me how I see the world and what color my anger is."

"They really ask you that shit?"

"No, I just made the last part up, but it's just as stupid as some of the shit he always wants to talk about. My dad breaks it down much simpler in ways that you can understand."

Andy cracked a smile.

"What's so funny?" asked Don.

"This is where my dad would say something like, 'oh you were listening.'" He paused for a second and then said, "Let me give you an example. The doctor says shit like, 'why do you think this and why that?, It gets on my nerves so bad. My dad, on the other hand, says shit like, 'You have to be willing to die to live.'"

"What the hell does that mean?"

"I think it means that you have to be willing to go out and do something that may kill you to feel alive," said Andy. "To really be alive and not just a blip on the earth taking up space."

He stopped for a second and then said, "Another one of his sayings that I like is, 'Everything in this universe is revolving around one little speck, and today you are not that speck.' That is one of my favorites. My point is that he makes me think about shit and doesn't just say 'this is what's wrong with you, and this is how to fix it.' He makes me want to grow mentally as well as everything else. He wants me to understand that everyone on this planet is going through something, even him, and it's not how we deal with it that makes us better, but it's how we deal with everyone else because of our shit that makes us a great or not so great human being. I've adopted his philosophy about one thing in particular. It's not how many friends you have, but how many people show up to your funeral. The doctor would never say anything that made that much sense."

"I need to talk with him, I think." Don paused and then added, "I mean, someone like your dad."

"It's okay, dink. I'm sure he would be happy to chew your ear off, too."

"I'm sorry, Andy. I'm sorry I left you there like I hated you. The only person I really hated was me."

Don stood up and cleared his throat. "The reason I came up here today was to tell your parents something. I wanted them to know that you didn't save my life. You didn't jump in front of a bullet or dive onto a grenade. You didn't save my life—you changed it. And to me, that's the same thing."

"Wow, Don," Andy said with a smile, "that was some deep shit."

"I rehearsed it over and over on the way up here."

"*And* you ruined it."

"Practiced or not, Andy, it was sincere."

"I know it was, Donny boy," said Andy. "I know it was."

"I hate myself so much for leaving like I did. I've just wandered and existed, like you said, ever since I've been home. I knew this was the only good thing that I could do before I put that bullet in my brain."

"I know. I know very well," said Andy. "My parents keep me from catching that particular disease almost daily."

Andrew could see that his friend was hurting and desperately looking for someone who would tell him that everything would be okay. He knew Don had probably been wandering like a nomad ever since he'd been home. "Have you been seeing anyone to help push those ghosts and demons out for good?" he asked.

"I was at first, at the V.A.," said Don, "but that guy was a veterinarian, I think. He must have been, because he didn't do shit for me."

"Well, I would recommend my doctor, but I think he's birthed a few calves too."

"What are you doing right now?" Don asked suddenly. "I mean, let's go do something. Get a burger or something." Don paused to evaluate Andy's expression, and then he continued, "Too soon?"

"No," said Andy, "but I'm helping Dad paint the rest of the barn. I had just come in to go to the bathroom when you came in."

"Oh."

"What? Cripples take craps too, you know."

"I'm sure they do." Don fumbled with his words. "Do you think I could help?"

"I already went," Andy joked.

"Not with your ass, you ass," said Don. "I mean with the barn."

"Well…"

"Too soon?" Don said again.

"No, I was just going to say, well, we do need someone to hold the paint can," said Andy. "Someone who we won't have to worry about their hand getting tired."

He chuckled and then said, "Too soon?"

"No, not at all," said Don. "If I get tired, I can sit on your lap."

"Only if you want something to poke you in the butt."

"Does that thing still work?" Don thought he might be treading on a sensitive subject, but *fuck it*, he thought. Might as well go all the way.

"Oh, yeah," said Andy, making his voice sultry. "Just sit right here and find out. The two of us get acquainted a lot." Andy started to giggle.

"Thank God I didn't shake your hand," said Don. "And I'm glad that it seems you can still crack yourself up as usual."

Andy raised his left hand and held it up in front of Don's face. "This is the one I use most often," he said. "She has a sexy accent. I call her Brigitte."

He cracked himself up again, and this time Don joined in.

"You sick bastard," said Don. "You really are a sick pup."

"Don't act like your hand doesn't have a sweet little French accent."

"Actually, its Swedish. Ya, big boy."

They both busted out laughing at the same time. Tears of laughter, reprieve, joy, and mostly relief brimmed the whites of their eyes.

Mike and Marie came in through the kitchen door to see the two guys laughing as though they'd just seen the funniest movie ever made. Mike had a smile from ear to ear, as did his wife. Mike said, "What the heck is so funny up in here?"

Marie chimed in, "Yeah, what's so funny?" She didn't really care; she was just glad to see Andy smiling and laughing. It had been a while since she had seen that expression on his face.

"Nothing, Mom," said Andy. "We just told a funny story about Burnside, is all."

"Okay, honey."

Andrew cleared his throat. "Dad, Don wants to know if he can help us finish painting the barn?"

"I have a better idea, son," said Mike. "Why don't you two finish the barn so that I can finish fixing up that chicken coop." Mike figured he would only be a third wheel and wouldn't understand most of Andy's and Don's jokes anyway.

Andy looked at Don seriously. "You're getting all the high parts."

"Uh, duh," said Don. He got up and pushed his chair back in under the old wooden table. "Let's go, wheels."

"Okay, crabby." Andy hurriedly added, "Too soon?"

"If I flip you over like a turtle, you'll know."

Mike watched the two men joking together and figured that this was probably the absolute best thing that could happen to both of their recoveries. Meanwhile, Andy pushed himself away from the table. "Get the door, Donny boy."

Before the two could escape to the barn, Marie blurted out to Don, "You're staying for dinner, right?"

Andy answered for Don. "He would be delighted. Thanks, Mom."

Don nodded his head in agreement. "How big is this barn?" he asked.

"It's huge. I already did my half, though," he added with a grin. Then he turned his wheelchair back so that the two could see each other. "Oh, and we need to get you a haircut."

"Uh, thanks for worrying about my grooming needs," said Don.

"You'll like this barber shop," said Andy. "Trust me."

The two young men went out the door, Don pushing his friend's wheelchair in front of him as they walked outside toward the barn.

Marie closed the door gently shut behind them. "Mike, will Andy be okay?" she asked, watching Andy and Don through the window.

Mike answered with his arm around his wife's shoulders. "For the first time since he's been home, Marie," he said, "I can honestly say that I think he will."